M.D. Anderson Volunteers Cooking For Fun

M.D. Anderson Cancer Center
Houston, Texas

Proceeds from the sale of **M.D. Anderson Volunteers Cooking For Fun** will be donated to the Volunteer Endowment Patient Support Fund, which provides programs for cancer patients at M.D. Anderson Cancer Center.

ISBN 0-9630631-0-3

1st Printing	5,000 copies	October, 1991
2nd Printing	5,000 copies	January, 1993

Printed in the USA by
WIMMER BROTHERS
A Wimmer Company
Memphis • Dallas

Introduction

M.D. Anderson Volunteers Cooking For Fun is a joint effort of volunteers and volunteer staff at M.D. Anderson Cancer Center. Proceeds from the sale of these books go to the Volunteer Endowment Patient Support Fund (VEPS), which supports innovative patient programs.

VEPS funds are used to purchase wigs and supplies for the hospital's Beauty/Barber Shop, as well as toiletries and pajamas. The Patient/Family Library receives radios, audio-cassette players and tapes, games and a wide selection of magazines in English and Spanish.

New services from cookbook proceeds will include a craft area, laundry room, exercise equipment, free newspaper delivery and additional beauty/barber services for patients and family members. Art and music therapy programs will also be implemented with monies earned from cookbook sales.

Volunteers and volunteer staff continue to look for opportunities to serve the thousands of patients, family members and visitors at M.D. Anderson. Proceeds from the cookbook will help these opportunites be realized.

Cookbook Committee

Dianne Ibenthal, Chairman

Shirin Blackwell
Diana Horowitz
Estelle Kastleman
Linda Manzione
Louise Perlitz
Sandy Schmelzer
George Vietor
Linda Young

Photographer
Jeffrey Arnim

Clerical Assistants
Janice Barnett
Susan McClellan Gibbs
Elva Lopez
Marsha Thompson

Staff Advisor
Dora Hughes

Marketing Advisor
Leslie Friedman

A special acknowledgement to M.D. Anderson's Nutrition and Food Service Department for their contribution of recipes for a healthy lifestyle.

Also, grateful appreciation to the professional chefs from around the country who shared their expertise.

Additionally, we wish to acknowledge members of M.D. Anderson's administrative staff for their assistance in obtaining the proper approvals.

Many others have aided and abetted this committee in compiling this cookbook. Without the wholehearted efforts of the volunteers and volunteer staff, we would have no book. Our many thanks to all who have given time and recipes so graciously.

Table of Contents

Dedication

This cookbook is dedicated to **Page Lawson**, Director of Volunteer Services at M.D. Anderson Cancer Center from 1973 until her retirement in 1991.

Her creativity and dedication inspired more than fifty innovative volunteer programs to provide services for patients, their families and cancer center staff. The Volunteer Endowment Patient Support Fund, which will receive the proceeds from sales of this cookbook, is one of the many programs made possible through Page's vision.

With infectious enthusiasm and indomitable determination, Page led her team of volunteers and staff to great heights of achievement. She maintained a glorious sense of humor and a grand "joie de vivre," which made all encounters with her just plain fun.

So, thinking of Page, we hope, with this cookbook, you have hours of just plain fun and delicious eating.

Organization

More than 2,600 men, women and teenagers provide special services during the day, evening and weekend, for cancer patients and their families at M.D. Anderson Cancer Center. They participate in nearly 50 different programs. These volunteers — who comprise the largest volunteer force of any health care institution in Texas — offer compassionate support to the more than 32,000 patients who come to M.D. Anderson annually.

Many volunteers are former patients who understand firsthand the needs and feelings of cancer patients. Other volunteers, having lost loved ones to cancer, are involved to offer support for patients and their families. They, too, understand the emotional devastation of the disease.

Volunteer roles vary from floor hosts to scientific research assistants; from patient escorts to those who clip roses in the garden; from gift shop operators to bilingual visitors.

Several volunteer-inspired programs address special patient needs. For example, the Adopt-a-Friend Program involves volunteers who offer ongoing companionship to patients from out-of-town. The Concierge Desk volunteers assist patients and family members with directions to appointments and ideas for local recreation and entertainment.

The Anderson Network is an innovative outreach program matching new patients with volunteers who are cancer patients themselves. Also unique to M.D. Anderson is the Patient/Family Library, which includes a Health Information Center with books on cancer and other health topics. The library also supplies books, magazines, newspapers, audiocassettes, radios, puzzles and games for patients and their families.

Perhaps M.D. Anderson's single largest volunteer initiative is the Children's Christmas Card Project, which offers holiday cards designed by young cancer patients undergoing treatment at M.D. Anderson. Since 1974, more than 25 million cards have been sold generating more than five million dollars in revenue. These proceeds have funded numerous programs designed to meet the educational, recreational and emotional needs of thousands of young patients.

Volunteers play an important role at M.D. Anderson, and new volunteer programs are developed each year to meet changing patient needs.

APPETIZERS

Hot Artichoke Dip I

1 (4 ounce) jar pimentos, diced
1 (14 ounce) can artichoke hearts, drained and chopped
1-1/2 cups mayonnaise
2 (7 ounce) cans green chilies, drained and chopped
4 ounces Monterey Jack cheese, shredded
1/2 cup Parmesan cheese
tortilla chips or crackers

Preheat oven to 325 degrees. Drain pimentos and reserve 2 teaspoons for garnish. In a medium bowl, mix pimentos, artichokes, mayonnaise, green chilies, Monterey Jack cheese, and Parmesan cheese. Spread mixture into a shallow 1-1/2 quart baking dish. Sprinkle with additional Parmesan cheese and reserved pimentos. Can be made ahead. Cover and refrigerate. Bake uncovered for 30 minutes. Serve with tortilla chips or crackers. Variation: Add two 6 ounce packages of frozen crabmeat.

Yields 20 appetizers

Elaine Davenport

Hot Artichoke Dip II

1 (16 ounce) can artichoke hearts
1/2 cup mayonnaise
1/2 cup drained plain yogurt
1 cup grated Parmesan cheese
dash paprika

Drain artichoke hearts and mash well. Add next 3 ingredients; mix with fork and put into baking dish. Sprinkle paprika on top. Bake at 350 degrees for 30 minutes. Serve with pita bread, cut into triangles, wheat crackers or crackers of your choice. This dip is also good cold.

Yields 2 cups

Sophia Papas

Artichoke Spread

1 (15 ounce) can artichoke hearts, well drained
3/4 cup Parmesan cheese
3/4 cup Hellman's Real Mayonnaise
1/4 teaspoon garlic powder
dash cayenne pepper
paprika

Finely chop artichoke hearts and mix well with remaining ingredients except paprika. Spread into small baking dish sprayed with Pam and cover entirely with paprika. Bake at 375 degrees for 25 minutes. Serve hot with crackers.

Serves 6-8

Catherine Arlinghaus

Avocado Spread

1 (8 ounce) package cream cheese, softened
1 package Good Seasons Italian Salad Dressing mix
1 tablespoon mayonnaise
juice of 1/2 lemon
1 avocado, chopped
1 tomato, chopped
dash of Tabasco

Mix all ingredients together. Refrigerate until ready to use. Serve with crackers.

Yield: approximately 2 cups

Sally Root

Hot Bean Dip

2 (8 ounce) cans red kidney beans
4 slices bacon
2 cups sour cream
2 tablespoons chopped green pepper
2 tablespoons minced onion
1/2 teaspoon salt
1/4 teaspoon garlic
1/4 teaspoon pepper

Drain liquid from beans. Mash beans and set aside. Fry bacon until crisp and drain. Stir beans into bacon drippings and cook over low heat. Mix in other ingredients and blend well. Sprinkle with bacon. Serve warm.

Kathy Blevins

Beau Monde Dip

1 cup sour cream
1 cup mayonnaise
1 tablespoon parsley flakes
1 tablespoon dehydrated onion
1 teaspoon dill weed
1 teaspoon Beau Monde seasoning (can be found on grocery shelf along with other spices)

Combine all ingredients and let stand overnight in refrigerator. Serve with raw vegetables such as celery, carrots, broccoli or cauliflower.

Serves 6

Linda Stearns

Easy Blue Cheese Vegetable Dip

1 pint cottage cheese
1/2 cup mayonnaise
1/4 teaspoon Worcestershire sauce
2 dashes Tabasco sauce
1 teaspoon garlic salt
celery seed to taste
1 (5 ounce) jar Kraft roka at room temperature

Blend the cottage cheese in the blender until smooth. Be careful not to process too much, it should be sour cream consistency. Blend all the rest of the ingredients, putting in the roka last. Chill. Serve with vegetables.

Bob Burrill

Baked Brie

4 crescent rolls, unbaked
1 small Brie cheese

Carefully spread crescent roll dough out sealing holes with your fingers. Place Brie in center and fold dough over. Turn over so smooth side is on top. Bake according to directions on roll package. Serve with fruit or crackers.

Serves 4-6

Louise Perlitz

Texas Caviar

4 cans blackeyed peas, drained
4 medium tomatoes, chopped
8 green onions, chopped
4 cloves garlic, mashed
2 medium green peppers, chopped
1 cup onion, chopped
2/3 cup cilantro, chopped
2 cups Picante sauce, mild

Mix all ingredients together and serve with Doritos.

Anne Sullivan

Cheddar Bites

2 sticks unsalted butter, softened
1 pound sharp Cheddar cheese, grated
1 large egg yolk
1/2 teaspoon cayenne
2 teaspoons salt
2 cups all purpose flour
1 large egg white, beaten lightly with a pinch of salt

Cream butter and cheese until it is smooth. Add egg yolk, cayenne, and salt. Blend well. Add flour and blend until it just forms dough. Lightly butter baking sheet. Drop 1/2-3/4 teaspoon full, 2 inches apart. Brush tops with egg white glaze. Bake 375 degrees for 10 minutes or until puffed and lightly golden. Transfer to rack. They keep, sealed in an airtight container for 3 days. If desired, reheat in a preheated oven (300 degrees) for 5 minutes. Or freeze.

Liana Ornstein

Cheese Delight Snacks

1-3/4 sticks butter or margarine
1/2 pound Cheddar cheese, grated
1 teaspoon Tabasco sauce (optional)
2 cups flour
2 cups Rice Krispies

Leave butter and grated cheese in bowl until room temperature. Then add the rest of the ingredients, blending well. Shape into balls the size of a walnut. Press onto ungreased cookie sheet, and flatten with a fork. Bake 325 degrees for 20 minutes. May be baked and frozen. Reheat in oven for a brief time.

Serves 4-5 dozen

Catherine P. Arlinghaus

Holiday Cheese Spread

4 (8 ounce) packages cream cheese
2 jars sharp cheese spread
2 tablespoons onion flakes
1 cup chopped pecans
2 teaspoons Worcestershire
2 teaspoons (heaping) flaking parsley

Soften cream cheese slightly. Cream together with sharp cheese spread. Add remaining ingredients to creamed mixture. Mix well. Fill any type of holiday containers (I like the small plastic 4 ounce glasses) and cover with any type of plastic wrap. Serve with crackers.

Susan McClellan Gibbs

Green Chili Pie

2 (4 ounce) cans whole green chilies
1 pound Monterey Jack cheese
4 eggs
1 unbaked pie crust

Carefully remove chilies from can. Run finger along edge of chili to spread and remove seeds and vein. Do not use water to rinse chilies. Line pan with chilies. Grate cheese and lightly fill pan, do not mash down. Beat eggs well and pour over cheese. Bake for 24 minutes to 1 hour at 275 degrees. May look soft in center. Cut and serve like pie.

Serves 1 deep dish pie or 2-9 inch pies

Kathy O'Brien

Chili Con Queso

2 pounds Velveeta cheese
2 cans Rotel tomatoes
1 bunch green onions, chopped
1 package Monterey Jack cheese
2 tablespoons cumin seed

Melt and mix all ingredients over low heat or double boiler. Serves a lot.

Angela Wheat Cheves

Chili Dip

1 pound ground beef
1 roll jalapeno cheese
1 roll garlic cheese
1 can cream of mushroom soup
1 can diced chilies

Brown and crumble ground beef in skillet. Add cheeses, stirring until melted. Add soup and chilies mixing well. Serve in chafing dish with corn chips.

Jeanne Dean

Crab Mold

6 ounces softened cream cheese
2 green onions (chopped fine)
1 (10 ounce) can cream mushroom soup (undiluted)
1 cup mayonnaise
1 tablespoon unflavored gelatin (dissolved in 3 tablespoons cold water)
1 pound fresh lump crab meat
1/2 cup celery (chopped fine)

Oil mold lightly (with mayonnaise); heat soup; dissolve gelatin in water; add to soup and cool slightly; combine with other ingredients and pour into mold. Chill overnight. Serve with melba toast or crackers.

Mary Belle Wooddy

Hot Crab Dip

1 (8 ounce) package cream cheese
1 (6-1/2 ounce) can crabmeat
1 teaspoon horseradish
1 tablespoon milk or cream
2 tablespoons chopped onion
1/2 teaspoon salt
dash pepper
1/3 cup sliced almonds, toasted

Mix all ingredients, except almonds, together. Put into a greased pie plate and bake at 375 degrees for 15 minutes. Remove from oven and top with almonds.

Serves 6-8

Linda Stearns

Texas Crabgrass

1 (10 ounce) package frozen chopped spinach
1 medium onion, finely chopped
1/2 cup butter
8 ounces fresh or frozen cooked crabmeat, flaked
3/4 cup freshly grated Parmesan cheese
1/4 cup dry sherry or sauterne

Cook and drain spinach. Saute onion in butter. Add remaining ingredients and heat thoroughly. Serve in a chafing dish with crackers.

Serves 10

Sally Root

Stuffed Cucumbers with Feta Cheese

4 cucumbers, chilled and peeled
1 tablespoon mayonnaise
1/2 cup crumbled feta cheese
1 tablespoon minced parsley

Cut chilled cucumbers in halves lengthwise and hollow out the centers. Combine the crumbled feta cheese with mayonnaise; mash well. Stuff the cucumbers with the cheese mixture. Sprinkle with parsley, chill and serve. Depending on the size of the cucumbers, after you stuff them, you can cut them into bite size or larger.

Sophia Papas

Curry Veggie Dip

Veggies — yellow squash, celery, carrots, large mushrooms, cucumbers, cauliflower, broccoli, cherry tomatoes, etc.
1 teaspoon curry powder
1 tablespoon ketchup
1 teaspoon Worcestershire sauce
1 cup "lite" mayonnaise
1/2 medium onion, finely grated with juice and all

Wash and slice veggies on the diagonal, if possible, so you will have larger slices making it easier to pick up the dip. Mix all dip ingredients together and refrigerate for a few hours before use — it tastes better.

Rosine Chappell

Super Guacamole Dip

4 over-ripe avocados
3 tablespoons picante sauce (more or less)
1 tablespoon lemon juice
1 tablespoon dried onion flakes
1/2 teaspoon garlic powder
1/4 teaspoon pepper
dash of salt and MSG (optional)

Combine all ingredients, mash with potato masher or beat on low speed of electric mixer until well blended. Serve with your favorite chips or veggies. May be frozen and later defrosted in microwave on "defrost" for 5 minutes, let rest for 10 minutes.

Makes about 2 cups

Catherine Arlinghaus

Curry Dip

1 pint Hellman's mayonnaise
3 teaspoons curry powder
3 tablespoons Worcestershire sauce
1/4 teaspoon onion salt
1/4 teaspoon garlic salt
pepper and Tabasco to taste

Combine all ingredients and use as a dip for any kind of vegetable.

Carolyn Hamrick

Sweet and Sour Hotdogs

2 tablespoons prepared mustard
1/4 cup grape jelly
1/2 pound frankfurters
1 teaspoon butter or margarine

Combine mustard and jelly in a 1 cup measuring cup. Microwave covered with plastic wrap, for 2-1/2 minutes. Cut each frankfurter diagonally in 8-10 slices. Put in 1 quart baking dish with butter. Microwave covered for about 3 minutes. Pour grape jelly sauce over frankfurters. Cook, covered for 4 minutes. Let stand 2 minutes. Serve hot; use toothpicks in individual slices.

Serves 6-8

Ruth Tynes

Jalapeno Cocktail Pie

2 or 3 jalapeno peppers, chopped and seeded
1 pound sharp Cheddar cheese, shredded
6 eggs, beaten

Sprinkle peppers on bottom of well greased 9 inch square pan. Cover with cheese. Pour beaten eggs over cheese and bake at 350 degrees or until firm. Cut into 1 inch squares when cool.

Makes 6-1/2 dozen

Clara Dawson

Chicken Liver Pate

3/4 cup butter or margarine
1 pound chicken livers
1/2 pound fresh mushrooms
1/2 cup finely chopped onion
1 teaspoon salt
4 drops hot pepper sauce
1/2 cup white wine
1 clove garlic, mashed

Melt 1/4 cup butter in skillet; add chicken livers, mushrooms, onions and salt. Simmer 5 minutes. Add hot pepper sauce, wine and garlic, cover and cook slowly for 10 minutes, or until livers and mushrooms are tender. Cool slightly and whirl in blender until smooth. Blend in remaining butter. Taste and add more salt if necessary. Put in crock and refrigerate overnight.

Yields about 3 cups

Helen Harbeson

Malaysian Cocktail Meatballs

- 1 pound Louis Rich Ground Turkey Sausage
- 1 package Rice-a-Roni, any flavor
- 1/3 cup dehydrated onion flakes
- 1 teaspoon pumpkin pie spice
- 1 cup canned pumpkin
- 1/2 cup Sherry Wine
- 1 tablespoon low-salt soy sauce
- 1/2 cup water chestnuts, chopped
- 1/2 teaspoon granulated garlic
- flour or cornstarch

Mix all ingredients together EXCEPT for the packet of dry flavoring mix from the Rice-a-Roni. Form into cocktail-size meatballs. Roll in flour or cornstarch, just lightly coating. Spray a nonstick pan with Pam. Fry meatballs gently over medium heat. When browned on two sides, mix dry packet according to directions on Rice-a-Roni box. You may substitute wine for some of the water. Lower heat and cook until liquid is absorbed - about 20 minutes. Cover pan and check at ten minutes. Serve with Chinese Duck Sauce.

Linda Manzione

Crab Stuffed Mushrooms

- 3 ounces cream cheese, softened
- 2 tablespoons sour cream
- 1 or 2 drops sherry pepper sauce
- 1/8 teaspoon garlic powder
- 2 teaspoons lemon juice
- 1 egg yoke
- 3-4 teaspoons green onion, minced
- 1 can white crab meat
- 24 medium size mushrooms

Combine first 8 ingredients. Stuff mixture into mushrooms. Broil on cookie sheet placed on lowest rack of broiler. Broil slowly for 10 minutes. Twenty-four mushrooms (medium size) or more if smaller, can be made up before time and placed in broiler after guests arrive.

Anne Clark

Natchez Cheese Wafers

- 2 cups Cheddar cheese, grated
- 1/4 pound butter or margarine, softened
- 1/2 teaspoon salt
- pinch of cayenne
- 1-1/2 cups flour, sifted
- paprika

Combine grated cheese, butter, salt and cayenne. Gradually work in flour. Form rolls in wax paper and chill. Slice into thin wafers and decorate with paprika. Place on cookie sheet and bake at 350 degrees for 30 minutes. A perfect party snack, these wafers may be prepared in advance and baked minutes before company arrives!

Jackie Blackman

Chicken Nachos
(Appetizers or Main Dish)

- 2 cups shredded Cheddar cheese
- 1/2 cup sour cream
- 1-1/2 cups cooked and shredded chicken
- 1 (4 ounce) can diced green chilies, drained
- tortilla chips
- 1-1/2 cups shredded lettuce
- 1/2 cup chopped tomato
- additional sour cream
- guacamole
- salsa

In medium saucepan, combine cheese and 1/2 cup sour cream. Stir constantly over low heat until cheese melts. Add cooked chicken and chilies to cheese mixture, stirring until heated through. Heat tortilla chips on cookie sheet at 350 degrees for 10 minutes. Arrange half the tortilla chips on a serving platter and top with half the chicken mixture. Repeat layering with remaining chips and chicken mixture. Sprinkle lettuce and tomato on top. Garnish nachos with sour cream, guacamole, and salsa. Serve on a warming tray.

Serves 4-6

Ann Heyda

Piccadilly Dip

- 1 pound ground beef
- 1 pound HOT Jimmy Dean sausage
- 2 small onions, diced
- salt and pepper to taste
- 2 teaspoons oregano
- 1 tablespoon cumin
- 4 tablespoons chili powder
- 4 cloves garlic, minced
- 6 tomatoes, peeled and diced
- 6 green onions, diced
- 1-1/2 cups chopped pimentos
- 1-1/2 cups raisins
- 1 small can tomato paste
- 1 large can tomato sauce
- 1-1/2 cups toasted almonds
- green onions for garnish
- Fritos or other chips

Saute first 4 ingredients in a large skillet until meat is browned; drain fat. Add oregano, cumin, chili powder, garlic, tomatoes and green onions. Combine with pimentos, raisins, tomato paste and tomato sauce. Simmer for 2 hours and add almonds. Pour into a chafing dish, garnish with chopped green onions and serve with Fritos. This is a unique dip that is delicious!

Doris Blumenthal

Pickled Herring (Sursild)

1 big (or 3 small) herring
5 large onions, sliced
2 tablespoons peppercorns
1 bay leaf
3 tablespoons sugar
1/2 cup white vinegar
1/2 cup water

Cut herring into 1 inch pieces. Layer herring, onions and peppercorns in a large container. Mix together bay leaf, sugar, vinegar and water and pour over herring, covering the herring completely. Allow to set 24 hours, covered.

Walter Vetterick

Alison Perry's Favorite Pigs in a Blanket

2 cups plus 2 tablespoons all purpose flour
1 cup (2 sticks) butter, firm
1 (8 ounce) package cream cheese, firm
1 package Oscar Mayer Beef Smokies

Place flour, butter and cream cheese in bowl of food processor and process until a dough is formed. Remove from food processor, shape into a ball and wrap in wax paper. Chill. (Can be made several days in advance). Cut smokies into bite-sized pieces. Set aside. On lightly floured surface, roll out small portions of the dough at a time - keep remaining dough refrigerated until needed. Roll dough to about 1/4 inch thickness. Cut pastry into several 1-1/2x1 inch squares. Place smokie pieces on pastry squares and roll up. Put the "pigs" on an ungreased baking sheet and bake at 375 degrees until golden brown. Note: This pastry is extremely versatile. Makes a great pie crust. Also, can be filled with an array of goodies — including sweet things, such as preserves. Almost anything goes — be creative!

Shirin Shiekh Blackwell

Rye Rounds

2 ounces prosciutto ham, sliced thin
2 ounces mozzarella cheese
1/3 cup Parmesan cheese
1 cup mayonnaise
1 tablespoon brandy
1 tablespoon white wine
paprika
1 small loaf party rye bread, buttered and toasted

Dice ham and combine with mozzarella cheese, Parmesan, mayonnaise, brandy and wine. Spread on rye bread. Sprinkle with more Parmesan and paprika. Broil until hot, and serve.

Serves 8-10

Linda Stearns

Salmon Pate

1 (16 ounce) can salmon
1 (8 ounce) package cream cheese, softened
2 tablespoons chopped green onions
1 tablespoon lemon juice
1/2 teaspoon salt
1/8 teaspoon pepper
1/8 teaspoon dill weed
2 tablespoons capers

Remove skin and large bones from salmon. Blend all ingredients, except capers. Spoon mixture into a bowl and stir in capers. Refrigerate at least 3 hours before serving. Can be put together day before serving. Serve with crackers; I prefer Waverly.

Serves 8-10

Barbara Elstad

Sausage Appetizers

1 pound pork sausage
1 large onion, chopped
2 cups Bisquick
3/4 cup milk
2 eggs
1 tablespoon caraway or poppy seeds
1/2 cup sour cream
1/4 teaspoon salt
paprika

Cook sausage and onion; drain. Mix together the Bisquick, milk and one egg and spread in a greased 9 x 13 inch pan. Sprinkle seeds on sausage and onion mix and spread this mixture on top of Bisquick. Combine sour cream, salt and one egg and pour over sausage. Sprinkle with paprika. Bake in a 350 degree oven for 30 to 35 minutes; cool, cut into bite size squares.

Clara Dawson

Cheese Sausage Balls

1 pound Owens mild sausage
1 pound Cheddar cheese, grated
3 cups Bisquick

Mix all ingredients together. Make into balls. Bake at 350 degrees for 20 minutes. To make ahead, freeze on cookie sheet — drop into freezer bags and store in freezer until needed.

Louise Perlitz

Spirited Sausages

1 (14 ounce) bottle catsup
1 cup bourbon
1 cup dark brown sugar
1/2 cup minced onion
1 tablespoon yellow mustard
4 (8 ounce) packages of miniature sausages (or 2 (16 ounce) packages wieners cut in 1 inch chunks)

Mix first five ingredients in large saucepan, cover and simmer very slowly for about 15 minutes, stirring several times. Add sausages (or wieners) and simmer another 15 minutes until heated thoroughly. Spoon into chafing dish or other dish that can be kept warm. Use decorative toothpicks to serve.

Mark E. Shier

Salsa Mexicana

8 green peppers, chopped
1 onion, chopped
1 cup coriander
2 tomatoes, chopped
1/2 cup water
salt to taste

Place all ingredients in a bowl, add water and season with salt.

Mariam Rosas

Salsa Ranchera

2 tomatoes
3 green peppers
1 small onion, chopped
2 cloves garlic, or to taste
2 tablespoons oil
salt

Puree the tomatoes and the green peppers with the onion and garlic. Saute with oil until well cooked. Season with a pinch of salt.

Mariam Rosas

Shrimp Dip I

1 (8 ounce) package cream cheese
juice of 1 lemon
1/2 cup mayonnaise
1/4 cup catsup
1/2 cup chopped celery
1/4 cup chopped green onion
5 drops Tabasco sauce
white pepper
1 pound shrimp, boiled, peeled and chopped

Mix all ingredients together and refrigerate. Best made a day before ready to serve. Serve with crackers.

Serves 6

Linda Stearns

Shrimp Dip II

- 1-1/2 pounds shrimp, cooked, peeled and diced
- 8 ounces cream cheese, softened
- 1 teaspoon salt
- 1/2 teaspoon pepper
- 1 tablespoon grated onion
- 1 teaspoon garlic salt or garlic powder
- 1 tablespoon Worcestershire sauce
- 3 tablespoons mayonnaise
- dash of Tabasco sauce
- olives, parsley or whole shrimp for garnish

Combine all ingredients except garnish and serve with chips or fresh vegetables.

Lou Hilley

Shrimp Olive Dip

- 1 can cream of shrimp soup, undiluted
- 1 (8 ounce) package cream cheese, cut into chunks
- 1 (8 ounce) can chopped ripe olives, drained
- 2 tablespoons lemon juice
- 1 teaspoon Worcestershire sauce
- 3/4 teaspoon curry powder

Combine soup and cream cheese in a 1 quart casserole. Microwave covered for 4 minutes. Stir until cheese is well blended. Stir in remaining ingredients. Microwave covered for 2-3 minutes, or until piping hot. Place over a candle warmer to keep hot, and serve as a dip with corn chips.

Serves 2-1/2 cups

Ruth Tynes

Shrimp Remoulade Dip

- 4 tablespoons olive oil
- 2 tablespoons vinegar
- 1 teaspoon salt
- 2 teaspoons prepared mustard
- 6 green onions, minced
- 2 stalks celery, minced
- 1 teaspoon paprika
- few drops Tabasco sauce
- 3 sprigs parsley, minced
- 2 cups cooked shrimp

Beat oil, vinegar and salt together. Add next six ingredients and pour over shrimp. Let stand 4 hours.

Betty Lightsey

Spinach Balls I

2 (10 ounce) packages frozen chopped spinach
3 cups herb seasoned stuffing mix
1 large onion, chopped
6 eggs, well beaten
3/4 cup melted butter
1/2 cup grated Parmesan cheese
1 tablespoon pepper
1-1/2 teaspoon garlic salt
1/2 teaspoon thyme

Cook spinach according to package directions; drain well, squeezing out all liquid. Combine spinach and all remaining ingredients; mix well. Shape into balls and place on lightly greased cookie sheet. Bake at 325 degrees for 15-25 minutes.

Yield: 9 dozen

Dona Hinton

Spinach Balls II

2 (10 ounce) packages frozen spinach
4 eggs, beaten
1-1/2 sticks butter, softened
1/2 cup Parmesan cheese
2 cups herb stuffing mix
2 large onions, chopped
1/2 teaspoon thyme
1 tablespoon garlic salt
1/2 teaspoon pepper
1 jalapeno, minced (optional)
1 small jar pimentos, drained (optional)

Cook spinach and drain very dry. Mix with all the other ingredients. Roll into balls and bake 20 minutes at 350 degrees or bake as a casserole. Spray casserole with Pam. This is an easy, popular dish for entertaining.

Serves 8

Susan Scott

Pork-Shrimp Spring Rolls (Egg Rolls)

Pork-Shrimp filling:
3 tablespoons oil
1/2 pound pork, cut julienne
1/2 pound raw shrimp, shelled, deveined, and diced
8 water chestnuts, minced
8 thin scallions, sliced
1 tablespoon soy sauce
1 teaspoon salt
1 package spring rolls

Heat oil in a skillet. Cook the pork for 5 minutes stirring frequently. Add the shrimp, water chestnuts and scallions. Cook 4 minutes. Season with the soy sauce, and salt. Let cool 10 minutes. Place a tablespoon of the filling in the center of each pancake in an oblong pan. Fold in the opposite ends, then roll up. Heat the fat to 375 degrees just enough to fry a few rolls at a time. Drain, cut in thirds and serve hot with mustard or vinegar sauce.

Serves 9 spring rolls

Nelly and Maribel Orencia

Spinach Dip in Rye Bread

10 ounces frozen spinach
1 pint light sour cream
1 cup light mayonnaise
3/4 package Knorr dry leek soup
1 tablespoon dry Italian salad dressing mix
1/2 cup chopped parsley
1/2 cup chopped green onion
1 teaspoon dry dill weed
2 loaves round, unsliced Rye bread

Thaw, drain and squeeze water out of spinach. Mix all ingredients well, except bread. Chill at least 2 hours. Cut top off of one loaf of bread when ready to serve. Pull chunks (bite-size) of bread to hollow the loaf, leaving crust for serving bowl. Reserve chunks. May store bread in plastic bag for several hours before serving. Fill "bowl of crust" with dip and surround it with bread pieces. This is usually so popular that you will need to use a second loaf to satisfy the guests!

Serves 15-20

Betsy Mulligan

Chicken Spring Rolls (Egg Rolls)

Chicken Filling:
1 chicken breast
1 teaspoon cornstarch
1/2 teaspoon salt
1/2 teaspoon sugar
2 tablespoons soy sauce
2 tablespoons oil
3 scallions, chopped
1-1/2 cups bean sprouts
1/4 cup diced bamboo shoots
1 package spring rolls

Cut the chicken in as narrow as possible strips. Mix with cornstarch, salt, sugar, and 1 tablespoon soy sauce. Let stand 10 minutes. Heat 1 tablespoon oil in a skillet. Saute the scallions, bean sprouts, and bamboo shoots for 2 minutes. Season with the remaining soy sauce and remove from pan. Heat remaining oil in the skillet and saute the chicken 2 minutes. Return the vegetables and cook 2 minutes. Chill for 30 minutes. Place a tablespoon of the filling in the center of each spring roll wrapper. Fold in the opposite ends, then roll up. Heat the oil or fat to 375 degrees and fry a few rolls at a time. Drain, cut into thirds and serve hot with mustard and/or vinegar sauce.

Serves 4-5

Nelly and Maribel Orencia

Super Dip

1 can refried beans
2 cans frozen guacamole dip (defrosted)
1 can chopped black olives
tomatoes, chopped
green onions, chopped
Cheddar cheese, grated
nacho chips

Layer first 6 ingredients in order, in a shallow plate or pan. Use enough tomatoes and onions to cover one layer. Serve with nacho chips.

Jeanne Dean

Taco Dip

1 (8 ounce) package cream cheese
1 (8 ounce) carton sour cream
1 envelope taco seasoning mix
1/4 cup shredded lettuce
1 tomato, diced
1/4 cup shredded Cheddar cheese
1 large bag taco chips

Mix cream cheese, sour cream and taco mix in a bowl. Place in a mound at the center of a large plate. Cover with the shredded lettuce, tomato and cheese. Serve with the chips scattered on the plate surrounding the dip.

Elva Lopez

Tuna Beer Fondue

2 tablespoons butter or margarine
1/3 cup chopped onion
1/2 cup flour
1 cup milk
1 (12 ounce) container beer
1-1/2 cups (6 ounces) shredded Swiss cheese
1/2 cup grated Parmesan cheese
1 (6-1/2 ounce) can tuna in vegetable oil
1 teaspoon lemon juice
1/4 teaspoon salt
1/8 teaspoon pepper
1/8 teaspoon nutmeg
cubes of French bread

Melt butter or margarine in medium saucepan. Add onion and cook until tender. Gradually add the flour and mix over low heat. Stir in milk and beer. Cook until mixture thickens and comes to a boil, stirring constantly. Reduce heat and simmer for ten minutes, stirring frequently. Add the cheeses, tuna and seasonings and heat through. When thoroughly heated, transfer to a fondue pot and keep warm. Serve with cubes of French bread. The fondue can be prepared ahead and then reheated when you are ready to serve.

Serves 4

George Rimmey

Tofu-Peanut Butter Dip

6 ounces soft tofu
2/3 cup cottage cheese
2 tablespoons peanut butter
1 tablespoon honey
1 package sugar substitute
1 teaspoon vanilla
sprinkle of cinnamon to taste (optional)

Blend all ingredients until smooth. Use as dip with vegetables. Great!

Betty Griffith

Quick Tuna Dip

1 (7 ounce) can tuna
1 (8 ounce) package cream cheese, softened
1/2 cup sour cream
1 tablespoon fresh horseradish
2 tablespoons minced onion
1 clove minced garlic
1 teaspoon Worcestershire sauce

Mix all the ingredients and chill. Delicious and easy to serve with chips.

Bob Burrill

Mexican Spiced Walnuts

1 pound bag of walnut halves
1/4 cup vegetable oil
2 teaspoon chili powder
1/2 teaspoon ground cumin
1/2 teaspoon ground tumeric
pinch, cayenne pepper
salt to taste

In a large skillet combine vegetable oil with spices and cook over low heat until oil is hot. Turn heat off, add walnuts and stir until well coated. Remove walnuts to a shallow baking pan and bake in a 300 degrees oven 10 minutes or until walnuts are crisp. Sprinkle with salt. Pack in air tight containers.

Donna Murphy

SOUPS/SALADS

Avocado Soup

1 can chicken broth
2 medium avocados
1 thinly sliced onion
1/2 teaspoon salt
1/4 teaspoon cayenne pepper
1-1/2 cups milk
lime slices

Liquify the first 5 ingredients in a blender. Pour into a bowl and chill. Stir in 1-1/2 cups milk. Cover and chill. Serve with lime slices.

Serves 6

Dora Hughes

Bean Soup

1/2 bag dried beans
smoked ham bone
2 tablespoons margarine
1 can tomatoes (drained)
1 large onion (halved)
2 stalks celery (halved)
2 carrots (halved)
2 garlic cloves (minced)
1/2 cup wine (red)
Worcestershire sauce (to taste)
ham stock (see directions)
bouquet garni
salt, pepper

Soak beans 6-8 hours. Rinse, cover with cold water, bring to boil 10 minutes, cover and simmer 3/4 hour. Cover ham bone with water and simmer 1 hour (use for stock). Cool, remove bone, skim fat. In large soup pot melt margarine. Add 1 can tomatoes, onion, celery, carrots, garlic, 1/2 cup red wine, Worcestershire sauce, stock, bouquet garni, salt, pepper. Cook until almost tender. Cool. Blend in blender. Return to pot, add beans. Heat and serve.

Serves 6-8

Betsy Mulligan

Black Bean Soup

3-1/2 cups black beans
1-1/2 quarts chicken stock
1 large onion, finely chopped
2 large celery stalks, finely chopped
2 large carrots, finely chopped
1 cup green onions, chopped
4 cloves garlic, minced
2 tablespoons sweet basil
1/4 teaspoon dill weed
1/8 teaspoon brown sugar
salt and pepper to taste
sour cream
green onion tops

Soak beans for 1 hour; rinse. Combine beans with chicken stock and heat to boiling. When boiling, reduce heat and add all other ingredients. Simmer for 4 hours. Serve with rice; garnish with sour cream and green onion tops.

Serves 6-8

Jan Purzer Wallace

Bacon, Beer, and Cheese Soup

3/4 of a 2 pound Velveeta cheese, cubed
1 can Cheddar cheese soup
1 to 1-1/2 cups cream or milk
1/2 cup beer
4 slices bacon, chopped
1 large onion, chopped
4 stalks of celery, chopped
pepper
garlic powder

Saute onion, celery, and bacon. Drain grease and discard. Add to soup mixture. Season with pepper and garlic powder. Cook on low in a crockpot for 2 - 4 hours.

Serves 4

Dora Hughes

Puree of Carrot Soup

2 medium onions, chopped
2 tablespoons butter or margarine
1 tablespoon vegetable oil
1 pound carrots, chopped and peeled (use a food processor)
1 quart chicken stock (canned or homemade)
salt and white pepper to taste
parsley to garnish
croutons to taste

In a 3 quart saucepan, saute onions in butter and oil until golden. Add carrots and chicken stock. Simmer gently until carrots are very soft. Puree in food processor or blender. Return puree to saucepan and season to taste with salt and pepper. Add more broth to get desired consistency if needed. Serve hot with garnish. Note: Recipe can be doubled, using 4 cans of broth and 1 cup of water with 1 chicken bouillon cube to make 2 quarts.

Serves 3-4

J. W. Tilton

Cook pasta "al dente" which means when you bite into it there should be some resistance.

Cream of Carrot Soup

2 tablespoons butter
1-1/4 pounds carrots, scraped, trimmed and cut into 1/4 in rounds (about 4 cups)
1/4 pound potatoes, peeled and cut into 1/4 inch slices, (about 1/3 cup)
1 medium onion, peeled and cut into medium dice
4 cups rich chicken broth
1 cup water
1 bay leaf
salt and pepper to taste
1 cup heavy cream
1/8 teaspoon nutmeg (freshly grated)
pinch of cayenne

Heat the butter in a large saucepan and add the onion. Cook, stirring often until transparent. Add the carrots, potatoes, chicken broth, water, bay leaf, salt and pepper. Bring to a boil and then simmer for 20 minutes. Strain the solids and discard the bay leaf, reserving the liquid. Add the solids to container of food processor and blend to make a fine puree. Gradually add the strained liquid. Pour the mixture into a saucepan or mixing bowl and add the cream, nutmeg and cayenne. The soup may be reheated or chilled at this point and served hot or cold.

Serves 4

Bob Burrill

Onion and Carrot Soup

5 cups vegetable broth, made with carrots, onions, celery, leeks and turnips
5 large onions, sliced in 1/4 inch slices
2 tablespoons margarine
1 teaspoon honey
2 tablespoons flour
1/2 teaspoon dried thyme
3 medium carrots, sliced
Parmesan cheese for garnish

Prepare vegetable broth and set aside. Saute onions in margarine over low heat for 20 minutes. Add honey and flour and brown for 5 minutes. Add vegetable broth, thyme and carrots and simmer for about 30 minutes. Serve with sprinkling of Parmesan cheese.

Serves 6

Selma Gold

Cheesy Clam Chowder

2 (7 ounce) cans minced clams, reserve juice
1-1/3 cups water, including clam juice
2 chicken bouillon cubes
1/4 cup butter
1/4 cup chopped onion
3/4 cup chopped celery
1/4 cup flour
3 cups milk
1 cup shredded Monterrey Jack cheese
1 cup shredded Cheddar cheese
1 (16 ounce) can new potatoes, sliced
grated Parmesan cheese
chopped parsley

Drain clams; add enough water to clam liquid to make 1-1/3 cups. Heat to boiling and dissolve bouillon cubes. In large saucepan melt butter and saute onion and celery until tender. Blend in flour and cook 1 minute. Gradually add milk to bouillon mixture and cook, stirring until thick. Add clams, cheese and potatoes. Stir until cheese melts. Serve hot with topping of Parmesan cheese and parsley. Great with muffins or cornbread!

Serves 6

Kathy Blevins

Corn and Shrimp Soup, New Orleans Style

1/3 cup oil
3 tablespoons flour
2 medium onions, chopped
1 bunch green onions, copped
1 bell pepper, chopped
2 tablespoons parsley
1 pound peeled shrimp
1 (1 pound) can whole kernel corn, drained
1 (1 pound) can Ro-tel tomatoes, undrained
salt, black and red pepper to taste
1 cup water
1 cup whipping cream

Make a light tan roux with oil and flour in a Dutch oven. Add vegetables and saute until soft. Add shrimp and simmer until they turn pink (no more than 4 minutes) Add corn, Ro-tel tomatoes along with seasonings. Add water and cream. Let simmer on low heat at least one hour, adding more water gradually until desired consistency.

Serves 6

Claudette Perse

New England Fish Chowder

- 4 potatoes, diced
- 1 onion, diced
- 1 pound Haddock fillet
- 1 (12 ounce) can evaporated milk
- 12 ounces homogenized milk
- 1 tablespoon butter

Boil onion and potatoes together barely covered with salted water. When potatoes start to get soft, add fish, stirring once. Add canned milk, homogenized milk and butter. Simmer for 10-15 minutes.

Serves 6

Dianne Ibenthal

Florentine Cream Soup

- 1/4 cup butter or margarine
- 1/2 cup flour
- 4 cans (13-1/2 ounces each) chicken broth
- 1 medium onion, chopped
- 1 stalk celery, chopped
- 1/4 cup chopped parsley
- 1/4 teaspoon salt
- 2 packages (10 ounces each) frozen chopped spinach, cooked until thawed
- 2 egg yolks
- 1 cup heavy cream

In a saucepan melt butter and add flour; cook 2 minutes, stirring constantly. Add chicken broth and stir until smooth. Add onion, celery, parsley and salt and simmer until cooked, about 30 minutes. Skim fat, strain and discard vegetables. Add spinach. Beat egg yolks and heavy cream in a separate bowl. Stir in 1 cup soup to egg/cream mixture, then slowly add to soup, stirring constantly. Cook 3 minutes. DO NOT BOIL.

Serves 8

Ruth Crowe

Gazpacho

- 2 ripe tomatoes, peeled
- 1 cucumber, peeled
- 1/4 cup diced green pepper
- 1/4 cup diced onion
- 1 cup tomato juice
- 1 tablespoon olive oil or safflower oil
- 1-2 tablespoons cider vinegar
- liquid hot pepper sauce
- 1/4 teaspoon garlic
- dash of white pepper
- 1/2 teaspoon cumin
- 1/2 stalk celery

Boil tomatoes to loosen skin, cut tomatoes and cucumber into chunks; place all ingredients in blender. Run on high speed until mixture is as smooth as you like, not long. Chill at least 2 hours before serving. Garnish with lemon or lime slice. A dollop of sour cream is also good as well as a chunk of avocado.

Anne Clark

Gazpacho Soup

- 2 large cans tomato juice
- 3 peeled tomatoes
- 3 peeled and seeded cucumbers
- 3 green peppers
- 1-1/2 cups celery
- dash salt
- Tabasco sauce
- 1 carton sour cream

Finely chop all vegetables. Add to juice, season and refrigerate overnight. Top with sour cream.

Page Lawson

Mama Jean's Gumbo

- 1/2 pound sausage
- 1 pound shrimp
- 1 pound crab meat, flaked
- 1 pound crab claws or bodies
- 3 dozen oysters, at least
- 1/3 cup flour
- 1/2 cup drippings from sausage, bacon or butter
- 1 Hen or fat fryer
- 2 large onions
- bay leaves
- red pepper to taste
- 3 cloves garlic
- 4 stalks celery
- 2 small or 1 large bell pepper
- 2 (#303) cans tomatoes, drained
- 1 small can tomato paste
- 1 small bunch parsley
- 1 bunch of green onions
- 1 bag of frozen okra or 1 pound fresh
- 1 tablespoon Worcestershire sauce
- 1 teaspoon sherry pepper sauce
- Tabasco sauce to taste
- black pepper to taste
- 6-8 cups chicken stock

Cover hen with enough water to boil and have at least 6 to 8 cups of stock left. Add 3 bay leaves, black and red pepper. Boil until chicken falls off the bone. Remove and debone. Flake meat. Works great if you are short on seafood. Fry sausage, remove meat and add enough bacon drippings or butter to make 1/2 cup grease. When hot add flour and cook until the color of walnut wood, careful not to burn or it will taste bitter. Start over if necessary. Like Big Mom says "Practice makes Perfect." Add onions, garlic, bell pepper, parsley, green onions and cook until wilted. Add sausage, flaked chicken, oyster liquor, chicken stock, bay leaves, okra, canned tomatoes, tomato paste, red pepper, Tabasco, Worcestershire sauce, sherry pepper sauce and black pepper. Cook slowly at least 1/2 hour, longer is better. Simmer some of the liquid off to make room for seafood if necessary. This is where you need to taste and adjust to your liking. Add shrimp, oysters, crab meat, and claws. Cook 1/2 hour, no more. Let sit overnight if possible. This will ensure flavor of seafood will be at its peak. Just reheat as needed.

Anne Clark

Hearty Lentil Soup

- 1-1/2 cups dried lentils
- 5 slices bacon, finely chopped
- 1 cup chopped onions
- 1 cup diced carrots
- 2 cups chopped celery
- 1/2 clove garlic, finely chopped
- 2 cups diced raw potatoes
- 1/2 cup tomato puree
- 2 whole cloves
- 2 bay leaves
- 6 cups cold water
- 4 cups beef stock
- 1 tablespoon salt
- 1 teaspoon MSG (can omit)
- dash of pepper
- 2 tablespoons red wine vinegar
- 2 cups sliced garlic sausage
- 1 cup thinly sliced leeks

Cover lentils with water; soak overnight, then drain. Saute bacon in a 6-quart kettle. Add onions, carrots, celery and garlic. Cook for a few minutes. Add lentils, potatoes, tomato puree, cloves, bay leaves, water, beef stock, MSG, and pepper. Simmer, covered, for about 1-1/2 hours, or until lentils are tender. Add red wine vinegar, garlic sausage, leeks and additional salt and pepper to taste. Heat through and serve.

Serves 10-12

Karin Telfer

Meatball Soup

- 1-1/2 pounds ground beef
- 1/4 cup Parmesan cheese
- 2 slices bread, soaked in water and squeezed almost dry
- 1 small onion, minced
- 2 eggs
- 1/2 teaspoon salt
- 1/4 teaspoon pepper
- 1/4 teaspoon basil
- 1/4 teaspoon parsley
- 1/4 teaspoon oregano
- 1 clove garlic, minced
- 1 can beef broth
- 1 can chicken broth
- dried parsley flakes, if desired

Combine all ingredients except beef broth, chicken broth and dried parsley. Shape into 1 inch balls. Heat broths together and bring to a boil. Add meatballs a few at a time so that broth does not stop boiling. After all the meatballs have been added, reduce heat, cover pot and let soup simmer 30 minutes. Add more seasoning and dry parsley if desired. Additional water can be added to broth if necessary.

Serves 4.

Lou Bruno

Mushroom Bisque

- 1 pound fresh mushrooms, sliced
- 1 small onion, chopped into 8 pieces
- 3 tablespoons butter or margarine
- 1/4 cup flour
- 2 cups Half & Half
- 1/3 cup chopped chives
- 2 tablespoons Brandy
- Salt to taste

Simmer mushrooms and onions in enough salted water to cover for 1/2 hour or until tender. Puree the liquid and vegetables in blender. Melt the butter or margarine in large saucepan. Gradually add the flour and mix until smooth over low heat. Slowly add the Half & Half, stirring constantly. Continue cooking until mixture is thick and smooth. Add the puree, chives and brandy. Reseason with salt, about 1/2 teaspoon. Heat before serving, but do not boil.

Serves 6

George Rimmey

Mushroom Cheese Soup

- 4 cans cream of mushroom soup
- 2 cups Half and Half
- 2 cups homogenized milk
- 8 ounces sour cream
- 8 ounces Velveeta cheese, cubed
- 1/2 teaspoon cayenne pepper
- 1 pound fresh mushrooms, trimmed and sliced
- 1/4 cup dry white wine

Combine soup, Half and Half, milk, sour cream, Velveeta and pepper. Stir well. Cook over medium heat until cheese is melted, stirring constantly. Stir mushrooms into soup mixture. Cook over low heat for 20-30 minutes stirring frequently. Add wine and serve. For advance preparation, omit last step. Let soup cool and refrigerate. Reheat and add wine before serving. To save calories use skim milk instead of Half and Half and homogenized milk. Use light sour cream.

Serves 8

Karen Ortegon

If you have no reason to throw a party, it's fun to think of one — the first tomato in your garden, the last day of summer, a friend's birthday, your baby's first tooth, your mother-in-law has just left after a 2 week visit, etc.

Peanut Butter Pumpkin Soup

4 tablespoons unsalted butter
4 cups pumpkin pie filling
2 cups pureed sweet potatoes, 3 large potatoes baked and skinned
1 cup smooth peanut butter
6 cups chicken broth
1 teaspoon ground pepper
1/2 teaspoon salt
sour cream
chives

Melt butter in soup pot over medium heat. Stir in pie filling, pureed sweet potatoes and peanut butter. Add broth, pepper and salt. Stir well. Reduce heat and simmer 20 minutes. Garnish with a blob of sour cream on top of each serving, and a liberal sprinkling of chives. No one will ever guess that one of the ingredients is a cupful of peanut butter! Bet $10.00. If you win, send 1/2 of your winnings to VEPS!

Serves 12

George Vietor

Split Pea Soup

1 package dried split peas
3 quarts water
4 carrots
4 stalks celery
3 medium onions
3 beef bouillon cubes
4 slices uncooked bacon, optional
2 tablespoons chopped parsley
2 cloves garlic
salt and pepper to taste

Place peas in a colander and wash under running cold water. Place all ingredients in a large soup pot and bring to a boil. Lower heat to medium low, cover and cook for 2-1/2 hours. Process all ingredients in a food processor or blender. Return to soup pot and season with salt and pepper. Serve plain or with sliced hot dogs or croutons.

Serves 8 to 10

Estelle Kastleman

When choosing appetizers, be sure that they won't be too filling, since they are meant to stimulate, not dull the appetite.

Sunny Splits Soup

1/2 cup green split peas
1/2 cup yellow split peas
1/2 cup red lentils
8 cups water
1/2 teaspoon caraway seed
1 onion, thinly sliced
2 stalks celery, cut 1/2 inch diagonal slices
2 carrots cut in 3/4 inch chunks
3 medium size Jerusalem artichokes cut in 1 inch chunks
1/2 teaspoon salt
roasted sunflower seeds

Rinse peas and lentils to remove surface dirt. Soak beans in water up to 8 hours. Soak beans in refrigerator if weather is hot. Using same soaking water, bring beans to a boil and skim off any foam that accumulates. Add caraway, onions, celery and carrots. Reduce heat and simmer covered for about 1 hour. Add artichokes and salt to taste. Simmer an additional 10 minutes until artichokes are tender, crisp. Garnish soup with sunflower seeds.

Serves 6

Selma Gold

Tortilla Soup

2 small onions, chopped
2 (4 ounce) cans chopped green chiles, drained
2 cloves garlic, crushed
2 tablespoons vegetable oil
1 cup peeled and chopped tomatoes
1 (10-1/2 ounce) can condensed beef bouillon
2 cups shredded chicken
1 (10-1/2 ounce) can condensed chicken broth
1-1/2 cups water
1-1/2 cups tomato juice
1 teaspoon ground cumin
1 teaspoon chili powder
1 teaspoon salt
1/8 teaspoon pepper
2 teaspoons Worcestershire sauce
1 tablespoon bottled steak sauce
3 corn tortillas, cut in 1/2 inch strips
1/4 cups shredded Cheddar cheese
sour cream
avocado wedges

Saute onion, chilies and garlic in oil until soft. Add tomatoes, bouillon, chicken, chicken broth, water, tomato juice, cumin, chili powder, salt, pepper, Worcestershire and steak sauce. Bring soup to a boil, lower heat and simmer covered 1 hour. Top with fried tortilla strips, cheese, sour cream and avocado wedges.

Leslie Friedman

Cheesy Vegetable Chowder

- 1/2 cup chopped onion
- 1 clove garlic, minced
- 1 cup sliced celery
- 3/4 cup sliced carrots
- 1 cup cubed potatoes
- 3-1/2 cups chicken broth
- 1 can (17 ounce) whole kernel corn, drained
- 1/4 cup butter or margarine
- 1/4 cup all-purpose flour
- 2 cups milk
- 1 tablespoon prepared mustard
- 1/4 teaspoon white pepper
- 1/8 teaspoon paprika
- 2 tablespoons diced pimento
- 2 cups (8 ounces) shredded Cheddar cheese

Combine first 6 ingredients in a large Dutch oven; bring to a boil. Cover, reduce heat, and simmer 15 to 20 minutes or until potatoes are tender. Stir in corn; remove from heat. Melt butter in a heavy saucepan over low heat; add flour, stirring until smooth. Cook 1 minute, stirring constantly. Gradually add milk; cook over medium heat, stirring constantly, until thickened and bubbly. Stir in remaining ingredients. Cook just until cheese melts, stirring constantly. Gradually stir cheese mixture into vegetable mixture. Cook over medium heat, stirring constantly, until thoroughly heated. Serve immediately.

Yield 2 quarts

Sr. Alice Potts

Chicken Vegetable Soup

- 4 quarts water
- 1 (2 pound) fryer, cut into serving size pieces
- 1 can tomato soup
- 4-6 carrots, peeled and sliced
- 6 stalks celery, sliced
- 1 onion, sliced
- 2 potatoes, cubed OR 1/2 cup uncooked rice
- cauliflower and/or any other vegetables of your choice
- juice of 1/2 lemon
- 1 tablespoon sugar
- Salt and pepper to taste

Bring chicken to a boil and skim surface foam (I prefer to remove skin and fat from chicken before boiling it). When surface is clear of foam, add tomato soup and all other ingredients. Cook for about 1 hour.

Serves 10-12

Rosine Chappell

Country Turkey Soup

- 1 onion, chopped
- 1 clove garlic, minced
- 1 pound cooked turkey, cut in chunks
- 3 cups water
- 1 can tomatoes
- 1 can cream of tomato soup
- 1 can red kidney beans
- 1/2 head cabbage, chopped
- 3 carrots, sliced
- 3 stalks celery, sliced
- 2 tablespoons rice
- 2 chicken bouillon cubes
- 2 teaspoons salt
- 1/4 teaspoon pepper
- 1 bay leaf
- 1/2 teaspoon thyme

In 2 or 3 quart pan cook onion and garlic until onion is transparent. Add remaining ingredients and mix well. Stir for 30 minutes or until vegetables are done.

Serves 6 to 8

Linda Stearns

Zucchini Soup (Cold)

- 5-6 small to medium size zucchini
- 1 large onion, peeled and thinly sliced (about 1 cup)
- 1-1/2 teaspoons curry powder, or to taste
- 3 cups chicken broth
- 1 cup heavy cream
- 1/2 cup milk
- salt and freshly ground pepper
- chives or scallions, finely chopped

Cut 1 cup zucchini into match-like strips. Place in saucepan and cold water to cover. Boil 3-4 minutes. Drain and set aside. Cut remaining zucchini into 1-2 inch pieces and place in heavy kettle. Add onion, curry powder and chicken broth. Stir; bring to a boil, then simmer covered about 45 minutes. Blend this mixture in a blender (should be about 4 cups). Add cream, milk, salt and pepper. Add zucchini strips. Chill thoroughly, covered. Before serving sprinkle with chives.

Serves 4 to 6

Helen Harbeson

Zucchini Soup

- 3-4 medium zucchini
- 1 cup chicken broth
- 1 large onion, chopped
- 1/4 pound corn oil margarine
- 1 can mushroom soup
- 1 cup milk
- salt and pepper to taste

Cook zucchini until barely tender in chicken broth. Saute onion in margarine. Dump everything in a blender and puree. Can be thinned with milk if too thick. Good hot or cold.

Serves 4

Karen Harrison

Hawaiian Ambrosia

6 oranges, peeled and diced
4 bananas
1 can (#2-1/2) pineapple chunks
1 cup coconut
1 small jar maraschino cherries
1/4 cup granulated sugar, or to taste
1/2 cup slivered almonds or finely chopped walnuts

Combine peeled and diced oranges, sliced bananas and pineapple chunks. Add remaining ingredients and stir gently. Cherry juice may be added for coloring as well as for flavoring.

Helen Harbeson

Apricot Pecan Salad

1 (20 ounce) can crushed pineapple
1 (8 ounce) package cream cheese, softened
1/2 cup chopped pecans
1 (3 ounce) package apricot gelatin
1 large jar apricot baby food
1-1/3 cups frozen Cool Whip, thawed

Combine all ingredients and chill.

Lynn Miller

Beet Salad Mold

1 large can beets
1 package (6 ounce) lemon gelatin
2 cups boiling water
1 teaspoon horseradish
1 tablespoon white vinegar
1/8 teaspoon salt

Blend beets, with juice, in blender until very fine. Set aside. Combine gelatin with boiling water and then add all other ingredients, including beets, to gelatin. Mix well and pour into greased mold or 8x8 pyrex dish.

Serves 8-10

Selma Leff

For decorative cucumber slices, score unpeeled cucumber lengthwise with the tines of a fork and then slice.

Blueberry Salad I

Salad:

- 1 large (6 ounce) box raspberry jello
- 1 cup boiling water
- 1 large can blueberries with juice
- 1 small can crushed pineapple with juice

Prepare jello with fruit and water in usual manner. Let set.

Topping:

- 1 (8 ounce) package cream cheese, softened
- 1 (8 ounce) sour cream
- 1/2 cup sugar
- 1 teaspoon vanilla
- chopped pecans

Blend first 4 ingredients and spread over the set jello. Chill again. Sprinkle with pecans before serving. This is a little unusual but very delicious and nice for a luncheon or supper. Easy to make ahead; easy to serve.

Serves 8

Susan Scott

Blueberry Salad II

- 2 (3 ounce) packages black raspberry jello
- 2 cups boiling water
- 1 (20 ounce) can crushed pineapple, undrained
- 1 can blueberry pie filling

Topping:

- 1/2 cup sour cream
- 1 (8 ounce) package cream cheese, softened
- 1/4 cup sugar
- 1 teaspoon vanilla
- 1/2 cup chopped pecans

Dissolve jello in water. Add pineapple and pie filling. Mix together, put into bowl and refrigerate. After it has congealed spread with topping. To make topping mix sour cream, cream cheese, sugar and vanilla together; spread on top of salad. Sprinkle top with chopped pecans.

John Gardner

Broccoli-Cauliflower Salad

- 1 bunch broccoli
- 1 head cauliflower
- 4 fresh green onions, chopped
- 1 cup mayonnaise
- 2 tablespoons vinegar
- 2 tablespoons sugar

Finely chop broccoli and cauliflower, or break into tiny sprigs. Add chopped green onions. Combine mayonnaise, vinegar and sugar. Mix all together and refrigerate several hours.

Serves 8-10

Jean Alloway

Broccoli and Cauliflower Salad

1 pound broccoli, flowerettes only
1-1/2 cups cauliflower, broken into small pieces
1/2 pound mushrooms, sliced
1 bunch green onions, chopped
1/2 cup sugar
1/2 cup Mazola oil
2 tablespoons white vinegar
1 teaspoon celery seeds
3/4 teaspoon salt
1 teaspoon paprika

Combine first four ingredients in a large bowl. Mix together sugar, oil, vinegar, celery seeds, salt and paprika and pour over salad. Marinate overnight.

Serves 4-6

Kay Laro

Perfect Caesar Salad

3 cloves garlic
3 anchovy fillets, drained & minced
2 large egg yolks
1 tablespoon white wine vinegar
1-1/2 teaspoon Dijon mustard
1 teaspoon Worcestershire sauce
1/4 teaspoon salt
1-1/2 teaspoons fresh lime juice
3/4 cup extra virgin olive oil
2 heads romaine lettuce, washed, patted dry, & torn into bite size pieces
1/4 cup freshly grated Parmesan cheese (or more, to taste)
1 cup garlic croutons with thyme (recipe follows)

Mince & mash garlic cloves with anchovy fillets to form a paste. In a bowl, whisk together the garlic/anchovy paste, egg yolks, both vinegars, mustard, Worcestershire sauce, salt and lime juice. Add olive oil in a stream, constantly whisking until it is emulsified. In a wooden salad bowl toss the romaine with the Parmesan cheese and croutons. Add dressing and toss all to combine well.

Garlic Croutons with Thyme:
2 garlic cloves, halved
2 tablespoons butter
1 cup of 1/2" cubes of bread
1/2 teaspoon dried thyme, crumbled well

Rub a heavy skillet with the cut side of the garlic, and in same skillet cook garlic in butter over low heat, stirring for approximately 5 minutes or until garlic is golden brown. Discard garlic. Add bread cubes and thyme. Cook croutons until lightly toasted on all sides. Sprinkle croutons with salt to taste and drain on paper towels.

Serves 4-6

Beverly Loftis

Cabbage Slaw

- 1 small head cabbage, shredded thin
- 1 red onion, chopped
- 1 cucumber, chopped
- 1 yellow squash, chopped
- 1 green bell pepper, chopped
- 2 stalks celery, chopped
- 5-6 radishes, chopped
- 6 tablespoons salad oil
- 6 tablespoons white vinegar
- 1 teaspoon salt
- 1 scant tablespoon sugar or Sweet 'n Low

Mix first 7 ingredients together. Combine oil, vinegar, salt and sugar and pour over vegetables, mixing well. Refrigerate overnight.

Selma Leff

Mom's Most Requested Coleslaw Recipe

- 1 head of cabbage, chopped
- 4 green onions, chopped
- 3/4 cup sliced almonds
- 1/2 cup sesame seeds
- 1-1/2 cups Top Ramen noodles (about 2 packages), crumbled
- 1/2 stick butter
- 1 cup vegetable oil
- 1/3 cup rice wine vinegar (no substitutions)
- 1/2 cup sugar
- 1-1/2 teaspoons salt
- 1 teaspoon pepper

Mix together the cabbage and green onions, set aside. In a medium saucepan, saute the almonds, sesame seeds, noodles and butter until light golden brown. Set aside. In a shaker jar, combine the oil, vinegar, sugar, salt, and pepper. Just before serving the salad, combine all ingredients.

Shirin Shiekh Blackwell

Crunchy Cabbage Salad

- 1 medium head cabbage, shredded
- 6 teaspoons sesame seeds
- 1-1/2 packages Ramen noodles
- 1 small package slivered almonds

Dressing:

- 1/4 cup oil
- 1/3 cup vinegar
- 4 tablespoons sugar
- 1 teaspoon salt
- 1 teaspoon pepper

In dry skillet brown Ramen noodles (do not use the seasoning packet and do not boil first), almonds, and sesame seeds. The sesame seeds brown quickly, so it is a good idea to add them a little later and stir very frequently. Add the browned ingredients to the shredded cabbage. Pour all the dressing over the salad and mix well. Refrigerate.

Serves 10-12

Rebecca Phifer

Cherry Coke Salad

1 (#2) can Bing cherries, seeded and drained, reserving juice
1 (#2) can crushed pineapple, drained, reserving juice
2 cups fruit juice and water, combine reserved juices and add enough water to make 2 cups
1 (3 ounce) package black cherry gelatin
1 (3 ounce) package raspberry, strawberry or cherry gelatin
12 ounces cold coke
2 (3 ounce) packages cream cheese, softened
1 cup celery, finely diced
1 cup nuts, coarsely chopped
1/2 cup flaked coconut, optional

Heat fruit juices and water to boiling; pour over gelatin and stir until dissolved. Add coke; chill until slightly thickened. Break up or beat cream cheese and add to fruits and nuts; fold into gelatin and chill until firm.

Serves 12

Kathy O'Brien

Chicken Noodle Salad

2 whole chicken breasts, cooked, boned and cut into small chunks
1/2 large head cabbage, sliced
1 package Ramen noodle soup mix, chicken flavor
1/3 cup slivered almonds
1/4 cup sesame seeds

Dressing:
2/3 cup salad oil
1/8 cup sugar
1-1/2 teaspoons salt
1/4 cup rice vinegar

Combine chicken and cabbage. Break up noodles in small pieces and cook according to package directions. Add flavoring from soup mix, almonds and sesame seeds to chicken mixture. Mix dressing ingredients and pour over salad. Marinate overnight. Keeps well in refrigerator.

Serves 8

Joyce Mansen

Carrot Raisin Mallow Salad

3 cups shredded carrots
1-1/2 cups Kraft miniature marshmallows
2/3 cup raisins
1/2 cup Miracle Whip salad dressing
1/2 cup celery slices
1/4 cup coarsely chopped walnuts

Mix all ingredients together lightly and chill. Prep time 10 minutes plus chilling.

Serves 8-10

Marie Brown

Special Chicken Salad

- 6 chicken breasts
- 1 large can artichokes, drained and rinsed
- 1 can water chestnuts, drained and rinsed
- 1 can Chinese vegetables, drained
- 1 tablespoon celery, diced
- 1 tablespoon onion, chopped fine
- 1 teaspoon salt
- 1/2 cup Kraft Miracle Whip Salad Dressing (DO NOT SUBSTITUTE)
- 1/2 cup mayonnaise
- 1 teaspoon lemon juice
- lettuce (to be used when ready to serve salad)

Cook chicken, cool and cut into bite size pieces. Cut artichokes into quarters and slice water chestnuts. Mix all ingredients together EXCEPT Miracle Whip, mayonnaise and lemon juice. Combine these three together separately and add to chicken mixture. Refrigerate. Better if made a day ahead. Serve on lettuce. This salad is delicious and you'd never guess the ingredients!

Serves 8 and can easily be doubled

Jeanne Dean

Scheherazade Chicken Salad

- 2 cups diced, cooked chicken (or more)
- 1/2 cup brazil nuts, walnuts, or almonds
- 1/2 cup chopped celery
- 1/2 cup chopped fresh mushrooms
- chopped green pepper
- pimento
- 1/2 teaspoon lemon juice
- 1/2 teaspoon grated lemon rind
- 2 avocados, cut up
- salt and pepper to taste

Can have all ingredients chopped and mixed the day before, then add the avocado shortly before serving. Looks beautiful on lettuce, tomato or red cabbage.

Serves 6-8

Angela Wheat Cheves

Sweet and Sour Chicken Salad

Salad:
1 head romaine lettuce
2 chicken breasts, boiled & shredded
4 scallions, chopped
4 ounces fresh mushrooms, sliced
1 cup sliced almonds
1 cup Chinese chow mein noodles
Dressing (recipe follows)

Combine first 4 salad ingredients in a bowl. Chill. Make dressing. Just before serving toss salad with almonds, noodles and dressing. (Note: chicken is best if boiled in highly seasoned water containing celery tops, carrots, onions, basil, marjoram, parsley, sage, bay leaf, salt and pepper.)

Sweet & Sour Dressing:
3/4 to 1 cup sugar
1/2 cup apple cider vinegar
1 cup oil
1 teaspoon celery seeds
1 teaspoon paprika
dash of salt

Combine sugar and vinegar in saucepan. Bring to a boil. Remove from heat and add remaining ingredients. Mix well and chill.

Serves 4

Beverly Loftis

Cranberry Salad I

1 pound fresh cranberries
2 cups sugar
2 cups seedless grapes
1 cup chopped pecans
2 cups miniature marshmallows
1 cup heavy cream, whipped, or 2 cups thawed frozen whipped topping

Wash and drain cranberries. Grind in food processor or blender. Add sugar and refrigerate overnight (or at least 4 hours). Add grapes, pecans and marshmallows. Fold in whipped cream; refrigerate until serving time.

Serves 15. Note: recipe can be halved

Tim Lassiter

Cranberry Salad II

2 cups fresh cranberries
1-1/4 cups water
1 cup sugar
1 package (3 ounce) cherry jello
3/4 cup celery, chopped fine
1/2 cup chopped apple
1/4 cup nuts, chopped fine

Combine cranberries and water and bring to a boil; add sugar and boil for 5 minutes. Stir in jello; let cool. Add celery, apple and nuts. Chill until firm.

Serves 6-8

Marilyn Healy

Crab Salad Supreme

- 1 package frozen puff pastry shells
- 1 pound crab meat
- 1 cup finely chopped celery
- 2 tablespoons finely chopped green pepper
- 1 tablespoon minced onion
- 1 teaspoon lemon juice
- 6 pitted ripe olives
- 1/2 cup mayonnaise
- salt and pepper to taste

Prepare frozen puff pastry shells according to package directions. Combine remaining ingredients, tossing together lightly with fork. Taste for seasoning. Chill. Just before serving, generously fill warm pastry shells with salad. Garnish with whole olives. Serve with fruits in season.

Serves 6

Susan Scott

Cranberry Salad III

- 3 cups fresh cranberries
- 2 cups granulated sugar
- 1-3/4 cups liquid - can use water or pineapple juice
- 2 packages (3 ounces each) cherry or strawberry gelatin
- 1 cup crushed pineapple, drained
- 1 cup diced celery
- 1 cup chopped pecans

Boil cranberries, sugar and liquid for 7 minutes. Add gelatin, pineapple, celery and pecans. Mix well and refrigerate.

Selma Leff

Daiquiri Salad

- 1 cup boiling water
- 1 package (6 ounce) lime flavored gelatin
- 1 can (6 ounce) frozen limeade concentrate
- 1/2 cup ginger ale (approximately)
- 1 can (20 ounce) pineapple tidbits or chunks in juice, drained (reserve juice)
- 1/2 cup light rum
- salad greens
- honeydew melon balls

Pour boiling water on gelatin in 2 quart bowl. Stir until gelatin is dissolved. Stir in frozen limeade concentrate. Add enough ginger ale to reserved pineapple juice to equal 1-1/4 cups. Stir pineapple juice, ginger ale mixture and rum into gelatin mixture. Refrigerate until slightly thickened, about 1 hour. After thickened, stir in pineapple. Pour into 5 cup mold and refrigerate until firm, at least 3 hours. Unmold on salad greens. Garnish with melon balls. If desired serve with whipped topping.

Serves 8-10

Barbara Chester

Hot Fruit Salad

- 1 (16 ounce) can sliced pears
- 1 (16 ounce) can pineapple chunks
- 1 (16 ounce) can sliced peaches
- 1 (16 ounce) can apricot halves
- 3/4 cup pecans (broken)
- 1 small jar stemmed maraschino cherries
- 1-1/2 cups juice from fruit
- 1 cup brown sugar
- 2 tablespoons cornstarch
- 1/2 cup butter or margarine
- pinch of nutmeg and cinnamon

Drain all juice from canned fruit. Save 1-1/2 cups of juice. Pour all fruit into 9 x 13 baking dish. Place pecans and cherries on top of fruit. Heat juice, brown sugar, cornstarch, butter, and spices until well blended. Pour mixture over fruit and bake at 350 degrees for 30 minutes.

Serves 8-10

Kathy Blevins

Millionaire Salad

- 1 (11 ounce) can mandarin oranges, drained
- 1 cup flaked coconut
- 1/2 cup miniature marshmallows
- 1 cup diced pineapple
- 2 tablespoons commercial sour cream

Mix oranges, coconut, marshmallows, and pineapple. Moisten with sour cream and chill.

Yield 4 to 6 servings

Bet Lindgren

24-Hour Fruit Salad

- 2 eggs, well beaten
- 1/4 cup fresh lemon juice
- 2 tablespoons sugar
- dash of salt
- 1 cup whipping cream, whipped
- 2 cups miniature marshmallows
- 2 cups pineapple tidbits
- 2 cups pitted Royal Anne cherries, drained
- 1 cup seedless grapes, halved
- 1/4 cup chopped blanched almonds (optional)

Combine eggs, lemon juice, sugar and salt and cook over very low heat until thick (or cook in double boiler). Cool. Fold cream into cooled mixture. Fold in marshmallows, well-drained fruits and nuts. Chill 24 hours. Can be prepared well in advance of serving time and can also be served as a light dessert.

Makes 12 servings

Marilyn Healy
Ruth Tanner

Ice Cream Jello Salad

1 package red or lime jello
1 cup hot water
1 pint vanilla ice cream
1 small can of strawberries or crushed pineapple

Dissolve jello in hot water. Add vanilla ice cream: stir until blended. Chill until jello is partially congealed. Add fruit and chill until set.

Margo Cannom

Bea Rizer's Holiday Salad Mold

1 (6 ounce) package strawberry jello
1 cup boiling water
1 (10 ounce) package frozen sliced strawberries, thawed, drained, juice reserved
1 (12 ounce) can pineapple chunks, drained, juice reserved
1/2 cup white wine
1/2 cup chopped walnuts
1/2 pint sour cream

Dissolve jello in boiling water. Using drained juices from berries and pineapple, combine to fill 1 cup. Add to dissolved jello. Add wine and mix well. Blend in the strawberries, pineapple and walnuts. Pour 1/2 of the jello mixture into a 6 cup mold, refrigerate 2 hours or until set. Spread the sour cream over the molded jello. Top with the remaining 1/2 of jello mixture. Refrigerate until top layer is set.

Serves 8-10

Shirin Shiekh Blackwell

Jicama Salad

1 small jicama
1 small red bell pepper
1 small yellow pepper
2 small zucchini
1 small carrot
4 tablespoons peanut oil
3 tablespoons lime juice
salt
cayenne

Peel jicama. Finely julienne all vegetables. Toss all ingredients together in a mixing bowl and season to taste.

Serves 4-6

Selma Gold

Mandarin Salad

1/2 cup sliced almonds
3 tablespoons sugar
1/2 head red tipped lettuce
1/2 head romaine lettuce
1 cup chopped celery
2 whole green onions, chopped
1 (11 ounce) can mandarin oranges, drained
1 avocado

Dressing:
1/2 teaspoon salt
dash of pepper
1/4 cup vegetable oil
1 tablespoon chopped parsley
2 tablespoons sugar
2 tablespoons vinegar
dash of Tabasco sauce

In a small pan over medium heat, cook almonds and sugar, stirring constantly until almonds are coated and sugar dissolved. Watch carefully as they will burn easily. Cool and store in air-tight container. Mix all dressing ingredients and chill. Mix lettuces, celery and onions. Just before serving, add almonds, avocado and oranges. Toss with the dressing.

Tyrrell Hill

Mango Salad

4-6 firm, ripe mangoes
1 sweet onion, thinly sliced
4 fresh jalapenos, seeded and slivered
1/4 cup light oil
3/4 cup cider vinegar
salt and pepper, to taste
dash of sugar

To prepare mangoes: Cut a slice off each end. To peel, stand mango on larger flat end and cut from top to bottom in a rounded curve with a sharp knife. Cut flesh away from the flat, oval seed using the same technique: Slice from top to bottom in a rounded curve on either side of seed. Cut remaining slices from the sides; do not cut too close to seed. Slice mango, or cut in chunks. Combine mango and onion slices with jalapeno. Make a dressing by stirring the oil, cider vinegar, salt, pepper, and sugar together. Mix gently but well with mangoes. Let stand 2 hours or more before serving.

Serves 8

Leah Whitty

Pasta Salad I

1 (20 ounce) can Dole pineapple, chunks in natural juice
3 cups cooked spiral pasta
2 cups snow peas
1 cup each: sliced cucumber, red bell pepper, carrots, bean sprouts
1/4 cup cilantro or parsley
1/4 cup black olives sliced (optional)
1 can Starkist water packed tuna, (drained) or 1 cup cooked, cubed chicken or turkey
1/2 cup bottled Kraft fat-free Italian salad dressing

Drain pineapple, reserve 1/4 cup juice. Combine pineapple and reserved juice with remaining ingredients. Chill.

Serves 6 to 8

Sharon Pyle

Pasta Salad II

3-4 cloves garlic (or more), some to be minced and some to rub salad bowl
1 (12 ounce or 16 ounce) package elbow, shell or corkscrew macaroni
1 package Good Seasons Italian Dressing, mixed to directions
1 can artichoke hearts, drained and chopped
1 small can chopped mushrooms, drained
1 small can black olives, sliced
3-4 stalks celery, chopped
1 small cucumber, chopped
salt, pepper and seasoned salt to taste
1 small jar stuffed green olives
Parmesan cheese

Rub salad bowl generously with a clove or 2 of minced garlic. Set aside. Cook macaroni according to package directions, making sure not to overcook; drain. Put hot macaroni into salad bowl that has been rubbed with garlic. Add remaining ingredients and mix well but gently. Don't be afraid to use plenty of garlic and Parmesan cheese! Refrigerate. Better when made the day before.

Lou Bruno

Orange Salad

- **45 Ritz crackers, crushed**
- **3/4 cup sugar**
- **1/2 cup margarine, melted**
- **2 (9 ounce) containers Cool Whip**
- **1 (6 ounce) can frozen orange juice concentrate, thawed**
- **2 cans Mandarin oranges, drained**

Combine first 3 ingredients; reserve one-fourth of mixture to sprinkle on top. Layer the mixture on the bottom of a 9x13 inch pan. Combine Cool Whip, juice and oranges in a bowl, mix well and pour over crust. Sprinkle top with cracker mix that has been saved. Refrigerate a few hours. This can be used as a dessert, if desired.

Serves 12-18

Joyce Johnson

Frozen Peach Salad

- **3 cups peeled, crushed peaches**
- **2 cups miniature marshmallows**
- **1/2 cup crushed pineapple, drained**
- **1/4 cup maraschino cherries, quartered**
- **1/2 teaspoon almond extract**
- **1/8 teaspoon salt**
- **2 cups commercial sour cream**
- **few drops red food coloring**

Combine all ingredients. Spoon into an 8 inch square pan. Cover with foil and freeze; When ready to serve, cut into squares.

Yield 6 to 8 servings

Jane McFaddin

Crunchy Pea Salad

- **1/2 cup Hellman's Lite mayonnaise**
- **1/4 cup Kraft "Zesty" Italian Dressing**
- **1 cup celery, chopped**
- **1/4 cup red onion, chopped**
- **1 package frozen peas, thawed and drained**
- **8 slices cooked bacon, crumbled**
- **1/2 cup tomatoes, chopped**
- **1 cup cashew nuts, chopped**

Mix mayonnaise and "Zesty" dressing together. Set aside. Combine celery, onion and peas and mix lightly. Add dressing. Before serving add bacon, tomatoes and cashews and toss gently.

Serves 8

Bob Burrill

Artichoke Rice Salad

- 1 package chicken Rice-A-Roni
- 2 green onions, sliced
- 1/4 green pepper, chopped
- 8 pimento stuffed olives, sliced
- 2 jars (6 ounce each) marinated artichoke hearts
- 1/4 teaspoon curry powder
- 1/3 cup mayonnaise

Cook rice as directed on package. Put in bowl and add next 3 ingredients. Drain artichokes and reserve marinade. Combine marinade with curry powder and mayonnaise. Mix until blended. Add dressing and artichoke hearts to rice mixture. Mix lightly. Cover and refrigerate overnight. Serve cold.

Serves 10-12

Karin Telfer

Tally's Curried Wild Rice Salad

- 2 cups cooked wild rice
- 1/2 cup grated carrot
- 1/3 cup finely chopped green pepper
- 1/4 cup chopped green onions
- 6 pitted large black olives, sliced
- 2 tablespoons raisins
- 2 tablespoons cashew nuts or peanuts, chopped
- 1/2 cup reduced calorie mayonnaise
- 1/4 cup unsweetened crushed pineapple, undrained
- 1 tablespoon lemon juice
- 1 teaspoon curry powder
- lettuce leaves, if desired

Combine first 7 ingredients in a bowl. Combine mayonnaise, pineapple, lemon juice and curry powder; stir into rice mixture and chill. Spoon onto lettuce leaves, if desired.

Serves 6

Bob Burrill

Wilted Spinach Salad

- 1/2 pound fresh spinach
- 1/4 -1/2 head of lettuce
- 6 slices bacon, fried, drained and crumbled; reserve drippings
- 1/4 cup vinegar
- 2 tablespoons water
- 2 tablespoons sugar
- salt to taste

Wash, drain and break spinach and lettuce into salad bowl. Add vinegar, water, sugar, and salt to bacon fat in skillet. Bring to a boil and pour over spinach and lettuce. Toss and add crumbled bacon.

Marilyn Healy

Spinach Salad

Dressing:

1 cup vegetable oil
1/4 cup cider vinegar
1/2 cup sugar
1 tablespoon catsup
1 tablespoon Worcestershire sauce
1 teaspoon salt

Salad:

10 ounce package fresh spinach, torn into bite-size pieces
1 (8 ounce) can water chestnuts, drained and chopped
1/2 pound bacon, cooked and crumbled
6 fresh green onions, chopped

Combine dressing ingredients and refrigerate overnight. Place salad ingredients in large bowl and toss well. Serve with dressing.

Serves 12-15

Susan McClellan Gibbs

Grapefruit and Spinach Salad

Salad:

1-1/2 pounds fresh spinach
4 pink grapefruit (oranges can be substituted, if desired)
2 tablespoons crumbled Roquefort cheese
1/2 cup Sherry French Dressing
salt
cracked pepper

Dressing:

1 egg
1 teaspoon sugar
2 teaspoons salt
4 cups salad oil (half olive oil makes it even better)
1/2 cup vinegar
1/2 cup sherry
2 cloves garlic, barely crushed

Remove stems from spinach. Wash thoroughly and put in a closed plastic bag to crisp. This can be done the day before. Peel and section the grapefruit. Mix the Roquefort cheese with the dressing and toss with the spinach and fruit. Correct seasonings. Sprinkle with cracked pepper.

Serves 8.

To make dressing mix egg, sugar and salt together; add oil and vinegar alternately until all the oil is added, then drip sherry in slowly. Add garlic cloves, and store in a Mason jar until ready to use. Toss among any collection of salad greens you may find, and your salad will be a success! This dressing has a special affinity for Roquefort cheese also.

Makes 5 cups

Karin Telfer

Taco Salad

- **2 pounds ground beef**
- **1 head lettuce, shredded**
- **1 large package Nacho Cheese Dorito Chips**
- **1 pound Cheddar cheese, diced**
- **1 pound can Pinto beans, drained**
- **4 tomatoes, diced**
- **1 small jar stuffed olives**
- **1 onion, chopped**
- **3-4 avocados, chopped**
- **mayonnaise**
- **picante sauce**

Brown ground beef and set aside. Combine next 8 ingredients. Add ground beef to ingredients and chill. Just before serving, add just enough mayonnaise to hold salad together. Toss and serve with picante sauce.

Serves 20

Clara Dawson

Yummie Tortellini and Vegetable Salad

- **1 pound spinach or egg tortellini, filled with cheese**
- **1 envelope Lipton Vegetable Recipe Soup Mix**
- **1/2 cup Miracle Whip or mayonnaise**
- **1/4 cup vegetable oil**
- **1 tablespoon lemon juice**
- **1 teaspoon dried basil leaves**
- **1 tablespoon finely chopped parsley**
- **1/4 teaspoon pepper**
- **1/2 cup sliced green onions**
- **1/2 cup chopped tomato**

Cook tortellini according to package directions; drain and rinse with cold water until completely cool. Set aside. In medium bowl, blend vegetable soup mix, miracle whip, oil, lemon juice, basil, parsley and pepper. Toss with tortellini, green onions and tomato. Chill.

Yields about 4 cups of salad

Shirin Shiekh Blackwell

Tuna-Mac Salad

4 ounces elbow macaroni, cooked
1 (6-1/2 ounce) can solid white tuna in water, drained and chopped
2 hard boiled eggs, chopped
1 large stalk celery, diced
2 green onions, sliced (including tops)
chopped olives
2 tablespoons relish

Dressing:
3/4 cup Hellman's Real Mayonnaise
1 teaspoon Worcestershire sauce
1 teaspoon lemon juice
dash Tabasco sauce
1-1/2 teaspoons prepared mustard
dash dill weed, paprika, pepper

Mix all salad ingredients in large bowl. In 2 cup measuring cup combine all dressing ingredients and blend well. Stir into salad and chill.

Serves 4

Catherine Arlinghaus

Cold Vegetable Salad

1 cup sugar
1 cup white vinegar
1/2 cup oil
1 can French style green beans
1 can LeSeur peas
1 can LeSueur white shoe peg corn
1 (4 ounce) jar sliced pimentos
1 medium green pepper, minced
1 cup celery, minced
1 bunch green onions, minced

Bring first 3 ingredients to a boil. Sugar must dissolve. Set aside. Drain green beans, peas, corn and pimentos. Put in bowl and toss gently. Add minced green pepper, celery and onions. Pour cooled salad dressing over vegetables and toss gently. Make day before — will last a week.

Eleanore Donnenworth

Zucchini Salad

5 medium zucchini, sliced very thin
1/2 cup celery, sliced
3 small sweet onions, sliced
2/3 cup sugar
1 teaspoon salt
1/2 cup salad oil
1/4 teaspoon pepper
1/2 cup cider vinegar
1/8 cup wine vinegar

Mix and refrigerate at least 24 hours. Exact amounts of vegetables not important. May add different color bell peppers.

Serves 8

Peggy Walker

BREADS/ROLLS

Apple-Raisin Bread

3 cups chopped, unpared apples
3 cups all-purpose flour
2-1/2 cups sugar
1-1/4 cups vegetable oil
4 eggs, beaten
1 tablespoon plus 1 teaspoon vanilla
2 teaspoons ground cinnamon
1-1/2 teaspoons salt
1-1/2 teaspoons baking soda
1 teaspoon cloves
1/2 teaspoon baking powder
2/3 cup raisins
1/2 cup chopped nuts

Heat oven to 325 degrees. Generously grease bottoms of 2 baking pans, 9x5x3 inches. Beat all ingredients on low speed, scraping bowl constantly, 1 minute. Beat on medium speed 1 minute. Pour batter into pans. Bake 1 hour or until wooden pick inserted in center comes out clean. Cool 10 minutes, then remove from pans to cool completely before slicing. Store in refrigerator.

Anita Chin

Banana Nut Bread - LOOK! - NO EGGS!

1/4 cup (4 tablespoon) melted margarine
3-5 large ripe bananas
1 cup sugar
1-1/4 cups flour
1 teaspoon baking soda
1/2 teaspoon salt
1/2 cup pecans, chopped

Melt margarine in a loaf pan. Mash bananas; add sugar and melted margarine. Mix well. Stir the dry ingredients together and add to banana mixture, mixing well. Add chopped pecans. Pour batter into loaf pan which is already greased from the melted margarine. Bake 1 hour and 25 minutes. Test with toothpick. Let bread sit a few minutes before removing from pan. Cut and eat — "guaranteed" to be the best!

Thommye Stewart

Mom's Banana Bread

1-3/4 cups flour
2 teaspoons baking powder
1/4 teaspoon baking soda
2 teaspoon salt
1/3 cup shortening
2/3 cup sugar
2 eggs
1 cup mashed bananas (about 3)

Mix all ingredients together and pour into greased loaf pan. Bake at 350 degrees for 1 hour.

Dianne Ibenthal

Beer Bread I

1 (12 ounce) can of Coors beer (open 30 minutes ahead — set at room temperature)
3 cups self-rising flour
3 tablespoons sugar (generous)

Mix ingredients together and pour into greased loaf pan. Bake at 400 degrees for 45 minutes to one hour. Set for 20 minutes.

Dora Hughes

Beer Bread II

1 stick corn oil margarine
1 warm beer
3 cups self rising flour
1/4 cup sugar
sesame seeds, optional

Grease loaf pan with end of margarine stick, then melt and set aside. Combine the rest of the ingredients and beat until smooth. Place in loaf pan and drizzle melted margarine over the top. Bake 350 degrees for 1 hour. If desired, add sesame seeds to top before baking.

Karen Harrison

Bubble Bread

1 package (24 count) frozen dinner rolls
1 small package (3 ounce) regular butterscotch pudding, not instant
1 cup brown sugar
1/4 cup granulated sugar
1 teaspoon cinnamon
1/2 cup melted butter
1/2 cup chopped nuts

Place frozen rolls in a bundt pan. Combine pudding mix with brown sugar and pour over rolls. Combine granulated sugar with cinnamon and sprinkle over pudding mixture. Pour melted butter over all and sprinkle with chopped nuts. Let stand overnight. Do not cover. Bake at 350 degrees for 30 minutes. Turn out on plate.

Serves 8

Linda Stearns

"He remains a fool his whole life long,
Who loves not women, wine and song."
—Martin Luther

Cheese & Chili Cornbread

3 ears fresh corn
1 cup yellow cornbread
1 teaspoon salt
1-1/2 teaspoons baking powder
1 cup sour cream
3/4 cup melted butter
2 eggs, beaten
1/4 pound Monterey Jack cheese
1 (4 ounce) can peeled green chilies

Scrape kernels from corn. Cut cheese into fine pieces. Drain and rinse chilies and chop. Combine all ingredients and mix well. Bake in greased 9x9 pan at 350 degrees for an hour or until set.

Yield 6-8 servings

Leslie Friedman

Jalapeno Cornbread

3 cups self-rising cornmeal
1 teaspoon salt (omit if cornmeal contains salt)
2 teaspoons baking powder
1 cup vegetable oil
3 eggs
1-1/2 cups milk
1 onion, chopped
2 tablespoons chopped jalapeno peppers
1 cup whole kernel corn, canned
1-1/2 cups grated Cheddar cheese

Preheat oven to 350 degrees. Grease muffin tins. In a bowl combine cornmeal, salt and baking powder. In a separate bowl, stir together the oil, eggs and milk. Quickly stir the liquid ingredients into the dry ones, mixing only until everything is moist. Stir in onion, jalapeno, corn and Cheddar. Evenly divide into prepared muffin tins. Bake until bread rises and turns brown, about 20 to 25 minutes.

Makes 18 muffins

Jane McFaddin

Mexican Corn Bread

2 eggs
2/3 cup cooking oil
1 cup sour cream
1 cup yellow cornmeal
1 cup yellow creamed corn
1 tablespoon baking powder
1-1/2 tablespoons baking powder
1-1/2 teaspoons salt
4 jalapeno peppers, seeded and finely chopped
1 cup grated sharp cheese

Combine eggs, oil, sour cream, cornmeal, corn, baking powder and salt. Add chopped peppers and half of the cheese. Spread in well-greased baking pan (12x8x2 inch) and cover with remaining cheese. Bake in 425 degree oven for 20-25 minutes.

Serves 8-10

Tyrrell Hill

Baking Powder Biscuits

2 cups sifted flour
3 teaspoons baking powder
1 teaspoon salt
1/3 cup oil
2/3 cup milk

Sift dry ingredients together. Combine oil and milk in mixing bowl. Add dry ingredients and mix together. Drop by spoonfuls onto baking sheet and bake at 400 degrees 12 to 15 minutes.

Dixie Talley

"Splendid" Ice Box Ginger Bread (because Mother said so!)

1 cup butter or margarine
1 cup sugar
4 eggs
1 cup molasses
2 teaspoons baking soda
1 cup buttermilk
4 cups flour
1/4 teaspoon allspice
1/4 teaspoon cinnamon
2 teaspoons (level) ginger
1 cup pecans, chopped
1/2 cup raisins (optional)

Cream butter and sugar. Add eggs, one at a time, and beat thoroughly. Add molasses; beat well. Add baking soda to buttermilk. Mix flour with spices. Add milk mixture and flour mixture alternately to batter. Mix well. Add pecans and raisins (if desired). This fills a large mixing bowl. Cover with wax paper and refrigerate; it will keep for a long time. When ready to bake I use small muffin tins (so great for a party or "drop ins"). Bake at 400 degrees 15 to 20 minutes. Large tins can also be used if desired.

Makes about 6 dozen small muffins

Thommye Stewart

Lemon Bread

1 cup sugar
1/2 cup shortening
1/8 teaspoon salt
2 eggs, beaten
1/2 cup milk
1-1/2 cups flour, sifted
1 teaspoon baking powder
3/4 cup nuts, finely chopped
grated lemon rind
1/2 cup sugar
juice of 1 lemon

Cream sugar, shortening and salt. Add eggs. Fold in milk, flour sifted with baking powder, nuts and lemon rind. Pour batter into a greased and floured loaf pan and bake in 350 degree oven for 45 minutes. Cool 5 minutes. Pour over mixture of 1/2 cup sugar and lemon juice. Let stand overnight.

Marilyn Healy

Buttermilk Biscuits

2 cups all purpose flour
2 tablespoons sugar
3 teaspoons baking powder
1 teaspoon salt
1/2 teaspoon baking soda
1/2 cup REAL butter, chilled
1 cup buttermilk

Heat oven to 450 degrees. In a medium bowl, stir together flour, sugar, baking powder, salt and baking soda. With a pastry blender cut in the butter until consistency of coarse crumbs. Add buttermilk and stir to mix. Turn onto a lightly floured work surface and knead three or four times. Roll dough to about 3/4 inch thickness. Cut with a 2-1/2 inch biscuit cutter dipped in flour. Bake on an ungreased cookie sheet for 12 to 15 minutes or until golden. Variations: Brush with melted butter before baking. Brush with melted butter and sprinkle with poppy or sesame seeds. Cut rolls in half, before baking, sprinkle with bacon bits, and gently press the top back on. To freeze biscuits, prepare but do not bake, and place in a single layer on a cookie sheet and freeze; when frozen, put into zip-loc bags and keep frozen until ready to use — then bake at 425 degrees for 15 to 18 minutes.

Yields 12 biscuits

Shirin Shiekh Blackwell

Monkey Bread

3 cans biscuits
1/2 cup sugar
1 tablespoon cinnamon
1 stick margarine or butter
1 cup brown sugar
2 teaspoons water
1/2 cup chopped pecans
3/4 cup raisins, optional (added to melted butter and sugar)

Cut biscuits into quarters. Combine sugar and cinnamon. Roll biscuits in sugar and cinnamon. Put into greased bundt pan. In saucepan, melt margarine and add brown sugar and water. Boil 2 minutes and pour over biscuits. Add pecans. Bake at 350 degrees for 25 minutes. Let cool for 10 minutes and unmold. Great with fruit and omelet for breakfast!

Serves 8

Kathy Blevins

Pull Apart Bread

1/2 cup pecan sprinkles
24 count Rich's frozen dinner rolls
1 box regular butterscotch pudding mix (not instant)
1/2 cup butter or margarine
1/2 cup brown sugar
cinnamon

Scatter pecans in bottom of well greased bundt pan. Add dinner rolls. Sprinkle pudding mix over rolls. Melt butter, add brown sugar and cinnamon. Pour over rolls in pan. Cover pan with towel and let stand over night in warm place. They will rise to top of pan or above. Next morning bake 25-30 minutes at 350 degrees. Don't underbake. Cover with foil last 10 minutes. Remove from oven and brush lightly with melted butter. Let stand 10 minutes before turning pan upside down on serving plate.

Serves 12

Walter E. Vetterick

Onion Muffins

1 cup self-rising flour, sifted
1 tablespoon mayonnaise
1/2 cup milk
1/2 cup chopped onion

In a large mixing bowl combine all ingredients and beat until almost smooth. Grease 8 muffin tins and fill 1/2 full with the batter. Bake in preheated 450 degree oven for 8-10 minutes.

Makes 8 muffins.

Lea Jones

Sour Cream Muffins

2 cups self rising flour
1 cup butter, melted and cooled
1 cup sour cream

Mix ingredients with a fork. Drop into ungreased muffin tins and bake in a preheated 400 degree oven for 20-25 minutes or until brown around sides and top. If using small muffin tins, reduce cooking time to 15 minutes. Make a bunch — they vanish fast!

Yield 12 regular or 24 small muffins

Louise Perlitz

Strawberry Surprise Muffin

- 1 cup buttermilk
- 1 cup rolled oats, uncooked
- 1 egg
- 1/4 cup honey
- 3/4 cups shredded coconut
- 1 cup whole wheat pastry flour
- 1-1/2 teaspoons baking powder
- 1/2 teaspoon baking soda
- 1/2 teaspoon salt
- strawberry preserves

Preheat oven to 400 degrees and grease muffin pans. Blend together milk and oats and let stand 30 minutes. Add egg, honey, and coconut, blending thoroughly. Blend dry ingredients together in a separate bowl. Add to liquid ingredients, just until mixed. DO NOT overmix. Fill muffin cups about half full. Place a scant teaspoon of jam in center of each muffin. Cover preserves with a dab of batter. Bake for 20 minutes. Cool 5-10 minutes before removing from pan.

Yield 10 medium muffins

Kathy Blevins

Pumpkin Muffins

- 2/3 cup instant nonfat dry milk
- 2 teaspoons pumpkin pie spice
- 1 teaspoon cinnamon
- 8 packages "Sweet and Low" (NOT EQUAL)
- 6 tablespoons flour
- 1 teaspoon baking soda
- 2 eggs, beaten
- 1 teaspoon vanilla
- 1 cup pumpkin
- 1/2 cup grated carrots
- 2 tablespoons raisins
- 2 tablespoons crushed pineapple

In medium bowl, combine dry ingredients. Set aside. In large bowl combine eggs, vanilla and pumpkin. Mix well. Add dry ingredients, carrots, raisins and pineapple. Divide dough evenly between 12 non-stick muffin tins. Bake at 350 degrees for 15 minutes.

Betty Griffith

Whole Wheat Muffins

- 2 cups whole wheat flour
- 2 teaspoons baking powder
- 1/2 teaspoon salt
- 1 egg, beaten
- 1/4 cup vegetable oil
- 1/4 - 1/2 cup honey
- 1 to 1-1/2 cups milk

Combine dry ingredients. Combine wet ingredients in another bowl. Fold wet into dry until moistened. Spoon into non-stick muffin tins, filling cup 1/2 the way. Bake at 400 degrees, about 20 minutes.

Serves 12 muffins

Betsy Mulligan

Sunshine Muffins

1 orange
1/2 cup orange juice
1 egg
1/4 cup oil
1-1/2 cups flour
3/4 cup sugar
1 teaspoon baking powder
1 teaspoon baking soda
1 teaspoon salt
1/2 cup raisins (optional)
1/2 cup chopped nuts (optional)

Cut orange into 8 pieces. Put cut orange (yes, the whole thing!), orange juice, egg and oil in blender and blend until smooth. In large mixing bowl combine flour, sugar, baking powder, soda and salt. Add orange mixture and blend well. Add raisins and nuts if desired and blend just until mixed. Pour batter into muffin tins and bake at 375 degrees 15 to 20 minutes.

Donna Murphy

Orange Nut Bread

2-1/2 cups flour
3 teaspoons baking powder
1 teaspoon salt
1 cup sugar
1/4 cup shortening
3/4 cup milk
1/4 cup orange juice
1 egg
3 tablespoons grated orange rind
1 cup chopped nuts

Combine first 4 ingredients in a bowl. Then cut next 4 ingredients into dry ingredients only enough to dampen dry ingredients. Add orange rind and nuts. Pour into greased loaf pan. Let stand for 20 minutes. Bake 350 degrees for one hour. Let stand 20 minutes and turn out. Store overnight before slicing.

Ann A. Corscaden

Cloud-Light Pancakes

1 cup flour
2 tablespoons sugar
2 tablespoons baking powder (yes, tablespoons)
1/2 teaspoon salt
1 egg
2 tablespoons cooking oil

Milk (approximately 3/4 cup, or enough to make the batter pour easily) Combine dry ingredients. Add egg, oil and milk. Mix lightly — mixture will be bubbly and foamy. Bake on well-greased, hot griddle.

Ruth Crowe

Referring to French dressing, an old Spanish proverb "calls for a quartet to compost it, a spendthrift for oil, a miser for vinegar, a counselor for salt, and a madcap for mixing."

Pancakes

1/2 teaspoon soda
1 cup buttermilk
3/4 cup flour
1 teaspoon baking powder
1/2 teaspoon salt
1 egg
3 tablespoons butter, melted
1 tablespoon sugar

Dissolve soda in buttermilk. Mix in remainder of ingredients. Cook on hot griddle.

Scoot Harrison

World's Fluffiest Pancakes

2 Egg Beaters
1 teaspoon baking soda
2-1/2 - 3 cups buttermilk
2 cups sifted flour
2 teaspoons baking powder
2 teaspoons sugar
1/2 cup oat bran
1/3 cup unprocessed wheat bran
1/4 cup vanilla, or to taste

Whisk Egg Beaters with baking soda and then whisk in 2-1/2 cups of buttermilk. Add all the remaining dry ingredients and vanilla. Mix thoroughly but do not beat or overmix. If mix is very thick, add additional buttermilk. Ladle onto hot nonstick griddle. Blueberries, sliced bananas, nuts, raisins, granola, etc. may be sprinkled on each pancake before flipping.

Linda Manzione

Waffles

1-1/3 cups flour
1/2 teaspoon salt
2 teaspoons baking powder
2 eggs, separated
1 teaspoon sugar
1/4 cup melted butter or margarine
1-1/4 cups sweet milk
chopped pecans, if desired

Sift flour, measure, and sift with salt and baking powder. Beat egg yolks until foamy; add sugar and butter to yolks. Mix well, then add milk alternately with dry ingredients to egg mixture. Beat egg whites until stiff and fold into batter. Bake in hot waffle iron. Add chopped pecans to batter in waffle iron if desired.

Scoot Harrison

Over-salted soup may be de-salted by slicing a raw potato into it. Boil for a short time, then remove the potato.

Beverly Luke's Shredded Wheat Bread

3 packages active dry yeast
1/3 cup warm water (105-115 degrees)
3 large shredded wheat biscuits
1 tablespoon salt
3 tablespoons butter
3 cups boiling water
1/3 cup sugar
1/2 cup molasses, dark karo or honey
8 cups all purpose flour

Combine yeast with 1/3 cup warm water. Allow yeast mixture to foam. Set aside. In a large bowl, mix together shredded wheat, salt, butter and boiling water until "mooshy." Let cool to room temperature. Add sugar and molasses and mix well. Add yeast mixture. Add 4 cups of the flour and blend well. Add remaining flour, by hand, about 1 cup at a time until a firm and slightly sticky dough is formed. (If dough is hard to work with, put some oil on your hands.) Knead dough on lightly oiled OR floured work area. Put dough back into bowl, cover and place in a warm, draft-free area, until doubled. Punch down and shape into loaves. Place in greased pans (2 - 9x5 inch OR 3 - 8x4 inch). Let rise until dough comes to the top of the pans. Bake at 400 degrees for 15 minutes. Reduce temperature to 350 degrees and continue to bake for about 30 minutes or until tops are nicely browned. Remove from pan and cool. Note: this can also be baked in bowls OR mini-loaf tins, for a nifty gift.

Shirin Shiekh Blackwell

Pizza

Dough:
1 cup lukewarm water
1 package dry yeast
1 teaspoon sugar
1 teaspoon salt
2 tablespoons oil
2 cups flour
1/2 cup flour

Topping:
1 (26 ounce) jar favorite spaghetti sauce
1 pound mozzarella cheese
liberal sprinkling Parmesan cheese
oregano and oil

Favorite additional toppings may be pepperoni, mushrooms, cooked ground beef, sausage, green peppers, black olives, onion, etc. Combine first 6 dough ingredients in large bowl, dump mixture on 1-1/2 cups flour on counter top and knead until mixed. Return to bowl, cover and let rise 1 hour in a warm place. Grease 2 pizza pans, divide dough, press onto pans working from center to edges making an edge up the side of pan. Add sauce, divided, cover with mozzarella, divided, sprinkle with Parmesan, drizzle about 1 tablespoon oil and 1 teaspoon oregano per pizza. Cook at 425 degrees for 7 minutes, remove and add favorite ingredients. After adding favorite ingredients bake an additional 8 minutes.

Serves 2 pizzas

Catherine P. Arlinghaus

My Quick Pizza Dough

1 package active dry yeast
3/4 cup very warm water (105 degrees to 115 degrees)
2 cups flour
1/2 teaspoon salt
olive or vegetable oil
cornmeal

In a measuring cup, dissolve the yeast in water. In a large bowl, stir flour, salt, and yeast mixture until blended. Cover bowl with waxed paper; let rest 5 minutes. Remove dough from bowl and place on counter top which has been lightly sprinkled with oil. Knead a few times. Lightly oil a 12 to 14 inch pizza pan and sprinkle evenly with cornmeal. Press dough into and up sides of pan. Top, as desired, and bake at 425 degrees until top is hot and crust is browned. Note: Dough can be divided into smaller individual pizza crusts. Also, the dough is good for making breadsticks. Freezes well.

Shirin Shiekh Blackwell

Pumpkin Bread

3 cups flour
1 teaspoon cloves
1 teaspoon nutmeg
1 teaspoon cinnamon
1 teaspoon allspice
1 teaspoon baking powder
1/2 teaspoon baking soda
1/2 teaspoon salt, optional
1 cup salad oil
3 scant cups sugar
3 eggs, well beaten
1 teaspoon vanilla
2 cups canned pumpkin
1 cup pecans

Sift first 8 ingredients together. Combine next 4 ingredients with sifted ingredients. Mix well and add the last 2 ingredients. Grease and flour three 1 pound coffee cans. Pam works wonderful and 2 loaf pans work out nicely. Fill each container 1/2 full. Bake 1 hour at 350 degrees. Cool then wrap in plastic wrap. Can be stored in refrigerator or frozen.

Anne Clark

Meredith's Pumpkin Bread

3-1/2 cups flour
3 cups sugar
1-1/2 teaspoons salt
2 teaspoons baking soda
7 teaspoons nutmeg
1/2 teaspoon cinnamon
1/2 teaspoon ginger
2/3 cups water
4 eggs
1 cup pumpkin
1 cup salad oil
1 cup raisins
1 cup chopped nuts

Sift dry ingredients into large bowl. Add water, eggs, pumpkin, salad oil, raisins, and pecans. Stir well. Grease and flour 3 or 4 coffee cans. Fill cans two-thirds full of batter. Bake at 350 degrees for 1 hour until done.

Yield 3 loaves. Also good as cupcakes or mini cupcakes. Perfect with hot tea on a cold afternoon.

Leslie Friedman

Kraus Pumpkin Bread

3-1/2 cups sifted flour
2 teaspoons baking soda
1-1/2 teaspoons salt
1-1/2 teaspoons cinnamon
1-1/2 teaspoons nutmeg
1-1/2 teaspoons pumpkin pie spice
3 cups sugar
1 (16 ounce) can pumpkin
1 cup oil (not olive)
2/3 cup water
5 eggs
1/2 cup chopped walnuts
6 ounces chopped dried apricots
1/2 cup golden raisins

Combine flour, soda, salt and spices with sugar in large bowl; make a well and add pumpkin, oil, water and eggs. Mix thoroughly; lastly, add nuts, apricots and raisins. Pour batter into two 9x5x2 inch bread pans that have been greased and floured. Bake at 350 degrees for an hour and 20 minutes. Cool, remove from pans and continue cooling on racks. Bread freezes well up to a year.

Leslie Friedman

Spoonbread

1 cup cornmeal
1-1/3 teaspoons sugar
1-1/2 teaspoons salt
1-1/3 cups boiling water
3 eggs
1 tablespoon baking powder
1-1/3 cups milk
4 tablespoons butter, melted

Mix sugar and salt with cornmeal and blend well. Pour boiling water over meal, stirring constantly. Let stand until cool. Beat eggs until light, add eggs and baking powder to mixture. Add milk and butter. Pour mixture into a 2 quart buttered pan or baking dish. Place in shallow pan of hot water in 350 degree oven. Bake about 35 minutes.

Serves 8

Donna Murphy

Beer Party Rolls

3 cups biscuit mix
3 tablespoons sugar
1 (10 ounce) can cold beer
2 tablespoons melted butter

Preheat oven to 450 degrees. Mix all ingredients except butter. Lightly grease small party muffin tins. Fill muffin tins and drizzle melted butter over batter. Bake 10 to 12 minutes.

Makes 2-1/2 dozen rolls

Claudette Perse

Butter Rolls

1-1/2 cups sifted flour
1/2 teaspoon salt
1/2 cup shortening or butter
ice water
2 tablespoons butter, more or less
1 cup sugar, or as needed
1 pint sweet milk
1/4 teaspoon nutmeg
1 teaspoon vanilla

Sift the flour and salt together. Add the shortening (or butter) and blend to a crumbly stage. Add enough ice water to make a stiff dough. Form the dough into five balls. Roll each ball of dough into a circle the size of a saucer, dot with butter, and sprinkle with enough sugar to cover top. Roll each circle as you would a jelly roll. Place side by side in a square baking dish. Bake in a 350 degree oven until brown. Remove the rolls from the oven. Combine milk, nutmeg and vanilla; pour over the roll. Put the rolls back into the oven for an additional 5 minutes. Serve warm.

Jane McFaddin

Meredith's Mom's Dinner Rolls

2 packages dry yeast
2 cups lukewarm water
3/4 cup sugar
1 teaspoon salt
6-7 cups flour
3 tablespoons cooking oil
2 eggs

Dissolve yeast in water. Add sugar and salt; stir well. Mix in 2 cups flour. Add cooking oil and mix. Add 2 more cups flour and eggs. Mix well and beat 100 strokes. Mix in 2 more cups flour. Add up to 1 cup more flour to make dough right consistency. Cover and let rise 1 1/2 hours at room temperature. Put on flour board and knead 1 minute. Make out rolls and place in greased pan. Cover with tea towel and let rise 2 hours more or until double in size. Bake at 375 - 400 degrees for 10 minutes. Yield 4-5 dozen rolls. These may be frozen in the pan. Allow a little longer for rising if frozen. This recipe takes some time, but the rolls are worth the effort. Great with dinner or at breakfast with jam.

Leslie Friedman

Double Quick Dinner Rolls

1 package dry yeast
1 cup warm water
2 tablespoons sugar
1 teaspoon salt
1 egg, beaten
2 tablespoons oil
2-1/2 cups flour

Dissolve yeast in warm water in large bowl. Add sugar, salt, egg, oil and 1 cup flour. Beat until smooth. Stir in remaining flour. Continue to stir until smooth. Scrape sides of bowl, cover and let dough rise in warm place until doubled in size (about 30 minutes). Stir down batter. Spoon into 12 greased muffin pans (large size). Fill each about half full, let rise until batter reaches top of cups. (About 20-30 minutes). Bake at 400 degrees for 15 minutes.

Serves 12

Euna Bell

Refrigerator Rolls

- 1 cup shortening
- 1 scant cup sugar
- 2 teaspoons salt
- 1 cup boiling water
- 1 cup cold water
- 2 eggs, well beaten
- 2 cakes yeast
- 6 cups flour, measure flour before sifting

Pour boiling water over shortening, sugar and salt and let cool to lukewarm. Add eggs. Dissolve yeast in cold water and add flour. Stir, do not knead. Place in refrigerator for at least 4 hours. This dough keeps for days in refrigerator. Simply pinch off what you want to bake; make into desired rolls; place in greased pan and let rise 3 hours. Bake 400 degrees. These are easy and marvelous. You can't miss!

Susan Scott

Ice Box Yeast Rolls

- 1 quart milk (I use skim milk)
- 1/2 cup warm water
- 1 cake of yeast
- 5 to 6 cups flour
- 2 sticks corn oil margarine, softened
- 1 tablespoon salt
- 1 heaping tablespoon baking powder
- 1 scant teaspoon soda
- 1 cup sugar

Heat milk to boiling point. Cool. Add yeast dissolved in warm water. Add enough flour to form a soft dough. Let rise 2 hours or until doubled. When ready add other ingredients and beat into a smooth dough. Roll out as needed and cut into rolls. Dough will keep in the refrigerator up to two weeks. Keep well covered. Allow 2 hours for cut rolls to rise. Bake 375 degrees.

Serves 90 party size rolls

Karen Harrison

My Favorite Gingerbread

- 1/4 cup sugar
- 1/4 cup butter, softened
- 1 egg, well beaten
- 1/2 cup molasses
- 1/2 cup boiling water
- 1-1/4 cups all purpose flour
- 1/2 teaspoon cinnamon
- 1/2 teaspoon ginger
- 1/4 teaspoon cloves
- 1 teaspoon baking powder
- 1 teaspoon soda

Cream sugar and butter. Add egg, molasses and boiling water. Set aside. Sift together dry ingredients and add to butter-molasses mixture. Beat well. Pour into small, lightly greased, loaf pan (8x4 inch). Bake at 325 degrees about 35 minutes.

Shirin Shiekh Blackwell

Scottish Scones

2 cups flour
3 tablespoons sugar
2 teaspoons baking powder
3/4 teaspoon salt
1/2 teaspoon baking soda
5 tablespoons butter
1/2 cup currants
1 (8 ounce) carton sour cream
1 egg, separated
1 teaspoon sugar
1/8 teaspoon ground cinnamon

Combine dry ingredients. Cut in butter until mixture resembles coarse crumbs. Stir in currants. In small bowl blend sour cream and egg yolk. Add all at once to crumb mixture, stirring just until dough clings together. On lightly floured surface knead dough gently 10 to 12 strokes. Pat or roll to 9 inch circle, about 1/2 inch thick. Cut with a 4 inch round cookie cutter. Slice each circle completely through into quarters, but do not separate. Place on ungreased baking sheet. Brush with egg white and sprinkle with sugar and cinnamon. Bake in 425 degree oven 15 to 18 minutes, or until light brown.

Ann A. Corscaden

Sugar Plum Loaf

1-3/4 cups sugar
3/4 cup margarine, softened
4 eggs
3/4 cup buttermilk
1 teaspoon orange extract
1 tablespoon lemon juice
1 (3-1/2 ounce) can coconut
8 ounces chopped dates
1 cup orange slice candy
1-1/2 cups chopped pecans
4 cups all purpose flour
1 teaspoon baking soda
dash of salt, optional
glaze, recipe follows

Cream sugar, margarine, and eggs until light and fluffy. Stir in buttermilk, orange extract, and lemon juice and set aside. Combine coconut, dates, orange slice candy and pecans. Combine flour, soda, and salt. Sprinkle flour mixture over fruit mixture and mix well. Stir flour mixture into creamed mixture — mixing well. Grease two 9x5x3 loaf pans. Spoon batter into pans and bake 300 degrees for 1 hour and 50 minutes, or until tests done. Cool in pan 5 minutes. Punch holes in top and drizzle glaze over top. Wrap each loaf tightly in foil to store.

Glaze:

1 cup powdered sugar
3 tablespoons orange juice

Marie Brown

Soup garnishes: popcorn, toasted croutons, crisp cereal, minced parsley, lemon slices, hard-cooked egg slices, chopped nuts, shredded cheese.

VEGETABLES

Jennie's Baked Beans

- **1 pound beans (yellow eye, soldier or Great Northern)**
- **1 medium onion, chopped**
- **1/4 cup molasses**
- **1/4 cup dark brown sugar**
- **1/4 cup ketchup**
- **1 teaspoon dry mustard**
- **1/2 teaspoon brown gravy mix**
- **2 tablespoons margarine**
- **salt and pepper to taste**

Soak beans overnight in just enough water to cover them. Next morning, par-boil beans for 15 minutes. Put beans and water into crock pot along with remaining ingredients. Cook on low all day. Dinner will be ready when you get home in the evening!

Dianne Ibenthal

Swiss-Style Green Beans

- **2 tablespoons butter**
- **2 tablespoons flour**
- **1 teaspoon salt**
- **1/4 teaspoon pepper**
- **1/4 teaspoon instant minced onion**
- **1 teaspoon sugar**
- **1 cup sour cream**
- **4 cups French-style green beans, cook and drained**
- **2 cups (1/2 pound) grated Swiss cheese**
- **Topping: 1/2 cup corn flake crumbs, 2 tablespoons butter, melted**

For topping, mix corn flake crumbs with melted butter. Set aside. Melt the 2 tablespoons butter in large saucepan over low heat; stir in flour, salt, pepper, onion and sugar. Add sour cream; stir until smooth. Increase heat to medium and cook sauce until bubbly and thickened, stirring constantly. Remove from heat. Fold green beans into sour cream sauce. Spread in greased 10x6x2 (1-1/2 quart) baking dish. Sprinkle cheese evenly over green beans. Add topping. Bake in 400 degree oven for 20 minutes or until heated through.

Serves 6. (This recipe has been in my family for years, and we never seem to tire of it.)

Beverly Loftis

Lemons have roughly the same amount of vitamin C as oranges, and four times the amount found in limes.

Barley and Mushroom Casserole

4 tablespoons butter
1 onion, chopped
1-1/2 cups barley
3 cups chicken broth
1/2 pound firm white mushrooms
1/2 cup finely chopped toasted almonds

Melt 3 tablespoons butter and saute the onions until soft. Add barley and brown. Place mixture in a 2 quart casserole and add 1-1/2 cups chicken broth. Cover and bake in a 350 degree oven for 30 minutes. Saute mushrooms in remaining butter and then add to casserole with remaining chicken broth and bake another 30-45 minutes until barley is tender. May need to add more broth. Sprinkle almonds on top.

Serves 6

Selma Gold

Green Beans Supreme

2 packages frozen green beans
2 tablespoons butter
1/4 cup chopped onion
1 tablespoon minced parsley
2 tablespoons flour
1 teaspoon salt
1/4 teaspoon pepper
1 cup sour cream
1/2 teaspoon grated lemon rind
1/2 cup grated Cheddar cheese
1/2 cup dry bread crumbs
2 tablespoons melted butter

Cook green beans and drain. Cook onion and parsley in butter until tender but not brown. Add flour, salt and pepper to onions and cook a minute or so but do not brown flour. Add sour cream and grated lemon rind to mixture, mix well, then add cooked beans and stir over low heat until heated through. Turn into baking dish. Top with cheese. Combine bread crumbs with melted butter and sprinkle over cheese. Broil at low heat until cheese melts and crumbs brown or bake in a 375 degree oven for about 20 minutes.

Serves 6

Mary Belle Wooddy

Green Beans Oregano

- **6 cups green beans (frozen are fine)**
- **6-8 slices low-sodium bacon, crisply cooked and crumbled**
- **2 (10-3/4 ounce) cans cream of mushroom soup (can use low-sodium)**
- **2 (3 or 4 ounce) cans mushroom slices**
- **1/2 envelope onion soup mix**
- **1/4 to 1/2 teaspoon oregano**

Cook beans until barely done in unsalted water. Drain. Reserve 2 or 3 slices bacon for garnish. Mix beans with crumbled bacon, soup, mushrooms, soup mix and oregano. Refrigerate overnight to blend flavors (very important). Bake in a 3 quart casserole at 350 degrees 30 to 40 minutes.

Serves 10 to 12

Margaret E. Harris

Broccoli Casserole I

- **butter**
- **1 onion, chopped**
- **2 packages frozen chopped broccoli**
- **1-1/2 cups rice**
- **1 can cream of chicken soup**
- **1 can cream of mushroom soup**
- **1 small jar Cheese Whiz**
- **1 stick margarine**

Saute onion in butter; cook broccoli and drain well. Cook rice and mix together with broccoli, soups, Cheese Whiz and margarine. Put mixture into a casserole dish and bake at 375 degrees for 45 minutes.

John Gardner

Broccoli Casserole II

- **3 (10 ounce) boxes frozen, chopped broccoli**
- **1 small can evaporated milk**
- **1 can cream of mushroom soup**
- **1 cup grated cheese, Cheddar or Velveeta**
- **1 can French fried onion rings**
- **salt and pepper, to taste**

Cook broccoli according to package directions, but not quite done. Drain well, then season with salt and pepper. Place in 11-3/4x 7-1/2 inch Pyrex dish. Mix evaporated milk and soup, and pour over broccoli and stir. Add more salt and pepper if desired. Sprinkle a layer of grated cheese over the broccoli mixture. Bake 25 minutes at 350 degrees in preheated oven. Then top with a layer of the canned fried onion rings and bake an additional 5-10 minutes, just until rings are crisp not too brown. Note: Fresh broccoli, partially cooked and cut into bite size pieces, can be used instead of frozen broccoli.

Serves 10-12

Dorothy McCormick

Creamy Broccoli

- 1-1/2 pounds fresh broccoli (or 2 (10 ounce) packages frozen broccoli spears)
- 1 can cream of mushroom soup
- 1/4 cup milk
- 1/2 cup shredded Cheddar cheese
- 1 cup Bisquick mix
- 1/4 cup firm butter or margarine

Cook broccoli in salted water until almost tender; drain. Place broccoli, cut into pieces, in an ungreased 1-1/2 quart casserole. Beat soup and milk until smooth and pour over broccoli. Sprinkle with cheese. Combine Bisquick mix and butter until crumbly and spread over cheese. Bake in preheated 400 degree oven until crumbs are light brown.

Serves 6-8

Les Lawrence

Broccoli Supreme

- 1-1/2 tablespoons margarine
- 2 medium onions, sliced thinly
- 1 bunch fresh broccoli, broken into flowerettes
- 1 (10-3/4 ounce) can cream mushroom soup
- 1/2 cup cream (I use milk)
- salt and pepper to taste
- 1 cup grated Swiss cheese

Heat margarine in frying pan. Add onions and broccoli and saute 2-3 minutes. Add soup, cream (or milk) and seasonings. Bring to boil and cook on low 5 minutes. Spoon into buttered, ovenproof dish and sprinkle with cheese. Place in upper half of 350 degree oven until cheese has melted, approximately 20 minutes.

Serves 4-6

Betsy Mulligan

Dilly Brussel Sprouts

- 2 packages frozen brussel sprouts
- salt and pepper to taste
- 1 cup Italian dressing
- 1 teaspoon dill weed
- 2 tablespoons of shredded green onions

In seasoned and boiling water, cook brussel sprouts until just tender. Drain and add remaining ingredients and chill in covered container over 12 hours.

Serves 10-12

Marie Sullivan

Curried Cabbage

1/2 head cabbage, chopped
small onion, chopped
1 tomato, diced
1 tablespoon oil
1 teaspoon curry powder
salt to taste

Boil ten minutes, in a large pot.

Rebecca Phifer

Stir Fry Cabbage

1 medium cabbage, chopped
2 stalks celery, sliced
1 medium onion, chopped
1 small bell pepper, chopped
2 tablespoons butter or margarine
1/2 teaspoon salt
1/8 teaspoon pepper

Stir fry cabbage, celery, onion, bell pepper, in margarine or butter in heavy Dutch oven for 5 minutes over high heat. Cover and remove from heat, let steam until cabbage is tender (5-10 minutes). Stir in salt and pepper.

Serves 8

Ann McFadin

Celery Bake

4 cups (1/2 inch diagonally sliced) celery
1 (2 ounce) jar sliced pimento, drained and chopped
1 (8 ounce) can water chestnuts, drained and sliced
1 can cream of chicken soup
1/4 cup water
1/2 teaspoon salt
salted nuts for garnish

Cook celery in 1 inch of boiling salted water, in tightly covered saucepan for 5 minutes. Drain. Mix all ingredients in ungreased 1-1/2 quart casserole. Cover and bake at 350 degrees about 45 minutes. Stir before serving and garnish with salted nuts. To serve as a main dish add cooked chicken breasts cut into medium size pieces.

Serves 6-8

Marilyn Healy

Flavored butters are great for homemade muffins. Combine 8 tablespoons of softened butter or margarine with 1/2 honey or your favorite jam.

Red Kal (Red Cabbage)

1 (3 pound) red cabbage
2 tablespoons vinegar
1/4 cup butter, melted
1/4 cup sugar
1 teaspoon salt
1 peeled, cored, cubed apple
1/2 cup currant jelly

Quarter cabbage and remove core. Chop and sprinkle with vinegar. Melt butter in skillet, stir in sugar and salt. Add cabbage and mix well. Cook (low heat) 15 minutes, tossing frequently. Add jelly and apple; toss. Cover and simmer for 2 hours, tossing frequently.

Dora Hughes

Copper Pennies

2 pounds carrots, sliced
1 bell pepper, finely chopped
1 onion, finely chopped
1/4 - 1/2 cup oil
1 teaspoon dry mustard or 1 tablespoon prepared mustard
1 can cream of tomato soup
1/2 to 3/4 cup vinegar*
1 cup sugar
1 tablespoon Worcestershire sauce

Cook carrots, making sure they remain firm, and drain. Add bell pepper and onion. Mix remaining ingredients in a saucepan; heat to just boiling and pour over carrots. Cover tightly and refrigerate. Keeps several days. This will surprise you; it is an unusual dish.

*Serves 15 to 20. *Taste as you add vinegar; 3/4 cup may be too sour for your taste.*

Margaret E. Harris

"The Men Love It" Corn

2 cans whole kernel corn, or large package frozen
2 tablespoons margarine, melted
1 teaspoon chicken seasoning or one chicken bouillon cube
1 teaspoon Season All
1 teaspoon dry mustard
2 teaspoons freeze-dried chives
1 teaspoon parsley flakes
1 cup sour cream
salt and pepper to taste
1 green pepper, sliced

Drain corn thoroughly. Add melted margarine with chicken flavoring and seasonings; stir in sour cream. Pour into buttered casserole, 1-1/2 quart size, and place in 325 degree oven for 30 minutes or until hot and bubbly. Garnish with green pepper slices.

Serves 6-8. Use 3 large cans or one six pound can corn for 16 people.

Thommye Stewart

Jewel's Mexican Corn Casserole

- 1 cup dry small elbow macaroni
- 1 (15 or 16 ounce) can whole-kernel corn, undrained
- 1 (15 or 16 ounce) can cream-style corn, undrained
- 1/2 cup melted margarine
- 1/2 cup chopped onions
- 1 can Ro-Tel tomatoes with green chilies
- salt and pepper, to taste
- 1/2 cup grated Velveeta cheese (regular or Mexican-style)

In a bowl mix together the macaroni, corn, margarine, onions, tomatoes, salt, pepper and cheese. Pour mixture into a 9x13x2 inch glass casserole dish which has been sprayed with Pam. Bake uncovered 30 minutes at 350 degrees, then cover and continue to bake another 30 minutes.

Shirin Shiekh Blackwell

Corn Pudding

- 2 (8-1/2 ounce) cans corn
- 2 eggs, slightly beaten
- 3/4 cup evaporated milk
- 2 tablespoons butter, melted
- 1 teaspoon salt
- 1/8 teaspoon pepper

Mix all ingredients well. Pour into a greased 1-1/2 quart baking dish. Bake at 350 degrees for 45 minutes or until firm.

Serves 6-1/2 cup servings

John Gardner

Shoe Peg Corn Casserole

- 1 (12 ounce) can shoe peg (white) corn
- 1 (16 ounce) can french green beans
- 1/2 cup diced celery
- 1/2 cup diced bell pepper
- 1/2 cup diced onion
- 1/2 cup grated sharp Cheddar cheese
- 1/2 cup sour cream
- 1 can celery soup
- 1 stick butter, softened
- 1-1/2 cups crushed Ritz crackers

Drain corn and green beans. Combine next 6 ingredients with corn and green beans and mix well. Mix crackers with softened butter and spread on top. Bake 350 degrees for 45 minutes.

Serves 6-8

Virginia Van Horn

Eggplant Parmesan

- 1 large (1-1/2 pounds) eggplant
- 2 eggs, beaten
- 1-1/4 cups Italian seasoned bread crumbs
- 1 cup olive oil or salad oil
- 1 (28 or 32 ounce) jar tomato sauce
- 1/2 pound mozzarella cheese, sliced
- 2 tablespoons grated Parmesan cheese

Pare eggplant and cut into 1/4 inch slices. Dip slices in eggs, then into bread crumbs, coating completely. Heat 1/2 cup oil in large skillet. Saute eggplant slices, a few at a time, until golden brown — about 3 minutes on each side. Add more oil as needed. Drain slices on paper towels. In 12x8 baking dish layer half of eggplant slices; top with half of tomato sauce and half of mozzarella cheese slices. Repeat. Sprinkle top with Parmesan cheese. Bake, uncovered, in preheated 400 degree oven for 15 to 20 minutes or until cheese is melted and sauce is bubbly.

Serves 6 to 8

Lou Bruno

Turkish Stuffed Eggplant

- 2 medium onions, chopped
- 2 tablespoons oil for saute
- 2 garlic cloves, crushed
- 3 medium tomatoes, peeled and chopped
- 3 tablespoons chopped parsley
- salt and pepper to taste
- 2 medium sized eggplants
- 2 teaspoons sugar
- 3 tablespoons lemon juice
- 1/2 cup olive oil

Saute onions in oil. Add the garlic, tomatoes, parsley, salt and pepper and cook until mushy. Cut the stem ends off each eggplant. Make 3 lengthwise slits, almost from end to end. With your hand hold each slot apart and spoon the onion mixture into each cavity. Arrange eggplants in a baking dish. Sprinkle with sugar, lemon juice and olive oil. Bake, covered, in preheated 350 degree oven for 40 minutes or until tender. Serve hot, or as they do in Turkey, serve cold with yogurt.

Serves 4 to 6

Ruth Crowe

Lettuce is a member of the daisy family.

Caponata

1 to 1-1/2 pounds eggplant, peeled and cut into 1 inch cubes
2 green bell peppers, cut into 1 inch pieces
2 large onions, diced
2-3 cloves garlic, minced
2-3 stalks celery, diced
1 (28 ounce) can tomatoes, cut up, undrained
1/2 cup olive oil
1/3 cup red wine vinegar
2 tablespoons sugar
2 tablespoons capers
2 tablespoons tomato paste
1-2 teaspoons salt
1/2 cup fresh parsley
1/2 cup pimento-stuffed green olives, rinsed and sliced
1/2 teaspoon black pepper
2 teaspoons crumbled dried basil
1/2 cup pine nuts, sauteed in olive oil (optional)

In a large heavy saucepan combine eggplant, bell peppers, onions, garlic, celery, tomatoes and olive oil and cook for 20 to 30 minutes, or until vegetables are barely tender. Add wine vinegar, sugar, capers, tomato paste, salt, parsley, olives, pepper and basil. Cover and simmer 15 minutes. Add pine nuts if desired and serve warm (not hot), at room temperature, or cold. May be refrigerated for as long as 3 weeks. This dish is good served as an accompaniment to almost any meal, but also can be served as an appetizer with pita bread or crackers. Adjust the ingredients to your taste. I usually use more stuffed olives and capers and sometimes add a red and yellow bell pepper in addition to the green pepper.

Estelle Kastleman

Baked Cheese Grits

2 eggs, beaten
3/4 cup grated Cheddar cheese
4 tablespoons butter, melted
2 teaspoons dry mustard
1/2 teaspoon salt
1 clove garlic, finely minced
2-1/2 cups cooked grits, kept warm

Preheat oven to 350 degrees. Mix eggs, cheese, butter, mustard, salt and garlic. Stir into grits and pour into a well-buttered 4-6 cup casserole. Bake uncovered for 50 minutes. Serve immediately.

Serves 4-6

Lea Jones

Company Hominy

1 stick margarine
1/4 cup chopped onion
3 (No. 2) cans yellow hominy
1 (8 ounce) jar jalapeno Cheese Whiz
1 can cream of mushroom soup
1-1/2 cups crushed corn chips

Saute onion in margarine. Add hominy, Cheese Whiz and soup. Pour into casserole dish and top with corn chips. Bake at 350 degrees for 20 minutes or until heated through.

Lea Jones

Marinated Vegetables

1 large (15 ounce) can sliced carrots
1 large (15 ounce) can small peas
1 large (15 ounce) can cut green beans
1 large (15 ounce) can yellow corn
celery, onion and green pepper (chopped to your taste)

Sauce:
3/4 cup sugar (or less)
3/4 cup vinegar
1/2 cup oil
1/2 teaspoon salt
1 teaspoon water
paprika

In a large bowl, combine the vegetables. Set aside. In a small saucepan, bring the sauce ingredients to a boil. Remove from heat and allow to cool. Pour over reserved vegetables. Allow to marinate 8 hours (or longer).

Serves 12-16

Page Lawson

Mushroom Roll Up

12 tablespoons butter, room temperature
2 tablespoons chopped chives
1/2 teaspoon sweet basil
1/2 teaspoon marjoram
8 medium mushrooms, chopped
bread slices, with crusts removed

Whip all ingredients together. Spread on slice of bread. Roll slices starting at corner. May be frozen at this point. Bake on cookie sheet at 350 degrees for 25-30 minutes.

Serves 18-20

Michael Kunc

"That Mushroom Thing"

- 1/2 to 1 pound fresh mushrooms, diced
- 2-3 tablespoons butter
- 1/3 cup onion, chopped
- 1/2 cup mayonnaise
- 1/3 cup celery, chopped
- 1/2 cup chopped green pepper
- 3/4 teaspoon salt
- 3/4 teaspoon pepper
- 8 slices white bread, buttered
- 2 eggs, slightly beaten
- 1-1/2 cups milk
- 1 can cream of mushroom soup

Saute mushrooms in butter. Add onion, mayonnaise, celery, green pepper, salt and pepper. Cut bread into 1 inch squares; place in bottom of casserole dish. Spread mushroom mixture on bread squares. Cut 3 more slices of bread into squares; place on top of mushroom mixture. Mix eggs and milk and pour over bread and mushroom mixture; refrigerate overnight (or at least one hour). Spoon can of undiluted mushroom soup over all; top with 2 more bread slices prepared as above. Bake at 300 degrees for 60 to 70 minutes or at 325 degrees for 50 to 60 minutes.

Serves 6 to 8

Ruth Crowe

Noodle Mushroom Pudding

- 1 (12 ounce) package medium size noodles
- 2 tablespoons butter or margarine
- 1 (8 ounce) package fresh mushrooms, sliced
- 1 bunch green onions, chopped
- 4 sprigs parsley, chopped
- 3 large eggs, well beaten
- salt and pepper to taste

Cook noodles as directed on package; drain and set aside. In a saucepan, melt butter and saute mushrooms and green onions until limp. Add chopped parsley to mixture and remove from heat. Mix vegetables and noodles together; fold in beaten eggs, salt and pepper. Pour mixture into lightly greased casserole or mold. Bake at 350 degrees for 25-30 minutes or until set and light brown on top.

Selma Leff

Since 1976 broccoli consumption in the USA has increased 169%!

1015 Onion Casserole

1/4 cup butter
3 medium 1015 super sweet onions, chopped
2 cups grated Swiss cheese, divided use
1 cup crushed saltine crackers, divided use
2 eggs
3/4 cup light cream (or half and half)
1 teaspoon salt
1/8 teaspoon pepper
2 tablespoons melted butter

Melt 1/4 cup butter in large skillet and saute onions until tender. Place half the onions in a 1-1/2 quart deep dish pie pan. Sprinkle 1 cup Swiss cheese and 1/2 cup cracker crumbs over onions. Repeat layers of onions and cheese. Beat eggs with cream, salt and pepper. Pour evenly over onion mixture. Melt 2 tablespoons butter in skillet and stir in remaining cracker crumbs. Lightly brown, then sprinkle crumbs over casserole. Bake at 350 degrees for 25 minutes. An excellent accompaniment to roast or ham.

Serves 6-8

Barbara Elstad

Pepperonata

olive oil spray (by Pam)
1 large onion, sliced
1 clove garlic, minced
2 large all-purpose potatoes, pared and cut into 1/2 inch cubes
2 large tomatoes, peeled, seeded and cut in large chunks
3 large bell peppers (mix colors), halved, seeded and cut in strips
3/4 teaspoon salt
1/2 teaspoon dried leaf oregano, crumbled
1/4 teaspoon dried leaf thyme

In large non-stick skillet spray Pam olive oil spray over medium heat. Saute onion and garlic until onion is limp. Stir in potatoes; cover and cook 10 minutes, stirring occasionally. Stir in tomatoes, peppers, salt, oregano and thyme. Cover and cook 10 minutes longer, until potatoes and peppers are crisp-tender. This is delicious as is but seasonings can easily be adjusted to suit your own taste.

Serves 4-6 High in Vitamin C, low in fat

Estelle Kastleman

Dilled Peas

1 carton sour cream
1/2 teaspoon curry powder, or less
1/2 cup fresh dill and chives, combined, chopped
1 or 2cans drained small green peas
salt
pepper

Combine all ingredients, gently mix and refrigerate.

Serves 4-8

Page Lawson

Snow Peas with Lemon-Anchovy Dipping Sauce

1-1/4 pounds fresh snow peas, blanched
Sauce:
2 egg yolks
3-4 tablespoons Dijon mustard
2 (2 ounce)cans anchovies, undrained
juice of 1 lemon
1 shallot, chopped fine
1 cup vegetable oil
1/4 cup sour cream
1 tablespoon capers, rinsed and drained
salt and pepper to taste

String peas and "crisp" in ice water; drain. Combine egg yolks, mustard, anchovies, lemon juice and shallot in food processor; process until "foamy" and pale. With processor running, add oil until absorbed. Pour into a bowl and stir in sour cream by hand. Season to taste. Gently fold in capers. Cover and refrigerate. Garnish with additional capers. Arrange snow peas in a "sunburst" pattern on a flat basket or platter. Place bowl of dipping sauce in center. This is also very good with blanched asparagus, green beans, etc.

Beverly Loftis

Peas With Wilted Lettuce

2 tablespoons no cholesterol margarine
1/2 medium head iceberg lettuce, thinly sliced
1 (10 ounce) package frozen green peas
1 teaspoon sugar or sugar substitute
1/2 teaspoon Mrs. Dash seasoning

Melt margarine in 4 quart saucepan over medium heat. Add lettuce and cook until wilted, about 5 minutes, stirring often. Add frozen peas, sugar, and Mrs. Dash; cook 5-6 minutes longer, stirring occasionally, and taste to be sure peas are tender. Note: This low calorie dish is ideal for buffets because the recipe can easily be doubled.

Serves 6

Mark E. Schier

Hash-Brown Casserole

1/2 cup chopped onion
2 tablespoons margarine
1 (8 ounce) package cream cheese, softened
2 cans cream of chicken soup
1 (8 ounce) carton sour cream
1 large package frozen hash-brown potatoes
stuffing mix, bread crumbs or crushed chips

Saute the onion in margarine and set aside. Combine cheese, soup and sour cream. Layer in a flat baking dish in the following order: hash browns, sauteed onion, cheese, soup and sour cream mixture, and stuffing mix, bread crumbs or crushed chips. Bake at 350 degrees until bubbly.

Serves 6 to 8

Ruth Crowe

Frozen Hashbrown Squares

2 pounds frozen hashbrown cubes, thawed
1 small onion, chopped
8 ounces sour cream
1 can cream of chicken soup
10 ounces grated cheese
topping recipe follows

Mix all ingredients well and pour into a 9x12 pan. Top with topping recipe and bake at 350 degrees for 1 to 1-1/2 hours.

Topping:
2 cups rice chex, crushed
1 stick margarine, softened

Combine ingredients and mix well.

Alberta Bain

Baked Potato Casserole

8 potatoes, boiled and peeled
1 pint sour cream
1 bunch green onions, chopped
1-3/4 cups Cheddar cheese, shredded
salt and pepper to taste
paprika
bacon bits

Grate cooked potatoes. Add sour cream, chopped green onions, half of cheese, salt and pepper. Put in buttered casserole. Sprinkle with rest of cheese. Top with paprika and bacon bits. Bake at 350 degrees for 30-40 minutes. This can be put together and refrigerated ahead of time.

Serves 6-8 or more

Linda Stearns

French Twice Baked Potatoes

8 medium sized baking potatoes
5 tablespoons butter
salt and pepper to taste
freshly grated nutmeg to taste
3 tablespoons cream plus additional cream or milk as needed
1/2 pound gruyere cheese, grated
1 egg
butter to dot on top

Bake potatoes in oven until they test done. Slit lengthwise down the center and empty the pulp in a large bowl, being very careful not to damage the skins. Mash potatoes with butter, salt, pepper, nutmeg, cream, cheese (save some to sprinkle on top of prepared potatoes), and egg. Add additional cream or milk as needed — final mixture should be fairly moist. Fill the emptied shells with the mashed mixture. Dot with butter and sprinkle with remaining grated gruyere. Bake in 375 degree oven approximately 30 minutes or until heated through and browned.

Serves 8

Karin Telfer

Candied Sweet Potatoes

6 medium sweet potatoes
1/3 cup firmly packed brown sugar
1/2 cup sugar
2 tablespoons all purpose flour
1 teaspoon cinnamon
1/4 teaspoon nutmeg
1/4 teaspoon allspice
3/4 cup pineapple juice
1/3 cup light corn syrup
2 tablespoons orange juice
1/4 cup margarine
1/2 cup chopped pecans

Cook sweet potatoes in boiling water until fork tender, 20 to 25 minutes. Let cool; peel and cut lengthwise into 1/4 inch slices. Set aside. Combine brown sugar and next 5 ingredients in a saucepan; stir in pineapple juice, corn syrup, orange juice and margarine. Cook over medium heat about 10 minutes, stirring occasionally. Place half of sweet potatoes in a lightly greased 13x9x2 inch baking dish. Pour half of sauce mixture over sweet potatoes; repeat layers. Sprinkle with pecans. Bake at 350 degrees for 30 minutes or until bubbly.

Serves 8-10

Jean Alloway

Start off cooking in cold water any vegetable that grows under the ground, such as potatoes, beets, carrots, etc. Start off cooking in boiling water any vegetable that grows above ground, such as corn, peas, beans, greens, etc.

Twice Baked Potato Casserole

- 36 ounces thawed hash browns
- 8 ounces sour cream
- 1/2 cup chopped onions
- 1 teaspoon salt
- 1 can cream of chicken soup
- 1 to 1-1/2 cups Velvetta cheese, diced
- 1/2 stick margarine, melted
- 1/4 teaspoon pepper

Mix all ingredients together and bake in buttered 9x3 pan at 350 degrees for 45 minutes. If you like it really cheesy, add some Velvetta to the top before baking.

Lynn Miller

Holiday Sweet Potatoes

- 3 cups cooked sweet potatoes, mashed (drain well if using canned)
- 2 eggs, beaten
- 1/2 cup sugar (use less, if desired)
- 1/2 stick butter or margarine, melted
- 1/2 cup milk
- 1/2 teaspoon salt
- 1-1/2 teaspoons vanilla

Topping:

- 1/2 cup brown sugar
- 1/3 cup flour
- 1 cup pecans, chopped
- 1/3 stick margarine, melted

Add eggs, sugar, butter, milk, salt and vanilla to mashed sweet potatoes. Mix well. Place in shallow 1-1/2 quart baking dish. Mix topping ingredients and spread over potatoes. Bake at 325 degrees for 30 minutes.

Serves 6

Liza Wright

Sweet Potato Casserole

- 6 cups cooked sweet potatoes
- 2 cups white sugar
- 1 teaspoon salt
- 4 eggs, beaten
- 1 stick margarine, melted
- 1 cup milk
- 1 teaspoon vanilla

Topping:

- 2 cups brown sugar
- 2/3 cup flour
- 2 cups chopped pecans
- 2/3 cup margarine, softened

Mash together cooked sweet potatoes, white sugar, salt, eggs, margarine, milk and vanilla. Put into greased casserole. Combine topping ingredients and spread on top of sweet potato mixture. Bake at 350 degrees for 35 minutes.

Selma Leff

Stuffed Pumpkin or Squash

6 small pumpkins or 3 large squash
2 zucchini, peeled and chopped
1 tomato, peeled and chopped
3 green onions, chopped
2 stalks celery, chopped
4 mushrooms, chopped
3 cloves garlic, minced
sunflower seeds
sesame seeds
oregano (to taste)
paprika (to taste)
salt, pepper (to taste)
1/2 cup bread crumbs
1/2 cup Parmesan cheese
Ritz cracker crumbs

Cut tops off pumpkins or half squash. Throw out seeds. Scrape as much vegetable out as possible leaving 1/4 inch shell. Put all vegetables together with pumpkin insides (add mushrooms for last 1 minute) in microwave dish. Cook on high 6 minutes, adding mushrooms after 5 minutes. Remove and cook pumpkin shells, cut side down, covered loosely with waxed paper, 5 minutes in microwave. Add bread crumbs to vegetables and 1/4 cup Parmesan cheese. Mix together with seeds. Stuff pumpkins. Cover with Ritz cracker crumbs and 1/4 cup Parmesan cheese. Bake in 325 degree oven 20 minutes until hot. (Serve with tops on pumpkins.)

Serves 6

Betsy Mulligan

Microwave Ratatouille

1 medium eggplant, peeled and cut into 1/2 inch cubes
1 large green pepper, cut into strips
1 large onion, thickly sliced
3 tablespoons olive or cooking oil
1 clove garlic, finely chopped
2 medium zucchini, sliced 1/4 inch thick
2 or 3 large tomatoes, peeled and cut into wedges or 1 (16 ounce) can tomatoes, drained
2 teaspoons minced parsley
1 teaspoon basil
1 teaspoon salt
1/2 teaspoon pepper
1 bay leaf

In 3 quart casserole mix eggplant, green pepper, onion, oil and garlic. Cover. Microwave on high 5 to 6 minutes until onions are transparent. Stir in zucchini and cover. Microwave on high 5 to 6 minutes. Stir in tomatoes, parsley, basil, salt, pepper and bay leaf. Microwave on medium 8 to 10 minutes, or until vegetables are barely tender.

Ruth Tynes

Brown Rice Casserole

- 1 large onion
- 1 stick margarine
- 1 can cream of mushroom soup
- 1 can beef consomme
- 1 cup rice

Tenderize onion in 1 stick of margarine. Mix cream of mushroom soup and beef consomme. Add to onion mixture and stir until not lumpy. Wash rice and put in a casserole and pour soup mixture over it. Put lid on. Bake 350 degrees for 30 minutes. Remove lid and stir with a fork. Put lid back on and bake another 30 minutes.

Serves 6

Joy Wiggins

Rice Augratin Supreme

- 4 cups cooked rice
- 1/2 cup onion, finely chopped
- 1/2 cup bell pepper, finely chopped
- 1/4 cup pimento
- 1 can cream of mushroom soup
- 1/2 cup milk
- 1/3 cup mayonnaise
- 2 cups grated Cheddar cheese
- 1 teaspoon salt
- 1/4 teaspoon black or white pepper

Combine rice, onion, bell pepper and pimento. Set aside. Blend soup, milk, mayonnaise, cheese and seasonings. Mix rice mixture and soup mixture together and turn into a buttered casserole. Bake at 350 degrees for 25 minutes or until bubbly.

Helen White

Brown Rice and Vegetables

- 1 (10 ounce) package frozen English peas
- 1/2 cup uncooked brown rice
- 1 medium zucchini, unpeeled and shredded
- 2 tablespoons chopped pimento
- 1 teaspoon dried whole basil
- 1 (1.3 ounce) package Italian reduced calorie dressing mix
- lettuce leaves

Cook peas according to package directions, omitting salt. Drain, set aside. Cook rice according to package directions, omitting salt. Combine peas, rice, zucchini, pimento and basil in large bowl. Make the salad dressing mix according to package directions. Pour over rice mixture and stir, combining gently. Cover and chill thoroughly. To serve, place on lettuce leaves using a slotted spoon.

Makes 7 servings

Bob Burrill

Frances Shiekh's "Company" Rice

1 large onion, sliced
1 cinnamon rind, broken in half
vegetable oil
1/2 - 3/4 cup blanched whole almonds
1/2 - 3/4 cup raisins, if desired
2 cups Uncle Ben's converted rice
1 teaspoon cumin
6 peppercorns
3 whole cloves
salt and pepper, to taste
2 (14-1/2 ounce) cans chicken broth
1/4 cup water

In large saucepan, saute onion and cinnamon rind in oil until onion is lightly browned. Remove the onions and set aside. Add almonds and raisins (if desired) to saucepan and saute until almonds turn light brown and raisins plump. Remove almonds and raisins and set aside. Add to saucepan, rice, cumin, peppercorns, cloves, salt and pepper. Saute until the rice gets "glossy" looking and very lightly browned. Add chicken broth, water and 1/2 of the reserved onions. Bring to a boil. Reduce heat and simmer until liquid is absorbed — about 20 minutes. Serve garnished with reserved almonds, raisins and remaining onions.

Shirin Shiekh Blackwell

Easy Mexican Rice

1 cup rice
2 tablespoons oil
1/2 cup chopped tomatoes, fresh or canned
1/4 cup chopped onion
1 garlic clove, crushed
2 carrots, diced
1/2 cup peas, frozen or canned
1/4 cup cilantro (coriander)
2 chicken bouillon cubes
2 cups chicken broth

Saute rice in a skillet with oil. Stir often to brown evenly and prevent burning. Add tomatoes, onion and garlic. Stir until onion is cooked, one or two minutes. Next, add carrots, peas, cilantro, bouillon cubes and chicken broth. Bring to a boil. Lower heat and simmer for approximately 20 minutes or until the liquid is absorbed.

Bea Quintero

"Cauliflower is nothing but cabbage with a college education."

— Mark Twain

Blanche and Connie's Spinach Casserole

2 (10 ounce) packages frozen spinach
1 (14 ounce) can artichoke hearts (optional), drained
1-1/4 sticks margarine
1 (8 ounce) package cream cheese
1 (8 ounce) can sliced water chestnuts
dash of garlic salt
1/2 cup croutons

Cook spinach according to package directions and drain well. Cut artichoke hearts in half and put aside. Melt 1 stick of margarine and add spinach, cream cheese, water chestnuts and garlic salt. Line bottom and sides of oblong (2 quart) greased baking dish with artichoke hearts and cover with spinach mixture. Sprinkle with croutons. Dot with remaining margarine. Bake 400 degrees for 20-25 minutes.

Serves 10

Sandy Schmelzer

Spinach-Cheese Squares

2 cups cooked, chopped spinach, drained
4 tablespoons butter
1 tablespoon minced onion
4 tablespoons flour
1 teaspoon salt (optional)
1/8 teaspoon pepper
2 cups milk
1 cup grated American cheese
2 eggs slightly beaten

Melt butter, add minced onion and cook over low heat until tender. Add flour and seasonings. Blend. Add milk and cook until sauce thickens. Add cheese. Blend. Slowly add hot sauce to the beaten eggs while stirring. Add spinach and mix. Pour into 8-inch square oven dish. Set in shallow pan of hot water. Bake at 350 degrees for 30 minutes or until firm.

Serves 6

Joyce A. Wagner

Zucchini Supreme

5 zucchini, approximately 2 lbs.
1 onion
1 (10-3/4 ounce) can cream of chicken soup
1 cup sour cream
1/2 cup margarine, melted
1 package chicken flavored stuffing mix
pimentos, optional

Dice zucchini and onion; boil until tender in small amount of water. Drain off liquid and stir in soup and sour cream. Mix well. In separate bowl pour margarine over stuffing mix and toss. Grease a large casserole. Place a layer of stuffing on bottom, then a layer of zucchini. Alternate layers, ending with stuffing mix. Add pimentos for color, if desired. Bake 350 degrees for 30 minutes.

Serves 6-8

Betty Tonnessen

Greek Spinach and Rice (Spanacorizo)

1 large onion, chopped
1/4 cup olive oil
2 (14-16 ounce) cans spinach, undrained
1 (14-16 ounce) can tomatoes, undrained
3/4 cup raw rice
plenty of salt, pepper and garlic salt to taste
2 teaspoons oregano leaves

Saute onion in the olive oil for a couple of minutes, in a large saucepan; then add all other ingredients. Cook on medium heat about 30 minutes until liquids are absorbed. Tastes great hot or cold.

Serves 6-8

Angela Wheat Cheves

Spinach Madeline

2 (10 ounce) packages frozen chopped spinach
4 tablespoons margarine
2 tablespoons flour
2 tablespoons chopped onion
1/2 cup vegetable liquid
1/2 teaspoon black pepper
1/2 cup evaporated milk
3/4 teaspoon celery salt
3/4 teaspoon garlic salt
salt to taste
1 teaspoon Worcestershire sauce
red pepper to taste
1 (6 ounce) roll jalapeno cheese, cubed

Cook spinach by package directions; drain and reserve liquid. Melt margarine in saucepan over low heat. Add flour, stirring until blended and smooth, not brown. Add onion and cook until soft, not brown. Add liquid slowly, stirring to avoid lumps. Continue stirring and cooking until smooth and thick. Add seasonings and cubed cheese. Stir until melted. Combine with spinach. Can serve immediately or top with buttered bread crumbs in casserole dish. Flavor is better by casserole method and refrigerated overnight. This is one of my favorites that I have used for years.

Jackie Blackman

Tomato Pudding

1 cup brown sugar
1 cup tomato puree
1/4 cup water
2 cups bread cubes, crust removed
1/2 cup butter, melted

Combine sugar, tomato puree and water in saucepan. Cook 5 minutes. While cooking sauce, put bread cubes in a casserole and pour melted butter over cubes. Pour hot tomato mixture over cubes. Do not stir. Bake at 325 degrees for 50 minutes.

Lou Bruno

Spinach Rice

3 tablespoons butter or margarine
1/2 cup chopped green onions
1/4 cup sliced almonds
2 cups Uncle Ben's converted rice
2 (14-1/2 ounce) cans chicken broth
1/2 teaspoon pepper
2 (10 ounce) packages frozen chopped spinach
2 cups shredded Cheddar cheese
1/2 cup chopped pimento
toasted sliced almonds

In a large saucepan, over medium heat, heat butter. Add onions, almonds and rice and cook until onions are tender, stirring constantly. Add broth and pepper. Heat to boiling. Reduce heat to low. Cover; simmer for 15 minutes. Add spinach. Cover; simmer 10 minutes or until liquid is absorbed, breaking up spinach with a fork. Add cheese and pimento, heat until cheese melts. Garnish with toasted almonds.

Makes 8 cups or 12 servings

Shirin Shiekh Blackwell

Squash Casserole I

2-3 pounds yellow squash
1/2 cup margarine
3/4 cup chopped onion
15 Ritz crackers, crumbled
2 eggs, beaten
salt and pepper to taste
dash of Tabasco sauce
1 cup grated sharp Cheddar cheese
1/2 cup seasoned bread crumbs
1 tablespoon melted margarine

Cut squash and boil until tender, 15 to 20 minutes. Drain and mash. Saute onions in margarine and mix with squash. Add remaining ingredients except bread crumbs and margarine. Mix well. Pour in 2 quart casserole dish. Mix bread crumbs and melted margarine and sprinkle over squash, to cover. Bake at 350 degrees for 35 minutes.

Serves 6-8

Betsy Mulligan

Zucchini and Cheese Casserole

3 cups finely grated zucchini
1 cup cracker crumbs
1 cup grated Cheddar cheese
2 beaten eggs
2 tablespoons chopped onions
bacon bits

Combine the first 5 ingredients and put into a well buttered casserole. Bake for one hour at 350 degrees. Top with bacon bits.

Dorothy McCormick

Squash Casserole II

1-2 pounds yellow squash, sliced
1/2 cup chopped onions
1/2 cup chopped green bell pepper
1/2 cup water chestnuts, sliced
1/4 cup butter
1/2 cup mayonnaise
1 teaspoon sugar
1/2 teaspoon red pepper
1 egg, beaten
1/2 cup grated Cheddar cheese
bread crumbs

Boil sliced squash until tender and drain. Saute onions, bell pepper and water chestnuts and add to the squash. Cool slightly. Add mayonnaise, sugar, pepper, beaten egg and grated cheese. Pour into a casserole dish and sprinkle bread crumbs on top. Bake at 350 degrees for 30 minutes.

Barbara Elstad

Squash Casserole III

1-1/2 pounds yellow squash
1 small can pimento
1 medium onion, chopped
1 cup sour cream
1 can cream of chicken soup
4 medium carrots, grated
1 (8 ounce) package Pepperidge Farm Herbed Seasoned Dressing
1 stick margarine

Cook squash in salted water. Drain squash and mash. Add all other ingredients, holding back 1/2 stuffing and mix well. Place in 2 quart casserole. Melt 1 stick margarine and mix with remaining stuffing. Sprinkle over squash. Bake 30-40 minutes at 350 degrees. May be prepared ahead and put in refrigerator. When ready to cook, bake 45 minutes to one hour at 350 degrees.

Serves 6-8

Euna Bell

Vegetable Medley

3 (16 ounce) cans mixed vegetables, drained or 3 packages frozen mixed vegetables
1/2 cup mayonnaise
1 can sliced water chestnuts, drained
1-1/2 cups Velveeta cheese, cut up
1 stick butter, melted
1 tube Ritz crackers, crushed

Mix vegetables with mayonnaise; add water chestnuts and cheese and pour mixture into a 9x13 inch baking dish. Combine butter with crushed crackers and spread on top. Bake at 350 degrees for 20 minutes.

Serves 6-12

Mary Miller

MAIN DISHES

Deviled Egg Casserole

6 hard boiled eggs
1 cup sour cream
2 teaspoons prepared mustard
salt, to taste
2 tablespoons butter or margarine
1/3 cup chopped onion
1/2 cup chopped green pepper
1 small can mushrooms, drained
1/4 cup chopped pimento
1 can cream of mushroom soup
1/2 cup shredded sharp Cheddar cheese

Slice eggs in half. Mix egg yolks, 3 tablespoons sour cream, mustard and salt. Stuff mixture into egg white shells. Melt butter and saute onion, peppers and mushrooms. Remove from heat. Stir in pimento, soup and remaining sour cream. Pour 1/2 mixture in baking dish. Arrange the stuffed eggs in a single layer. Cover with remaining mixture. Sprinkle with cheese. Bake at 350 degrees until hot, about 20 minutes. May be prepared ahead of time and then heated.

Serves 6

Peggy Walker

Eggs for Brunch

18 eggs
1 cup and 2 tablespoons half and half
1 can cream of mushroom soup
1/2 pound mushrooms, sliced
5 ounces shredded sharp cheese
10 slices bacon (crisp and crumbled)
1 green pepper, chopped
4 green onions, sliced

Beat eggs with half and half and scramble. Remove from heat. Saute green pepper, mushrooms, and onions in butter and add to soup. Put soup mixture and cheese into eggs. Pour into shallow greased 3 quart baking dish. Top with bacon and bake 250 degrees for 1 hour. May be made day ahead.

Serves 16

Mary Belle Woody

Salt your food with humor, pepper it with wit and sprinkle over it the charm of friendship.

Egg and Cheese Casserole

16 slices bread with crust removed
8 slices ham, 1/4 inch thick
8 slices Old English cheese
7 eggs
3 cups milk
1 teaspoon salt, optional
1-1/2 teaspoons dry mustard
3 cups cornflakes, crushed
1 stick melted butter

In casserole dish, make a layer of bread, a layer of ham, a layer of cheese and another layer of bread. Mix eggs, milk, salt and mustard and pour over top and let soak overnight. Next day place cornflakes over top and drizzle butter over mixture. Bake 1 hour at 325 degrees. This is excellent for brunch!

Serves 8 or more

Ruth Jahns

Cheese Egg Souffle

4 slices buttered bread with crusts cut off
1/2 pound rat cheese, grated
2 1/2 cups milk
4 eggs
1 tablespoon powdered mustard
1/2 teaspoon salt

In buttered souffle dish place half of the bread. Add half of the cheese. Mix milk with the eggs and mustard. Add half of the milk mixture to the souffle dish and repeat layering with rest of the ingredients. Put in refrigerator for an hour before baking. Bake 1-1/2 hours at 300 degrees.

Serves 6

Nohra Kellough

Reunion Egg Dish

4 or 5 slices of bread
1 pound sausage, hot or mild
8 eggs
2 cups milk
1 cup grated Cheddar cheese

Cover bottom of 2 quart flat casserole with bread slices. Crumble and cook sausage and spread over bread. Beat eggs and milk together and pour over bread and sausage. Sprinkle cheese over all and bake at 325 to 350 degrees until set.

Serves 6 to 8 people and is easily adjusted for more

Ruth Crowe

Waist Watcher's Brunch Omelette

1 container Egg Beaters
12 ounces nonfat yogurt
1 package frozen chopped greens (spinach or broccoli or collards)
1 teaspoon garlic powder
1 teaspoon onion powder
1/2 teaspoon dry basil
3/4 cup low-fat cheese (mozzarella, Cheddar, etc.)

Defrost frozen greens — do not cook. Drain thoroughly. Mix all ingredients together except cheese. Spread in a 9x13 baking dish which has been sprayed with Pam. Sprinkle with shredded cheese and dust with freshly ground pepper. Bake at 375 degrees for about 20-25 minutes or until cheese is light brown and omelette is puffy.

Linda Manzione

Fettucini Alfredo I

1 package wide egg noodles, cooked and drained
1 stick margarine
16 ounces sour cream
salt, to taste
pepper, to taste
parsley flakes, to taste
garlic powder, to taste
basil, to taste
grated Parmesan cheese, to taste

Cook noodles according to package directions and put aside. In a saucepan, melt margarine and add sour cream, mixing well. Add rest of ingredients, mixing well and pour over cooked noodles, mixing well once again. If sauce too dry you may add milk.

Helen Mascolo

Fettuccine Alfredo II

1 large package fettuccine
1 cup grated Parmesan cheese
1 egg, beaten
1 cup melted butter
1 cup half and half cream, warm
garlic, minced, to taste
salt and pepper to taste

Cook fettuccine according to package directions, making sure not to over cook. Drain noodles and leave a little moisture on them. Put into a hot serving bowl. Sprinkle with cheese and toss; add beaten egg and toss. Add melted butter and warm half and half and toss until noodles are evenly coated. Season with garlic and salt and pepper to taste.

Serves 6 to 8

Lou Bruno

Great American Lasagna

1 pound ground beef
1-1/2 tablespoons olive oil
1 clove garlic, minced
1 tablespoon parsley flakes
1 tablespoon basil
2 teaspoons salt
2-1/2 cups canned tomatoes
1 (6 ounce) can tomato paste
1 (10 ounce) package lasagna noodles
2 (12 ounce) cartons large curd cream style cottage cheese
2 beaten eggs
2 teaspoons salt
1/2 teaspoon pepper
2 tablespoons parsley
1/2 cup grated Parmesan
1 pound American cheese slices

Brown meat in hot oil. Add next six ingredients. Simmer uncovered until thick, about 1 hour, stirring occasionally. Cook noodles. Combine cottage cheese with next five ingredients. Place layer of noodles in 9x13 casserole. Spread 1/2 cottage cheese mixture over noodles, add 1/2 the cheese slices, cover with 1/2 of the meat mixture. Repeat layers. Bake 350 degrees 30 minutes or until hot.

Serves 8

Jeanne Dean

Lasagna

2 pounds ground chuck
2 cups chopped onion
2 cloves garlic, minced
2 teaspoons msg.
2 teaspoons salt
1/2 cup olive oil
2 (#2-1/2) cans tomatoes
4 (8 ounce) cans tomato sauce
2 teaspoons onion salt
1/2 teaspoon salt
1 (12 ounce) package lasagna noodles
oil
12 ounces mozzarella cheese
4 ounces ricotta cheese

Saute first six ingredients in olive oil. Add next five ingredients and simmer 2-1/2 hours. Boil lasagna noodles according to package directions. Oil lasagna pan. Put in a layer of noodles (about half), a layer of mozzarella cheese, a layer of ricotta cheese, and a layer of sauce. Then repeat the three layers. Top with Parmesan cheese. Bake at 350 degrees for 45 minutes. Let stand for 15 minutes.

Serves 10

Elizabeth Bourgain

Health Wise Marinara Meat Sauce for Pasta

- 1/2 to 3/4 pound round steak
- 2 tablespoons no cholesterol oil
- 1 (14.5 ounce) can chicken broth
- 1 (28 ounce) can whole tomatoes, chopped and drained (reserve liquid)
- 1 carrot, chopped
- 1 stalk celery, chopped
- 2 large cloves garlic
- 1 tablespoon oregano
- 1 teaspoon sweet basil
- 1 bay leaf
- 1/4 teaspoon thyme
- 1/8 teaspoon black pepper
- 1 or 2 dashes crushed red pepper
- 2 green onions, including tops
- 1 (1.5 ounce) package spaghetti sauce mix
- 1 (28 ounce) can Progresso crushed tomatoes with puree
- 1 onion, chopped
- 1 green pepper, chopped
- 1 (6 ounce) can tomato paste
- 4 ounces dry red wine (can delete and substitute water if desired)
- 3 tablespoons grated Parmesan cheese
- 1 tablespoon parsley
- 1 teaspoon sugar (or more, to taste)

Trim fat from steak and chop in a food processor. Brown meat in a 4 quart pot with oil for 2-3 minutes until meat is heated. Add chicken broth; cover pot and simmer for 5 minutes. Pour liquid into a jar. Cool until fat solidifies on top, then remove fat and discard. Put juice, drained from whole tomatoes, into a 2 quart pot with carrot and celery. Bring to a boil, cover and simmer for 5 minutes. After this cools slightly, pour liquid only into a blender, along with the garlic, oregano, basil, bay leaf, thyme and black and red pepper. Blend 20 seconds. Add carrots, celery, green onions and spaghetti sauce mix. Blend again for 20 seconds. Pour this mixture into the large pot with meat, and add the can of crushed tomatoes with puree and simmer. To this same pot, add onions, green pepper and chopped tomatoes. Place cooled broth fluid (from step 1) into blender and add tomato paste, wine, Parmesan cheese and parsley. Blend lightly and add to large pot. Simmer for 1-2 hours; add sugar to taste. Keep cover on pot for thinner sauce and off for a thicker sauce. You have now made the most health supporting marinara sauce possible and created a flavor that will exceed the best from Firenze to Napoli!

Serves 8   A low cholesterol and no salt recipe

Howard W. Andersen

Vegetable-Cheese Lasagna

1 tablespoon and 1 teaspoon margarine
3 cups thinly sliced mushrooms
1 tablespoon and 1 teaspoon olive oil
1 cup chopped onion
6 garlic cloves, minced
1-1/2 cups tomato sauce
1 cup canned Italian tomatoes (with liquid) drain and dice
11 ounces shredded Monterey Jack cheese, divided
1-1/2 teaspoons salt (divided)
1 teaspoon each, oregano leaves and Basil leaves
1/2 teaspoon pepper (divided)
1 bay leaf
2 (10 ounce) packages frozen spinach, thawed and well drained (about 2 cups)
2 cups part-skim ricotta cheese
1 egg beaten
8 ounces lasagna noodles (cooked)

In 10 inch skillet heat margarine over medium heat until bubbly and hot; add mushrooms and saute, stirring occasionally, until mushrooms are lightly browned and cooked 2-3 minutes. Remove from heat and set aside. In 3 quarter saucepan heat oil over medium heat; add onion garlic and saute until onions are softened (1-2 minutes). Add tomato sauce, tomatoes, 3/4 teaspoon salt, oregano, basil, 1/4 teaspoon pepper, bay leaf. Mix well. Reduce heat to low, cover, let simmer, stirring occasionally for 25 to 30 minutes, remove and discard bay leaf. In medium mixing bowl combine spinach, ricotta cheese, egg, remaining 3/4 teaspoon salt, remaining 1/4 teaspoon pepper, mixing well. Preheat oven to 350 degrees. In bottom of 13x9x2 inch baking dish spread 1/2 cup tomato mixture, arrange half of the lasagna lengthwise in dish — overlapping edges slightly. Spread half of the spinach mixture evenly over macaroni and top with half of mushrooms; spread 1/2 cup of the tomato mixture over mushrooms and sprinkle with half of Monterey Jack cheese. Arrange remaining macaroni crosswise in dish, cutting noodles to fit and overlapping edges slightly spread remaining spinach mixture over noodles — top with remaining mushrooms, tomato mixture, Monterey Jack cheese. Bake until lasagna is cooked through and cheese is lightly browned 40-50 minutes. Remove from oven and let stand 15 minutes before serving.

Serves 8

Leslie Hungerford

Moma's Manicotti

Sausage and Meat Sauce:
- **1 pound Italian sausage, each pricked in several places with a fork**
- **1 pound ground turkey or lean ground beef**
- **1 medium onion, finely chopped**
- **10 cloves garlic, minced**
- **4 cups pureed tomato**
- **6 ounces canned tomato paste**
- **1-1/4 cups water**
- **1 tablespoon basil**
- **salt and pepper to taste**

In a covered pot over medium heat, cook sausage in 1/4 cup water five minutes. Uncover and let water evaporate; brown the sausages well and drain on paper towels. Discard fat; brown meat, onions and garlic in the same pot. Stir in tomato puree, tomato paste, basil, salt and pepper and remaining water. Cover; simmer for 45 minutes. Cut sausages into bite-size pieces and add to the sauce. Cook 15 more minutes, stirring occasionally.

Pasta & Filling:
- **1/2 pound manicotti (16 shells), boiled and drained**
- **2 pounds sieved low-fat cottage or ricotta cheese**
- **1/2 pound mozzarella cheese, diced**
- **2 tablespoons chopped fresh parsley**
- **1 tablespoon dried basil**
- **1/2 teaspoon salt**
- **freshly grated Parmesan cheese**

Preheat oven to 375 degrees. In large bowl, combine the cottage cheese, mozzarella, parsley, basil and salt. Stuff this filling into the cooked manicotti shells. Spoon half the sauce into a 13x9 inch baking dish. Arrange half the stuffed shells in one layer on top of the sauce. Spoon most of the remaining sauce, reserving about 3/4 cup, over the shells. Top with the remaining shells in one layer. Spoon the reserved sauce over the top. Sprinkle with freshly grated Parmesan cheese. Bake 30 minutes in the preheated oven.

Doris Blumenthal

Pizza Genna (Italian Quiche)

- **12 eggs, separated**
- **3 pounds ricotta cheese**
- **1 pound mozzarella cheese, cubed**
- **1/4 pound provolone cheese**
- **Prosciutto (Italian ham)**
- **3 sticks pepperoni, sliced**
- **black pepper**

Mix ricotta cheese with beaten egg yolks. Add rest of the ingredients and pour into a lasagna baking pan. Fold beaten egg whites into mixture and bake approximately 2 hours.

Helen Mascolo

Shirin's Ravioli Casserole

2 tablespoons olive oil
1 medium onion, chopped
3 large cloves garlic, minced
1 teaspoon thyme
1/2 teaspoon oregano
1 teaspoon sugar
1/2 teaspoon pepper
1 (28 ounce) can Progresso Peeled Tomatoes (Italian Style with Basil), drained
1 (14-1/2 ounce) can Hunt's Stewed Tomatoes, drained
salt to taste
25 frozen jumbo cheese filled ravioli
olive oil
8 to 10 ounces Cheddar cheese, grated
8 to 10 ounces mozzarella cheese, grated
1/2 to 3/4 cup fresh grated Parmesan cheese

Heat oil in saucepan and add onions and garlic. Saute until onions become transparent. Add thyme, oregano, sugar, pepper, tomatoes and salt. Bring to boil; reduce heat and simmer for 20 minutes. Boil ravioli according to package directions for "al dente". Lightly oil 13x9 inch baking dish. Arrange ravioli in baking dish. Pour the tomato sauce over the ravioli. Sprinkle the cheese on top. Bake at 350 degrees until cheese melts and becomes bubbly. Note: if you are in a hurry, spaghetti sauce in a jar may be substituted for the tomato sauce.

Shirin Shiekh Blackwell

Spaghetti Carbonara

1 pound thin spaghetti
6-8 slices bacon
1/8 cup olive oil
1/4 medium size yellow onion, peeled and chopped
2 tablespoons butter, softened
1/4 cup chicken broth
salt and pepper to taste
1 egg, lightly beaten
1/8 cup chopped parsley
1/2 cup grated Parmesan cheese

Cook spaghetti according to package directions. Meanwhile, fry or microwave bacon until crisp. Heat oil in 12 inch skillet over moderate heat. Add and cook onion until soft, about 5 minutes. Add butter, chicken broth, salt and pepper. Heat through. Drain pasta and toss with sauce. Add eggs and toss. Add parsley and cheese then toss again. Crumble bacon over pasta and stir in.

Dianne Ibenthal

Asparagus and Salmon Casserole

1 pound fresh asparagus or 2 packages frozen asparagus spears
4 tablespoons butter or margarine
4 tablespoons flour
1-1/2 cups milk
1 (6 ounce) can red salmon, drained, cleaned and flaked
1/2 teaspoon salt
1/4 teaspoon pepper
1/4 cup Parmesan

Clean fresh asparagus, cut into 1 inch pieces and cook until tender. Drain asparagus and place in buttered baking dish. If frozen asparagus is used, cook according to package directions and drain. Melt butter in saucepan; blend in flour, one tablespoon at a time. Stir in milk slowly. Cook, stirring constantly until thick. Add the flaked salmon and salt and pepper. Mix well and pour this mixture over the cooked asparagus. Sprinkle the Parmesan cheese on top. Bake in preheated oven 350 degrees for 15-20 minutes.

Serves 6-8

George Rimmey

Baked Orange Ruffy

1 pound orange ruffy
salt and pepper to taste
lemon juice
1 medium onion, sliced
5 large mushrooms, sliced
8 ounces lowfat plain yogurt
1/2 cup Parmesan cheese
Italian bread crumbs

Line a baking dish with orange ruffy. Top with salt, pepper and lemon juice. Saute onion and mushrooms and place over fish. Mix yogurt and Parmesan cheese and spread over fish, onions and mushrooms. Top with bread crumbs, cover with foil and bake at 350 degrees for 30 minutes.

Mary Bellos

Crab Quiche

4 ounces Swiss cheese, shredded
1 unbaked 9 inch pie shell
1 cup crabmeat
2 green onions and tops, sliced
3 eggs, beaten
1 cup light cream or half and half
1/2 teaspoon salt
1/2 teaspoon grated lemon peel
1/4 teaspoon dry mustard
1/4 cup sliced almonds

Sprinkle cheese evenly over bottom of unbaked pie shell. Top with crabmeat and green onions. Combine eggs, cream, salt, lemon peel and dry mustard. Pour over crabmeat. Top with almonds. Bake at 325 degrees until set, about 45 minutes. Remove from oven and let stand 10 minutes before serving.

Serves 6

Mrs. Lloyd P. Zowarka

Perry's Deviled Crab

1-1/2 cups coarsely crushed cracker crumbs, divided
1-1/4 cups milk, divided
1 cup chopped celery
1 cup chopped green onions
1/2 cup chopped fresh parsley
1 pound fresh crabmeat
1/2 teaspoon salt
few dashes red pepper
1-1/2 teaspoons dry mustard
1/2 cup melted butter

Reserve about 1/2 cup cracker crumbs and 3/4 cup milk. Mix all ingredients together and combine well; put into baking dish and pour reserved milk over mixture. Top with reserved crumbs and bake at 350 degrees until delicately browned and bubbly.

Serves: 4-6

J. F. DeCell

Janson's Temptation

2 filets salt herring (fairly bonefree) or Scandinavian anchovies or canned kippered herring and anchovies
milk, if needed
4-5 potatoes
2 medium onions
2 tablespoons butter
1 cup cream or half and half

If fillets are very salty, soak overnight in milk. Rinse and remove coarse bones. Slice crosswise in 1/2 inch strips. Peel potatoes and cut into shoestrings. Slice onions thinly and saute in butter until golden. Arrange in casserole, layers of potatoes, herring, and onions: bottom and top layers should be potatoes. Pour cream over the dish to saturate lower half of mixture. Bake 50-60 minutes at 350-375 degrees. Look in after 30 minutes and add more cream if necessary. If freezing, bake only 30-40 minutes.

Walter Vetterick

When you are preparing dinner for six, make enough for twelve, serve only half and freeze the remainder!

Linda's Seafood Lasagna

- 8 lasagna noodles, cooked and drained
- 1 cup onions, chopped
- 2 tablespoons butter or margarine
- 1 (8 ounce) package cream cheese, room temperature
- 1-1/2 cups cottage cheese
- 1 egg, beaten
- 2 teaspoons dried basil, crushed
- 1/2 teaspoon salt
- 1/8 teaspoon pepper
- 2 cans cream of mushroom soup
- 1/3 cup milk
- 1/3 cup dry white wine
- 1 pound cooked shelled shrimp (cut in half if desired)
- 1 (7-1/2 ounce) can crab, drained, flaked (cartilage removed)
- 1/4 cup Parmesan cheese, grated
- 1/2 cup sharp Cheddar cheese, grated (2 ounces)

Place 4 noodles in greased 9x13 dish. Cook onion in butter until tender. Blend in softened cream cheese. Stir in cottage cheese, egg, basil, salt and pepper. Spread one-half of mixture on noodles. Combine soup, milk and wine. Stir in shrimp and crab; spread one-half on cottage cheese layer. Repeat layers. Sprinkle with Parmesan cheese. Bake uncovered at 350 degrees for 45 minutes. Top with Cheddar cheese and bake 2 to 3 minutes longer.

Serves 12

Bob Burrill

Trout Amandine

- 2 pounds fresh trout or snapper fillets
- 1/4 cup flour
- 1 teaspoon Lawry's seasoned salt
- 1 teaspoon paprika
- 1/2 cup melted margarine
- 1 cup sliced almonds
- 4 teaspoons lemon juice
- 8 drops Tabasco sauce
- 2 tablespoons chopped parsley, optional

Cut fillets into six portions. Combine flour, seasoned salt and paprika. Roll portions in flour mixture and place in a single layer, skin side down, in a well greased baking dish. Drizzle 2 tablespoons melted margarine over portions. Broil about 4 inches from source of heat 10-15 minutes or until fish flakes easily when tested with a fork. While fish is broiling, saute almonds in remaining margarine until golden brown, stirring constantly. Remove from heat and mix in lemon juice, hot pepper sauce and parsley. Pour over portions and serve at once.

Serves 4-6

Leah Whitty

Seafood Pasta DiFerrante

3 pints oysters
4 tablespoons butter
1 tablespoon olive oil
1-1/2 pounds medium, peeled shrimp
1 pound fresh lump crabmeat
1/4 cup fresh lemon juice
salt and freshly ground pepper
1 pound angel hair or green spinach noodles

Sauce:
1/2 cup olive oil
4 tablespoons butter
8 large cloves garlic, minced
1 heaping cut fresh parsley, chopped
1 bunch fresh basil, chopped
juice of 1/2 lemon
1/2 teaspoon salt
1/2 teaspoon pepper
Tabasco sauce, to taste

For sauce, melt butter and olive oil in heavy saucepan. Add minced garlic and saute for 3-5 minutes, but do not allow to darken or burn. Add parsley and basil at the end of cooking. Season with the lemon juice, salt, pepper and Tabasco sauce if desired. Set aside. Blanch oysters by putting them in boiling water, then turning off the heat. Leave in water for 3 minutes, then drain well. Melt butter in skillet with olive oil. Saute the shrimp 1-2 minutes. Add the crabmeat and the drained oysters. Season with the lemon juice and freshly ground pepper. Cook pasta of choice in rapidly boiling water according to package directions — 3-5 minutes for angel hair type. Drain well and toss. Add the sauce to the combined seafoods and toss around lightly. Serve steaming hot.

Serves 4-6 for main course

Stephen DiFerrante

Sauteed Fish with Tomato Sauce

1-1/2 pounds firm fish (sliced fillets or small, whole fish)
flour, seasoned with salt, pepper and garlic powder
1 tablespoon butter
2 tablespoons olive oil
1 clove garlic, minced
1 teaspoon minced parsley
1 cup canned Italian style tomatoes

Dip fish in seasoned flour. Heat together the butter and olive oil and saute fish, browning on both sides. Add garlic, parsley and tomatoes. Cook fish, covered, over low heat for about 10 to 12 minutes. Before serving sprinkle with additional minced parsley.

Serves 3 or 4

Lou Bruno

Tuna on a Shoestring

1 (6-1/2 ounce) can tuna
1 cup carrots, shredded
1 cup celery, diced
3/4 minced onion
3/4 to 1 cup salad dressing
1 (4 ounce) cup shoestring potatoes
lettuce leaves
parsley and carrot curls

Combine tuna, carrots, celery, onion and salad dressing in mixing bowl; mix gently. Cover and chill. Just before serving, fold in potatoes. Arrange in lettuce lined bowl. Garnish with parsley and carrot curls.

Dora Hughes

Deviled Tuna Pot Pie

2 tablespoons margarine
1/2 medium onion, chopped fine
1-2 cloves garlic, minced
1 large celery stalk, sliced thin
1 cup fresh or frozen whole kernel corn
1-2 tablespoons pimento, chopped
black pepper, to taste
2 tablespoons flour
1/2 cup milk
1 cup low salt chicken broth
2 tablespoons grated Parmesan cheese or cheese of your choice
2 teaspoons Dijon mustard
1 tablespoon lemon juice
2 (6-1/2 ounce) cans water packed white tuna, flaked including water
4 refrigerator whole wheat or oat biscuits, halved horizontally and slightly flattened

Preheat oven to 450 degrees. In a heavy saucepan, melt margarine and saute onions, garlic, and celery just until softened. Add next three ingredients and mix well. Blend flour, milk, and broth in another saucepan and cook until thickened. Add the thickened flour mixture to the corn mixture and blend well. Add cheese, mustard, and lemon juice to corn mixture, mixing well. Remove from heat. Fold in flaked tuna (water included, it contains nutrients). Transfer the mixture to an ungreased, shallow 5 or 6 cup casserole. Arrange biscuit halves on top and sprinkle with paprika. Bake uncovered until biscuits are golden, about 10 minutes.

Serves 5-6

A. Marion Webster

Mill Rice Scampi

1-1/2 cups uncooked rice
1 teaspoon salt
1/2 pound melted margarine
1 large onion finely chopped
1/4 teaspoon cayenne pepper
1/2 teaspoon Accent
1 tablespoon curry powder
handful of chopped parsley
1 medium can mushrooms with juice
1 pound cooked shrimp

Cook rice with 1 teaspoon salt. Saute chopped onions with margarine until transparent. Add the other ingredients and pour over rice. Keep hot until serving time over hot water.

Serves 6.

Joy Wiggins

Shrimp Cacciatore

1 tablespoon butter
2 tablespoons olive oil
1 onion, chopped
1 clove garlic, cut in half
2 cups Italian plum tomatoes
1 green bell pepper, cut into 8-10 slices
1/2 pound fresh mushrooms, sliced
1/2 cup dry white wine
1 pound raw shrimp, shelled and deveined

In a saucepan, heat together butter and olive oil. Add onion and garlic and saute until onion is soft and pale gold. Add tomatoes and bell pepper. Cook this sauce for about 15 minutes and then add mushrooms and wine. Continue to cook, covered, for about 20 minutes or until sauce is the consistency you like. Remove garlic, add shrimp and simmer in sauce 15 minutes or until done. Serve over rice or macaroni.

Serves 3 or 4

Lou Bruno

Shrimp Casserole with Angel Hair Pasta

- 1 pound shrimp, peeled
- 8 ounces angel hair pasta
- 2 (10-3/4 ounce) cans cream of mushroom soup
- 1 cup light sour cream
- 1/2 cup sliced green onions
- 1/4 cup chopped bell pepper
- 1/2 teaspoon dried dill weed
- 1/2 teaspoon pepper
- 1/2 cup shredded Cheddar cheese
- parsley sprigs for garnish

Simmer shrimp in boiling water for 2 minutes. Drain and rinse with cold water. Cook and drain pasta according to package directions. Combine pasta, soup, sour cream, onions, bell pepper, dill weed, and pepper. Mix well. Cut 1/4 of the shrimp into thirds and mix with shredded cheese and noodle mixture. Pour into shallow baking dish, cover and bake at 350 degrees for 20 minutes. Remove cover. Arrange remaining shrimp on top and return to oven for 10 minutes. Garnish with parsley sprigs before serving.

Serves: 6

Betsy Mulligan

Shrimp Casserole for a Crowd

- 1 green pepper, chopped
- 2 stalks celery, chopped
- 1 medium onion, chopped
- 2 cups water
- 1 small can pimentos, chopped, drained
- 3 pounds cooked, deveined shrimp
- 1 (7-1/2 ounce) can crabmeat
- 4 hard cooked eggs, thickly sliced
- 4 tablespoons butter
- 4 tablespoons all purpose flour
- 2 cups half and half
- 1 cup shredded sharp Cheddar cheese
- 1/2 teaspoon salt
- 1/8 teaspoon pepper
- 3/4 cup buttered bread or cracker crumbs

Combine green pepper, celery, onions and water. Cook until vegetables are tender. Add pimento, shrimp, crabmeat and eggs. Set aside. To make cheese sauce, melt butter and stir in flour until smooth. Gradually add half and half until mixture thickens, stirring constantly. Add cheese, salt and pepper. Add sauce to shrimp mixture and place in a greased 3 quart casserole. Sprinkle crumbs over the top and bake at 400 degrees for 15 minutes.

Serves 12-15

Nohra Kellough

Shrimp Casserole Harpin

2 pounds large shrimp
1 tablespoon lemon juice
3 tablespoons salad oil
3/4 cup raw rice
2 tablespoons butter or margarine
1/4 cup minced green pepper
1/4 cup minced onion
1 teaspoon salt
1/8 teaspoon pepper
1/8 teaspoon mace
dash cayenne pepper
1 can tomato soup
1 cup cream
1/2 cup sherry
1/2 cup slivered almonds (optional)
paprika

Early in the day, shell, devein, and cook the shrimp in boiling salted water. Drain. Place in a 2 quart casserole. Sprinkle with lemon juice and oil. Cook rice as directed and refrigerate. One hour and ten minutes before serving preheat oven to 350 degrees. Melt butter in skillet and saute green pepper and onion. Combine rest of the ingredients except 1/4 of the almonds and paprika. Add the rice, sauteed onions and green pepper and the rest of the ingredients to shrimp in the casserole. Top with almonds and paprika. Bake uncovered 55 minutes or until bubbly.

Serves: 6-8

Marie Sullivan

Shrimp Creole I

4 tablespoons butter
1 medium onion, cut fine
1 green pepper, cut fine
4 stalks celery, cut thin
2 tablespoons flour
1/2 teaspoon crushed sage (if you like sage; otherwise, omit)
1 teaspoon salt
1/8 teaspoon pepper
1 tablespoon lemon juice or vinegar
1 can tomatoes
1-1/2 pounds shrimp, cleaned and shelled

Heat butter in skillet to brown onions, peppers and celery. Blend in flour, sage, salt and pepper. Add lemon juice and tomatoes; cover and simmer 10 minutes. Add cleaned shrimp and bring to boil. Lower heat and simmer 8 minutes. Serve over bed of rice.

Serves 6-8

Mary Cypert

Shrimp Creole II

- 1-1/2 cups chopped onion
- 3 stalks celery, chopped
- 2 cloves garlic, minced
- 2 medium green peppers, chopped
- 1/4 cup butter
- 1 (15 ounce) can tomato sauce
- 1 cup water
- 2 teaspoons snipped parsley
- 1 teaspoon salt
- 1/2 teaspoon cayenne
- 2 bay leaves, crushed
- 1 pound fresh cleaned raw shrimp
- 3 cups hot cooked rice

Cook and stir onion, celery, garlic and green pepper in butter until onion is tender. Remove from heat; stir in tomato sauce, water, parsley and seasonings. Return to stove and simmer, uncovered, 10-15 minutes, adding more water if necessary. Stir in shrimp and heat to boiling. Cover and reduce heat to medium; continue cooking for 10 to 20 minutes or until shrimp are pink and tender. Serve over rice.

Serves 6

Jane McFaddin

Shrimp Divan

- 2 packages frozen peas
- 2 pounds cooked shrimp, shelled
- 2 cans cream of shrimp soup
- 1 cup Hellman's mayonnaise
- 1 tablespoon lemon juice
- 1 teaspoon curry powder
- 1/2 cup shredded sharp Cheddar cheese
- 1 cup soft bread crumbs
- 2 tablespoons margarine or butter, melted

Cook peas according to package directions. Place in greased 11x7x2 inch baking dish. Put shrimp on top of peas. Mix together soup, mayonnaise, lemon juice and curry; pour over shrimp. Sprinkle cheese on top. Combine bread crumbs with melted margarine and sprinkle over cheese. Bake in 350 degree oven for 25-30 minutes. Easy and delicious!

Serves 8

Kay Laro

Exposure to direct sunlight softens tomatoes instead of ripening them. Leave the tomatoes, stem up, in any spot where they will be out of direct sunlight.

Shrimp De Jonghe

1 cup butter, melted
2 cloves garlic, minced
1/2 cup parsley, chopped
1/2 teaspoon paprika
dash of cayenne pepper
2/3 cup cooking sherry
2 cups soft bread crumbs
5-6 cups shrimp, cleaned and cooked

To melted butter add garlic, parsley, paprika, cayenne and cooking sherry. Mix well and add to bread crumbs. Toss. Place shrimp in a baking dish or individual ramekins. Spoon the crumb mixture over shrimp. Bake at 325 degrees for 20 to 25 minutes, or until crumbs are brown. Sprinkle with additional chopped parsley before serving.

Lou Bruno

Shrimp New Orleans

1 large bottle Wish Bone Italian dressing
1 medium white onion
2 cloves garlic, minced
1/2 bell pepper, minced
juice of 1 fresh lemon
2 pounds dressed medium shrimp

Combine first five ingredients, mixing well. Add shrimp and marinate for 4-5 hours. After 4-5 hours, broil shrimp in dressing 20-30 minutes. Dressing will divide into oil and gravy. Use oil on tossed salad, gravy on mashed potatoes. Serve with white wine and French bread.

Serves 4

Pearlie Leger

Shrimp and Rice

2 cans cream of shrimp soup
1/3 cup raw rice
2 tablespoons margarine
2 celery stalks,chopped
1/4 green pepper, chopped
1 cup sliced water chestnuts
1 large jar pimentos
1 pound cooked shrimp
2 tablespoons sherry
1/2 cup Parmesan cheese
Tabasco and salt to taste

Warm cream of shrimp soup without adding water but do not boil. Cook rice according to package directions. Saute in margarine, celery, green pepper, water chestnuts and pimento. Add rice and sauteed ingredients to soup. Then add shrimp, sherry, Parmesan, Tabasco and salt to taste. Warm in casserole, in slow oven. Tends to get a little soupier as it is heating. For more guests add more shrimp.

Serves 8 or 2-3 couples

Nelly and Maribel Orencia

Wild Rice and Shrimp Casserole

1/2 cup flour
1 cup margarine, divided
4 cups chicken broth
1/4 teaspoon pepper
1 cup thinly sliced onions
1/2 cup thinly sliced green pepper
1 cup sliced mushrooms
2 pounds cooked shrimp
2 tablespoons Worcestershire sauce
2 drops Tabasco
4 cups cooked wild rice
buttered bread crumbs

Make sauce, gradually adding flour to half melted margarine, adding broth and seasonings. Set aside. Saute vegetables in remaining margarine. Combine all ingredients (except crumbs) and place in shallow 9x13 casserole. Top with buttered crumbs. Bake at 350 degrees for 45 minutes. Great party dish! Can be made ahead.

Serves 10

Jeanne Dean

Shrimp and Scallop Casserole

1 cup minced onion
1 stalk celery, chopped fine
1/2 stick margarine
2 tablespoons flour
1 (13 ounce) can evaporated milk
2 egg yolks, beaten
1 pound cooked scallops (or crabmeat)
1 pound cooked shrimp
3 tablespoons sherry
1/2 teaspoon cayenne
1/4 teaspoon pepper
1 teaspoon salt
1/2 pound grated Cheddar cheese

Saute onion and celery in margarine until wilted. Blend in flour. Combine milk and eggs, then gradually add to flour mixture, stirring constantly for 5 minutes. Combine scallops and shrimp in separate bowl; pour in sherry and seasonings, mixing well. Combine with all ingredients and turn into greased baking dish and sprinkle with cheese. Bake at 375 degrees or until cheese melts.

Serves 6.

Nathan Huang

Use as little water as possible when cooking vegetables to retain vitamins and minerals. Avoid violent boiling of most vegetables.

Shrimp Scampi

1 pound raw shrimp
1/4 cup butter
1 tablespoon lemon juice
1 teaspoon parsley
1 teaspoon chives
1/2 teaspoon tarragon
1/2 teaspoon dry mustard
3/4 teaspoon Season All
1/8 teaspoon red pepper
1/8 teaspoon garlic powder (can use equivalent of fresh garlic)

Shell and devein shrimp. Melt butter in skillet. Add lemon juice, seasonings, and shrimp. Saute shrimp until pink, about 8 minutes, depending on size, turning once.

Serves 2

Lila Poland

Tuna Cakes

12 saltine crackers (crumbed)
1 (6 ounce) can tuna, drained
1 egg, beaten
1/4 cup skim milk
1 teaspoon minced onion
1 teaspoon fresh parsley
1/4 teaspoon Worcestershire sauce
dash pepper
1 teaspoon margarine

In medium bowl combine all ingredients except margarine and shape into 6 equal patties. In 10 inch skillet heat margarine until bubbly and hot. Add patties and cook over medium heat, turning once, until browned on both sides.

Serves 2 (3 cakes each)

Leslie Hungerford

Sherried Artichoke Chicken

3 pounds chicken parts (use chicken thighs)
salt, pepper, paprika
6 tablespoons butter or margarine
1 can artichokes
1/4 pound mushrooms
3 tablespoons minced onions (use frozen ones)
3 tablespoons flour
2/3 cup chicken broth
1/4 cup sherry
1/2 teaspoon dried rosemary

Preheat oven to 375 degrees. Sprinkle chicken with salt, pepper and paprika. In a skillet melt 4 tablespoons butter and brown chicken on all sides. Put in casserole. Arrange artichoke hearts between chicken pieces. Add 2 tablespoons of butter to drippings in skillet. Add mushrooms and onions, saute until tender. Sprinkle flour over mushrooms, stir in broth, sherry and rosemary. Cook stirring for a few minutes. Pour over chicken and bake in 375 degree oven for 40 minutes.

Serves 4

Tibby Lloyd

Chicken Green Bean Casserole

1/2 cup chopped onion
1 can cream of mushroom soup
1/2 cup milk
1-1/2 cups shredded Cheddar cheese
1 teaspoon salt
3 cups cooked chicken, cut into chunks
1 can French style green beans, drained
1 can chop suey, drained
1 can onion rings (Durkee's)

Mix chopped onion, soup, milk and cheese together in saucepan. Add salt. Warm these ingredients. Add chicken, green beans and chop suey. Put in casserole dish and top with onion rings. Bake at 350 degrees for 1 hour.

Serves 6

Linda Stearns

Chicken Breasts with Artichoke Hearts

3 whole chicken breasts, halved
flour
vegetable oil
2 tablespoons butter or margarine
2 tablespoons flour
1 teaspoon salt
1/4 teaspoon white pepper
3 tablespoons brandy
2 teaspoons lemon juice
1-1/2 cups water
2 chicken flavor bouillon cubes
1 cup sour cream
2 (9 ounce) packages frozen artichoke hearts, thawed and drained

Coat chicken with flour. In skillet over medium heat lightly brown chicken in vegetable oil. Place in 12x9 baking dish and set aside. Preheat oven to 350 degrees. Melt butter or margarine in 2 quart saucepan, stir in 2 tablespoons flour with salt and pepper until smooth. Slowly stir in brandy, lemon juice, water and chicken bouillon; cook, stirring constantly until thickened and smooth; whisk in sour cream and pour over chicken. Cover tightly with foil and bake 45 minutes. Remove foil and add artichokes. Recover and continue baking 15 minutes longer.

Serves 6

Claudette Perse

Lemon cups filled with tartar sauce make an eye-appealing border for seafood.

Aunt Kate's Chicken

1 chicken or parts
margarine
1 onion, chopped
1 green pepper, chopped
1 (8 ounce) box mushrooms, sliced
1 cup tomato or V-8 juice
1 cup water
1/2 cup sherry
1 teaspoon paprika
1 teaspoon salt
1/4 teaspoon pepper

Brown chicken in butter and place in casserole. Saute vegetables in skillet. Add tomato juice, water, sherry and seasonings. Pour over chicken. Cover and bake at 375 degrees for 30-45 minutes. Serve with rice.

Serves 4-6

Jeanne Dean

Page's Chicken

12 slices Canadian bacon
6 chicken breasts, boned, skinned and split
3 cups yogurt
2 cans cream of mushroom soup

Place Canadian bacon in bottom of casserole. Arrange chicken breasts on top. Combine yogurt and soup. Pour over the chicken. Bake at 275 degrees for 2-1/2 to 3 hours. Cover with foil the first 2 hours. Then cook uncovered remainder of time.

Serves 8-10

Page Lawson

Apricot Chicken

4 skinless, boneless chicken breasts
4 tablespoons low sugar apricot jam
juice of 1/2 orange
1/4 teaspoon rosemary
1 teaspoon minced garlic
1/8 teaspoon cinnamon
1/4 cup raisins
1/4 cup water
pepper to taste

Place chicken in baking dish. Mix all ingredients together and pour over chicken, coating well. Bake at 400 degrees for 10 minutes. Turn chicken over; lower oven to 325 degrees and continue baking for 30 minutes. Good served with steamed carrot sticks.

Honey Epstein

Rip's Barbecued Chicken (Texas Style)

- 1 (5 ounce) bottle Worcestershire sauce
- 5 ounces water (halfway between 1/2 and 3/4 cup)
- 5 ounces vinegar
- 2 tablespoons margarine
- 2-3 slices uncooked bacon, chopped
- 1/2 teaspoon salt
- 1/2 teaspoon black pepper
- 1/2 teaspoon celery salt
- 1/2 tablespoon prepared mustard
- grated rind of 1/2 lemon
- 1-2 dashes Tabasco sauce
- 1-2 cloves garlic, crushed
- 3-4 chickens, about 1-1/2 pounds each
- salt and pepper

Combine first 12 ingredients and simmer for 30 minutes. In the meantime split chickens in half and season with salt and pepper. Place chickens on hot grill, skin down, and brown on both sides, turning occasionally. This takes about 15 minutes. Baste first with oily part of sauce that has floated to top. Continue basting and turning over gentle coals until chickens are done. They will be tender and a deep rich brown. This takes about 45 minutes.

Serves: 6-8

Roberta Torn

Baked Chicken Breasts

- 6 whole chicken breasts, boned, skinned, and split
- flour
- butter
- 2 (10 ounce) cans of cream of chicken soup
- 1 pint of sour cream
- 1 small can water chestnuts, sliced
- 2 (4 ounce) cans of mushrooms, drained and sliced
- 4 ounce package sliced almonds

Flour chicken breasts and brown in skillet with small amount of butter. When browned on both sides, layer chicken in a casserole dish. Combine soup, sour cream, water chestnuts, and mushrooms and pour over chicken. Sprinkle almonds over the top. Bake 1 hour in a preheated 350 degree oven. The chicken breast casserole can be made the night before, refrigerated and then baked prior to serving.

Margo Cannom

Chicken-Broccoli Casserole

2 packages frozen broccoli spears
6 chicken breasts, can use deboned
2 cans cream of chicken soup
1 cup mayonnaise
1 tablespoon lemon juice
1 teaspoon curry powder
1 cup grated cheese
croutons (onion-garlic flavor)
1/2 cup cheese, grated

Cook broccoli slightly and drain. Combine remaining ingredients except croutons and 1/2 cup cheese. Layer broccoli, chicken breasts, in a 9x13 inch pan, then pour mixture on top. Sprinkle 1/2 cup cheese and croutons on top. Bake uncovered 1 hour at 350 degrees.

Ann Heyda

Chicken Broccoli Quiche

3 cups grated Cheddar cheese
1-1/2 cups cooked chicken, diced
2/3 cup chopped onion
1 package frozen chopped broccoli, thawed and drained
1-1/3 cups milk
3 eggs
1/4 teaspoon pepper
3/4 cup Bisquick

Mix 2 cups of the cheese, chicken, onion, and broccoli in greased pie plate. Beat remaining ingredients except cheese with hand mixer until smooth. Pour over mixture in pie plate. Bake until knife inserted in center comes out clean. Bake 350 degrees, 20-30 minutes. Top with remaining cup of cheese. Bake until melted 1-2 minutes. Cool 5 minutes.

Serves: 6-8

Susan McClellan Gibbs

Broiled Chicken

3 onions, peeled and sliced
2 fryers, quartered, skin removed
juice of one lemon
black pepper to taste
Lawry seasoning, without salt
paprika, enough to make chicken look rosy

Lightly grease a baking pan and line with sliced onions. Place chicken, which has been seasoned with lemon and other seasonings, on top. Broil 25 to 30 minutes on each side. Spoon the juice from onions over chicken as it is broiling.

Selma Leff

Chicken Curry

- 1/2 cup chopped celery
- 1/2 cup chopped onion
- 1/4 cup oil
- 1/3 cup flour
- 2 cups chicken broth
- 1 cup tomato juice
- 1/2 teaspoon Worcestershire sauce
- 1 teaspoon salt
- 1/2 teaspoon pepper
- 1/2 teaspoon thyme
- 1-1/2 teaspoons curry
- 4 cups chicken, boiled and boned
- 4 cups cooked rice
- Toppings — see text below

Brown onions and celery in oil. Stir in flour and add chicken broth a little at a time, stirring constantly. Add tomato juice, Worcestershire sauce, salt, pepper, thyme, curry powder, and chicken. Let simmer 30 minutes to 1 hour. Serve over a bed of rice. In separate small bowls have available the following: flaked coconut, pineapple chunks, diced tomatoes, chopped onions, sliced bananas, dry-roasted peanuts, and raisins. Put a spoon or two of each over the curry and rice after the person has been served. This sounds like a strange combination; but, believe me, it is delicious. Alternative toppings can be chopped boiled eggs, diced bell peppers, grated cheese and chopped lettuce.

Serves 8

Rebecca Phifer

Chicken Breasts with New Potatoes and Shallots

- 3 tablespoons butter, softened
- 4 boneless chicken breasts
- 8 small scrubbed new potatoes
- 6 peeled shallots
- 1 tablespoon flour
- 1 cup chicken broth
- 1/2 teaspoon salt
- 1/8 teaspoon pepper

Heat oven to 375-400 degrees. Butter a roasting pan large enough to hold chicken breasts in single layer. Spread skin side of chicken with butter, and place in pan. Cut potatoes and shallots in half and scatter around chicken. Sprinkle all with salt and pepper. Cover pan with foil and bake 15 minutes. Uncover and baste and continue baking until chicken is brown and potatoes tender. Transfer to platter. Leave 2 tablespoons of drippings in pan, add flour, cook 3 minutes, stirring. Add chicken broth and simmer. Drizzle over chicken and vegetables.

Serves 4

Jeanne Dean

Chicken Cordon Bleu

- **4 whole chicken breasts, split, boned and skinned**
- **8 (1 ounce) slices boiled ham**
- **8 (1 ounce) slices Swiss cheese**
- **3 tablespoons minced parsley**
- **1/4 teaspoon pepper**
- **1 egg, beaten**
- **1/2 cup Italian bread crumbs**
- **1/4 cup butter or margarine**
- **1 (10.75 ounce) can cream of mushroom soup, undiluted**
- **1 (8 ounce) carton sour cream**
- **1/3 cup dry sherry**
- **1 (4 ounce) can sliced mushrooms, drained**

Flatten each piece of chicken to 1/4 inch thickness. Place 1 slice of ham and 1 slice of cheese in center of each chicken breast. Sprinkle with parsley, and pepper. Roll up lengthwise and secure with toothpick. Dip each roll in egg; coat with bread crumbs. Melt butter in heavy skillet; brown chicken on all sides. Remove chicken to 12x5x2 inch baking dish, reserving drippings in skillet. Add remaining ingredients to drippings and stir well. Pour over chicken. Bake uncovered at 350 degrees for 40-45 minutes.

Serves 8

Betty Tonnessen

Cranberry Chicken

- **1 can whole cranberry sauce**
- **1 package Lipton onion soup mix**
- **1 bottle french dressing or Italian Salad Dressing**
- **chicken parts (thighs, legs or breasts)**

Mix first three ingredients in baking dish. Add chicken and marinate at least 30 minutes, turning a couple of times. Bake in 350 degree oven for 1 hour or until done.

Herb White
May DeCell
Susan Bick-Binse

Chicken Cutlets with Wine and Cheese

- **4 boneless chicken breasts**
- **1 egg, slightly beaten**
- **seasoned bread crumbs**
- **2 tablespoons olive oil**
- **1/4 cup white wine**
- **Swiss cheese slices**

Dip chicken in beaten eggs and then in bread crumbs. Saute in olive oil, adding more if needed. Place in shallow casserole. When skillet has cooled add wine and stir to loosen any crumbs. Pour over chicken, adding extra wine if desired. Cover with cheese slices. Cover casserole with foil and let sit about an hour. Punch holes in foil and bake for 20 minutes at 325 degrees. Bake a few minutes uncovered.

Serves 4

Jeanne Dean

Winter Park Ski Lodge Chicken Enchiladas

- 1/3 cup half and half cream
- 2 (3 ounce) packages cream cheese, softened
- 2 cups cooked, chopped chicken
- 3/4 cup finely chopped green onions
- 1/2 teaspoon salt or to taste
- 3-4 cans Old El Paso green chile enchilada sauce
- 10-12 flour tortillas (8 inches round)
- 3/4 cup shredded Cheddar cheese
- 3/4 cup shredded Monterey Jack cheese
- sour cream
- olives
- lettuce
- tomatoes

Beat together half and half with cream cheese until smooth; add chicken, onions and salt. Set aside. Spoon a thin layer of enchilada sauce in 9x13 inch baking dish. On a flat surface spread each tortilla with a thin layer of enchilada sauce. Arrange about 1/4 cup of the chicken mixture down center of each tortilla. Roll tortilla and place, seam side down, on top of enchilada sauce. Spoon more enchilada sauce (to taste) over tops of tortillas. Cover dish with foil and bake in preheated 350 degree oven about 20 minutes or until hot. Remove foil and sprinkle top with cheese. Bake five minutes longer, or until cheese melts. Garnish with sour cream and olives; serve lettuce and tomatoes on the side.

Serves 6

Sally Kersting

Creamed Chicken Tacos

- 1 package flour tortillas
- chicken stock, heated
- 1 can cream of chicken soup
- 1 can cream of mushroom soup
- 1 large can evaporated milk
- 1 medium onion, chopped
- 1/4 cup chopped green chilies
- 3 cups boned chopped chicken
- 2 cups grated Cheddar cheese

Soften tortillas in chicken stock. Line a 9x13 dish with softened tortillas. Heat next 6 ingredients together. Layer this mixture with tortillas and cheese; repeat layers, ending with grated cheese on top. At this point either freeze or bake at 350 degrees for 30 minutes or until bubbly. Remove from oven and let stand 30 minutes before serving. Mexican rice goes great with this.

Marsha Thompson

Moe's Punjabi Chicken Curry

- 3 large onions, thinly sliced
- 1 fresh jalapeno pepper, chopped (use caution - these sting!)
- 6 whole cloves garlic
- 1/2 cup vegetable oil
- 1-1/2 tablespoons turmeric
- 1/2 teaspoon chili powder (more, if "hotter" is desired!)
- 1-1/2 tablespoons cumin
- 1-1/2 tablespoons Garam Masala (can be found in most Middle Eastern groceries)
- 10 whole cloves
- salt, to taste
- 8 cherry tomatoes OR 1-1/2 large tomatoes
- 2/3 cup water
- 2 whole chickens, skinned, washed, and cut into serving size pieces
- 2 pieces of ginger root (walnut size pieces), finely chopped
- cooked rice

In Dutch oven or heavy large pot, combine onions, jalapeno, garlic and oil. Saute until onions are light brown. Add turmeric, chili powder, cumin, garam masala, cloves, salt, tomatoes and water. Cook until oil separates from other ingredients or until thickened. Add chicken and ginger. Stir until well blended and bring to a boil over a medium heat. Lower temperature and simmer for 1 hour or until chicken is tender. Serve with hot rice.

Serves 8

Shirin Shiekh Blackwell

Baked Chicken and Rice

- 7/8 cup rice, uncooked
- 1 can cream of mushroom soup
- 1 can cream of chicken soup
- 1 can cream of celery soup
- chicken pieces, as desired
- pepper, to taste
- chopped chives or parsley (optional)

Put rice in greased shallow baking dish. Stir in undiluted soups. Put chicken on top and sprinkle with pepper. Top with chives and parsley if desired. Bake, uncovered, in 350 degree oven for about an hour. Note: The number this will serve varies according to the amount of chicken used. Recipe may be doubled to serve larger group. Chicken broth may be substituted for any of the soups, if desired, to cut down on calories.

Ruth Tanner

Lemon Broccoli Chicken

- 2 whole chicken breasts, split, skinned, and boned
- 1 tablespoon vegetable oil
- 1 can cream of broccoli soup
- 1/4 cup milk
- 2 teaspoons lemon juice
- 1/8 teaspoon pepper
- 4 thin lemon slices

Cook chicken with vegetable oil 10 minutes or until browned on both sides in skillet. Combine soup and milk, stir in lemon juice and pepper. Pour over chicken. Top each chicken piece with lemon slice. Reduce heat to low. Cover and simmer 5 minutes or until chicken is fork tender.

Serves 4

Wayne McHatton

Chicken Cacciatore

- 1 (2-1/2 pound), fryer cut up
- 1/4 cup flour
- 4 tablespoons olive oil
- 1 clove garlic, crushed
- salt and pepper
- 1 teaspoon oregano
- 1 teaspoon basil
- 1 teaspoon parsley
- 1 (16 ounce) can Italian style tomatoes
- 2 bay leaves
- 1/2 cup chopped onion
- 1/2 cup chopped green bell pepper
- sliced mushrooms, if desired

Coat chicken with flour. Heat oil and garlic in large skillet; add chicken and brown on one side. Before turning chicken sprinkle with salt, pepper, oregano, basil and parsley; turn. After chicken has been browned on both sides add tomatoes and bay leaves. Heat to boiling. Reduce heat and add onions and bell pepper. Simmer 30 to 40 minutes, covered. Remove cover and simmer a little longer if you like a thicker sauce. Can add mushrooms if desired.

Serves 4

Lou Bruno

Empress Chicken

- 8 chicken thighs, skin removed
- 1/3 cup soy sauce
- 2 tablespoons wine
- 4 teaspoons sugar
- 1 slice fresh ginger
- 2 cups water
- 4 green onions, chopped
- 1 can bamboo shoots
- 1 package frozen peas, thawed
- cooked rice

Fry chicken until it changes color. Add the rest of the ingredients except the peas and rice. Simmer covered 1 hour. Add peas and cook until done. Serve with rice.

Nathan Huang

Chicken Enchiladas Verdes

Filling:
- **5 whole chicken breasts, halved**
- **6 cups canned chicken broth**
- **2 carrots, coarsely chopped**
- **1/2 large onion**
- **4 garlic cloves**
- **4 parsley sprigs**
- **2 bay leaves**

Sauce:
- **6 tablespoons (3/4 stick butter)**
- **6 tablespoons all purpose flour**
- **1 tablespoon vegetable oil**
- **2-1/2 large onions, chopped**
- **2 spinach bunches, stemmed and coarsely chopped**
- **1-1/2 cups sour cream**
- **4 green onions, cut into pieces**
- **1 to 2 (4 ounce) cans diced jalapeno chilies, drained**
- **salt and freshly ground pepper**
- **1-1/2 pounds Monterey Jack cheese, grated**
- **vegetable oil**
- **24 (6 inch) corn tortillas**
- **sour cream**

For filling: Place chicken and broth in large saucepan. Add carrots, onion, garlic, parsley and bay leaves. Bring to boil. Cover and simmer 5 minutes. Turn off heat and let stand until chicken is cooked through, about 1 hour. Remove chicken from broth and cool slightly. Strain cooking liquid. Return to saucepan and boil until reduced to 3 cups. Skin and bone chicken. Shred meat and place in medium bowl. Chill.

For sauce: Melt butter in heavy medium saucepan over low heat. Add flour and cook until light brown, stirring frequently, about 5 minutes. Whisk in reserved chicken cooking liquid. Increase heat to medium and cook until sauce thickens, stirring occasionally. Cool. Heat 1 tablespoon oil in heavy large skillet over medium heat. Add onions and cook until soft, stirring occasionally, about 5 minutes. Add spinach and stir until wilted, about 2 minutes. Transfer to processor. Add sauce, 1-1/2 cups sour cream, green onions and 1 can chilies and puree until smooth. Season with salt and pepper. Add second can of chilies, if desired.

Butter two 9x13 inch baking dishes. Spread 1/2 cup sauce over bottom of each. Add 1 cup sauce to chicken. Mix into heavy medium skillet. Heat over medium-low heat. Add 1 tortilla and cook until softened, about 5 seconds. Drain on paper towels. Repeat with remaining tortillas and roll up. Arrange seam side down in prepared dishes. Spoon remaining sauce over. Cover with foil. (Can be prepared 1 day ahead. Refrigerate enchiladas to room temperature before baking.) Preheat oven to 400 degrees. Bake covered enchiladas until just heated through, about 10 minutes. Uncover, sprinkle with remaining cheese and bake until cheese melts, about 5 minutes. Serve with sour cream.

Chris Salazar

Fiesta Chicken Ole

6 chicken breasts
2 (10 ounce) cans tomatoes
1 small can jalapeno peppers
1 (2-1/2 ounce) can black olives, sliced
8 (8 inch) flour tortillas
2 large avocados, peeled and sliced
2 cups sour cream
1-1/2 pounds Monterey Jack cheese

Boil chicken, remove skin and bones and cut into chunks. Mix tomatoes and jalapenos in blender. Add sliced olives to mixture. Spread enough of this mixture to cover bottom of large baking dish. Place 4 tortillas on top and add more tomato mixture. Next, layer one-half the chicken and one-half the avocados. Spread 1/2 cup sour cream and sprinkle with cheese. Repeat until all ingredients are used. Bake uncovered at 325 degrees for 45 minutes. Serve with rice, salad and refried beans.

Serves 6 to 8

Kathy Blevins

Chicken Florentine (Light and Easy)

1 pound chicken breasts, skinned and boned
1/8 teaspoon pepper
3/4 cup chicken broth
2 tablespoons dry wine
1 pound fresh spinach
1 tablespoon water
2 tablespoons cornstarch
3 ounces Philadelphia light cream cheese
lemon juice
paprika

Place chicken in skillet. Sprinkle with pepper. Add broth and wine and bring to a boil. Cover and simmer 25-35 minutes. Remove chicken with slotted spoon. Cover and keep warm. Reserve broth in skillet. Meanwhile wash spinach. Place in large covered saucepan with just the water clinging to leaves. Reduce heat when steam forms. Cook 3 minutes. Set aside, keeping warm. Combine water and cornstarch and stir into broth. Cook until thickened. Add cream cheese, stir until melted. Arrange spinach on platter. Sprinkle with lemon juice. Top with chicken and sauce. Sprinkle with paprika.

Anne Sullivan

Chicken Fricassee

1 (4 pound) chicken, cut up
salt, pepper and flour
1 tablespoon shortening
1 onion, chopped
1 sprig thyme or 1/8 teaspoon dried
1 tablespoon minced parsley
1 bay leaf
3 cups boiling water

Season chicken with salt and pepper. Coat with flour. Brown in shortening. Add onion and saute. Add seasonings and water. Bring to a boil. Cover and reduce heat. Simmer until tender, about 45 minutes to an hour.

Serves 4-6.

Butsey Weinstein

Hot Chicken Casserole

6 cups cooked chicken breasts, cut up
1/2 cup chopped onion
1 cup chopped celery
1-1/3 cups evaporated milk
2 cans cream of mushroom soup
2 cans chicken with rice soup
1 (5 ounce) can chow mein noodles

Topping for Casserole:
2/3 cup butter or margarine
1/3 cup slivered almonds
1-1/2 cups Pepperidge Farm herb stuffing

Mix first seven ingredients and put into a 13x9 inch casserole. For topping, melt butter or margarine, add almonds and saute, but do not brown. Pour butter and almond mixture over the stuffing. Combine and put on top of casserole. Bake for 1 hour at 350 degrees. Watch so top does not brown. May fix and freeze ahead of time.

Serves 9-12

Carolyn Hamrick

Chicken Paprika

2 tablespoons butter
2 tablespoons oil
2 broiler-fryers, cut up
salt and pepper
3 medium onions, chopped
1 clove garlic, chopped
2 tablespoons paprika
2-1/2 tablespoons flour
1 cup chicken broth
2 cups sour cream

In casserole, heat butter and oil and brown chicken. Season with salt and pepper and remove chicken. In remaining fat, cook onions and garlic until translucent. Add paprika and flour and cook gently, stirring, for 3 minutes. Add broth, then sour cream, stirring constantly until sauce is smooth and thickened. Replace chicken. Bake, covered, in preheated 350 degree oven for 1 hour, or until chicken is tender. Good served over noodles or rice.

Serves 4 to 6

Ruth Crowe

Chicken Paprika with Dumplings

- **2 tablespoons vegetable oil**
- **1 (2-1/2 to 3 pound) broiler fryer chicken, cut up**
- **1 medium onion, chopped**
- **1/2 cup water**
- **1/2 teaspoon instant chicken bouillon**
- **2 tablespoons paprika**
- **1 teaspoon salt**
- **1/4 teaspoon pepper**
- **2 tablespoons chopped parsley**
- **1 cup dairy sour cream**

Heat oil in skillet. Add chicken pieces and brown on all sides. Remove chicken from pan. Cook and stir onions in same skillet until tender. Drain fat from skillet; stir in water, bouillon, paprika, salt and pepper. Loosen brown particles from bottom of skillet. Return chicken and heat to boiling; reduce heat to simmer, cover and cook 20 minutes. Add chopped parsley. Continue cooking until thickest pieces of chicken are done, about 10 to 15 minutes. Remove chicken to heated platter and keep warm. Skim fat from skillet. Stir sour cream into liquid in skillet and heat until just hot. Spoon sauce over chicken and serve with noodles or dumplings. Tip from a Texas Hungarian: Day before making paprika chicken, soak chicken in cool water at least 1 hour. Drain; lightly salt, and refrigerate overnight in bowl with piece of wax paper covering chicken. Omit salt during cooking and taste to see if you desire more salt.

Martha Warden

Herbed Chicken Rose

- **1/4 teaspoon garlic salt**
- **1/4 teaspoon paprika**
- **1 tablespoon flour**
- **4 large pieces frying chicken**
- **2 or 3 tablespoons shortening (half butter)**
- **1/4 teaspoon dried rosemary**
- **1/4 teaspoon dried basil**
- **1-1/2 teaspoons cornstarch**
- **1 tablespoon water**
- **1/2 cup California Rose**
- **1/2 cup sour cream**

Combine garlic salt, paprika and flour. Dredge chicken in flour mixture. Brown on both sides in hot shortening. Sprinkle with herbs; add wine; cover and cook slowly until tender, about 25 minutes. Skim any excess fat from pan liquid. Thicken liquid with 1-1/2 teaspoons cornstarch mixed with 1 tablespoon water, if desired. Stir in sour cream. Delicious and extremely easy.

Serves 4

Herb White

Ding-How Chicken

2/3 cup honey
3 tablespoons curry powder
3 tablespoons Dijon mustard
1 teaspoon ground ginger
6 chicken thighs with skin removed

Blend honey, curry powder, mustard and ginger in a stainless or glass bowl. Combine chicken with honey mixture and turn until it is well coated. Place in shallow 2 quart baking dish or foil-covered broiler pan. Bake in a preheated 350 degree oven until chicken tests done, 35 to 40 minutes. This recipe can be doubled, tripled or more. Leftovers are a real lunch-time treat served at room temperature with a light salad. Note: This recipe made enough honey mixture for at least 8 chicken thighs and produced a wonderful curried gravy.

Herb White

Good Party Chicken

12-14 skinned chicken breasts
salt and pepper to taste
1 (12 or 16 ounce) jar apricot preserves
1 package Lipton onion soup mix
1 (16 ounce) bottle (or a bit less) Thousand Island or French dressing
2 teaspoons to 1 tablespoon curry powder (optional)

Season chicken with salt and pepper. Arrange in baking dish. Combine remaining ingredients and pour over chicken. Marinade several hours; all day is better! Cover, bake at 400 degrees for 30 minutes; lower oven to 325 degrees and bake an additional 30-45 minutes, lifting cover the last 5-10 minutes. This is great served over rice.

Serves: 12-14.

Thommye Stewart

King Ranch Casserole

1 whole chicken, cut up
1 (8 ounce) can Rotel tomatoes
1 can cream of mushroom soup
1 onion, diced
salt and pepper, to taste
flour tortillas, torn into small pieces
Velveeta cheese

Boil chicken; skin and shred meat. Mix tomatoes, cut in small pieces, soup, onion, salt and pepper. Grease large casserole dish. Place layer of tortillas in bottom of dish. Layer chicken, tomato mixture and cheese until all ingredients are used. May top with additional cheese. Cover dish with foil and bake at 350 degrees for 50 minutes. Recipe can easily be doubled.

Serves 4-5

Darlene Hold

Chicken A La King

- **2 tablespoons butter**
- **1/3 green pepper, cut into strips**
- **1/4 pound fresh mushrooms, sliced**
- **1/4 cup flour**
- **1-1/3 cups cream or evaporated milk**
- **1-1/3 cups good strength chicken broth**
- **salt and pepper, to taste**
- **2 cups cold diced, steamed, skinless chicken**
- **1/2 pimento, in strips**

Melt butter in top of double boiler over direct heat, add green pepper and mushrooms and simmer for 5 minutes covered. Lift out pepper and mushrooms. Blend flour into the drippings, add cream or milk, broth, and seasonings and cook with constant stirring, still over direct heat, until sauce boils and thickens. Add chicken, pimento, green peppers, and mushrooms and place over boiling water, cover and cook until chicken is heated through. Serve hot over toast, baking powder biscuits, crisp noodles, or rice.

Serves 5

Marjorie Evans

No Mess Chicken Parmesan

- **4 boneless chicken breasts**
- **1 egg, beaten**
- **1 cup milk**
- **1 cup Italian bread crumbs**
- **2 packages mozzarella cheese, thin sliced**
- **1 large bottle of Ragu chunky garden style sauce**
- **Parmesan cheese**

Preheat 350 degree oven. Trim fat off, pound breast, mix 1 egg and 1 cup of milk, dip breast into egg and milk mix, then coat breast with bread crumbs until fully coated. Brown both sides of breast in skillet over medium heat. Add 1 tablespoon butter in skillet with breasts, should take 15 minutes. Spray casserole dish with Pam (light coat), lay one layer of mozzarella cheese on bottom of casserole dish, lay breast on top. Add 1/2 bottle of Ragu sauce on top to cover cheese and breasts. Lay another layer of cheese, use rest of sauce on top. Cut cheese thinly, lay diagonally over chicken, sprinkle Parmesan cheese over top. Bake 20 minutes. Note: Serve with garlic bread or French bread.

Serves 4

Michele Ingrando

Chicken Parmesan

1 clove garlic, crushed
2 tablespoons lemon juice
1/4 cup melted butter
1/2 cup bread crumbs
1/3 cup Parmesan cheese
2 tablespoons parsley
1-1/2 teaspoons salt
3/4 teaspoon pepper
2 chicken breasts, halved

Combine garlic, lemon juice and butter. Blend crumbs, cheese, parsley, salt and pepper. Dip chicken first in butter and then crumb mixture. Roll up and bake at 350 degrees for about one hour.

Serves 4

Virginia Van Horn

Chicken Imperial

2 cups bread or corn flake crumbs
3/4 cup grated Parmesan cheese
1/4 cup parsley, chopped
1 clove garlic, crushed
2 teaspoons salt
1/8 teaspoon pepper
1/4 pound butter, melted
1 large frying chicken, cut into serving pieces

Combine crumbs, cheese, parsley, garlic, salt and pepper and set aside. Dip chicken pieces in butter, then crumb mixture, coating well. Place pieces in baking dish; do not overlap. Dot with remaining butter and bake in preheated 350 - 375 degree oven for 1 hour or until fork-tender. Note: Instead of using butter for dipping chicken you can use 2 eggs, beaten, combined with 2 tablespoons water. If this method is used, grease baking dish well before placing chicken in to bake.

Serves 4-6

Les Lawrence

Oven Fried Chicken

6 chicken breasts
1 cup finely crushed crackers
1 cup Parmesan cheese
1/4 cup minced onion
3 tablespoons dried parsley
1 teaspoon salt
1/2 teaspoon pepper
1/2 cup butter, melted
2 tablespoons softened butter
sesame or poppy seeds, optional

Mix together crumbs, cheese, onions, parsley, salt and pepper. Dip each piece of chicken in melted butter, covering well. Roll each piece in crumb mixture to make thick coating. Arrange on shallow baking pan so pieces do not touch. Pat each piece with softened butter, then sprinkle with sesame or poppy seeds, if desired. Bake at 375 degrees for 1 hour, turning after 30 minutes.

Dora Hughes
Elva Lopez

Peachy Chicken

- boiling water
- 1-1/2 tablespoons soy sauce
- 2 beef bouillon cubes
- 2 cups minute rice
- 6 chicken breasts
- salt and pepper to taste
- 1/3 cup butter
- 1 cup peach halves
- 3 tablespoons flaked coconut
- powdered ginger

Add boiling water to soy sauce to make 2 cups. Add bouillon cubes. Pour over rice and let stand. Season chicken with salt and pepper and brown in butter. Save drippings. Spoon rice into center of 6 (12 inch) pieces of heavy duty foil. Top with chicken; spoon drippings over chicken. Close foil and bake 45 minutes at 400 degrees. Drain peaches. Uncover foil, place a peach half on each. Sprinkle with coconut mixed with ginger. Place under broiler until coconut is golden brown.

Herb White

Ritz Chicken Casserole

- 1 stack Ritz crackers, rolled to crumbs
- 1 stick butter, melted
- 1/4 cup chicken broth
- 1 can cream of chicken soup
- 1 small carton sour cream
- 1 medium jar sliced mushrooms
- 4-6 whole skinless, boneless chicken breasts, sliced
- shredded Cheddar cheese

Mix cracker crumbs with melted butter. Place most of mixture in bottom of 9x13 inch casserole dish (save some for topping). Mix together broth, soup, sour cream and mushrooms. Place chicken pieces over cracker crumbs and pour soup mixture over chicken. Sprinkle cheese over chicken and remaining crumbs on top. Bake at 325 degrees for 30 minutes or until bubbly. Serves 8. This dish freezes great, so make 2 while you're at it.

Phyllis Neu

Chicken and Rice

- 1 cup rice
- 1 can chicken broth
- 1 cup water
- 1 small can mushrooms
- 1/2 teaspoon Worcestershire sauce
- 1 teaspoon onion flakes
- 1/4 teaspoon garlic salt
- 4 chicken breasts, boned and skinned
- 4 tablespoons butter
- 1 teaspoon paprika
- 1 tablespoon parsley
- salt and pepper to taste

Put the first 7 ingredients into baking pan. Add chicken. Put 1 tablespoon butter on each piece of chicken. Add remaining ingredients. Bake at 425 degrees for approximately 45 minutes. Stir occasionally.

Serves: 4

Dianne Ibenthal

Swiss Chicken Cutlets

- 5 chicken breasts, split, skinned and boned
- salt
- garlic powder, if desired
- 2 eggs, beaten
- 1 cup fine dry bread crumbs
- 1/4 cup cooking oil
- 3 tablespoons butter or margarine
- 1/4 cup all-purpose flour
- 1/2 teaspoon salt
- 1/8 teaspoon pepper
- 2-1/4 cups milk
- 1/2 cup dry white wine
- 1 cup shredded Swiss cheese
- avocado slices
- tomato wedges

Place each chicken breast between 2 pieces of waxed paper and pound out to 1/4 inch thickness with meat mallet. Sprinkle chicken with salt and garlic powder. Dip in egg, then crumbs. Heat oil and brown chicken about 2 minutes on each side. Add more oil as needed. Set chicken aside. Melt butter; blend in flour, salt and pepper. Add milk slowly, then stir in wine and cook sauce until well blended. Pour 1/2 of sauce in a 13x9 inch dish. Arrange cutlets on top of sauce and top with remaining sauce. Cover and chill several hours or overnight. Bake, covered, in a 350 degree oven for about 50 minutes. Remove cover, sprinkle with cheese and top with avocado slices and tomato wedges. Return to oven, uncovered, for 2-3 minutes or until cheese is melted. Since the breasts are split in half this recipe will serve from 5 to 8 people. This dish has always been my children's most often requested "special" birthday treat!

Estelle Kastleman

Sour Cream Chicken

- 2 tablespoons fresh lemon juice
- 1 cup sour cream
- 2 cloves garlic, crushed
- 1-1/2 teaspoons salt
- 1-1/2 teaspoons celery salt
- 1 teaspoon paprika
- 2 teaspoons Worcestershire sauce
- black pepper, to taste
- 6 chicken breasts
- 1 cup fine dry bread crumbs
- 1 stick margarine, melted

Mix together first 8 ingredients. Coat chicken with mixture. Place skin side up in large, shallow, greased baking dish. Mix bread crumbs with margarine. Sprinkle over chicken. Bake at 350 degrees for 1-1/4 hours or until tender and golden brown.

Serves 6

Pam Bankerd

Chicken Spaghetti I

- 1 chicken hen
- salt and pepper
- 1 bay leaf
- celery leaves
- 1 large onion, minced
- 3 stalks celery, minced
- 1/2 green bell pepper, shredded
- 2 tablespoons minced parsley
- 1 stick butter, melted
- 1 large can tomatoes, drained, cut up
- 1 tablespoon Worcestershire sauce
- salt and pepper to taste
- dash cayenne
- 1 pint chicken broth
- 1 large can sliced nushrooms
- 1 cup ripe olives, sliced
- 1 package spaghetti, broken in pieces, cooked according to package directions
- bread crumbs, finely crushed

Cook hen until tender, adding salt, pepper, bay leaf and celery leaves during last 30 minutes of cooking. Let cool in broth, then remove skin and bones and cut into chunks. To make sauce add onion, celery, bell pepper and parsley to butter and saute until onion is pale yellow. Add tomatoes, Worcestershire, salt, pepper and cayenne. Stir in chicken broth and cook until a rich sauce is formed. Add sliced mushrooms and olives. In a 9x12 inch baking dish place a layer of cooked spaghetti, layer of sauce and a layer of chicken. Repeat until all ingredients are used. Dust lightly with bread crumbs and dot with butter. Bake, covered, in 350 degree oven for 45 minutes. Add more broth if needed; mixture should be very moist.

Serves 8

Les Lawrence

Chicken Spaghetti II

- 1 onion, chopped
- 1 medium green pepper, chopped
- 2 tablespoons butter
- 2 cups cooked chicken, cut in bite-size pieces
- 1/4 cup pimento, chopped
- 1 can cream of chicken soup
- 1 small can evaporated milk
- 1/2 teaspoon salt
- 1 cup chicken broth
- 1 small jar jalapeno Cheese Whiz
- 1 small jar regular Cheese Whiz
- 1/2 pound spaghetti, broken up and cooked
- 1 (6 ounce) package grated cheese

Saute onion and green pepper in butter. Add next 8 ingredients and warm over low heat. Transfer to large casserole and add cooked spaghetti. Bake at 350 degrees for 1 hour. Add grated cheese on top a few minutes before casserole is done.

Serves 6-8

Linda Stearns

Chicken Salad Casserole

1 box Uncle Ben's Wild Rice with Mushrooms
1 can French style green beans, drained
1 can cream of celery soup
1/2 cup mayonnaise
1/4 cup chopped onion
1 cup water chestnuts, drained and chopped
2 cans boned chicken or 2 to 3 cups cooked chicken or turkey
salt and pepper
1 cup grated cheese, optional

Cook rice as directed on package. Mix all other ingredients, except cheese, with rice and place in 8x12 greased casserole. Top with cheese, if desired. Bake at 350 degrees for 30 minutes. Note: You can use any left over meat such as ground hamburger or tuna. Also, you can use other vegetables as desired. Serve with a salad, rolls or bread sticks for a delicious meal!

Serves: 6-8

Dixie Talley

Spanish Chicken Rice

1 pound boneless skinless chicken, cut into strips
1 tablespoon olive oil
1 tablespoon crushed garlic
paprika
salt and pepper to taste
1 small onion, chopped
1 green pepper, chopped
1-1/2 cups chicken broth
1 can Rotel tomatoes, drained
1-1/2 cups minute rice, cooked
grated cheese

Saute strips of chicken in olive oil, garlic, paprika, salt and pepper. When cooked add green pepper and onions. Saute a few more minutes. Add chicken broth. Bring to a boil and add tomatoes and rice. Remove from heat. Let stand 5 minutes. Add grated cheese when serving.

Serves 6

Cher Longoria

Upside Down Pizza

1-1/2 pounds ground beef
1 medium onion
1 can or jar pizza sauce
1/2 teaspoon garlic salt
1/2 teaspoon oregano
8 ounces mozzarella
2 eggs
1 cup milk
1 tablespoon oil
1/2 teaspoon salt
1 cup flour
1/2 cup grated Parmesan

Preheat oven to 350 degrees. Meanwhile brown meat and onion together and drain off fat. Blend in pizza sauce, garlic salt, and oregano. Put mixture into greased 9x13 pan and sprinkle with mozzarella cheese. In small bowl mix eggs, milk, oil, salt, and flour. Pour over the top of the meat mixture and sprinkle with grated Parmesan cheese. Can add any other topping if you like; mushrooms, sausage, etc.

Serves 12

Mary Miller

Chicken Stroganoff

- 2 large whole chicken breasts, boned and skinned
- 2 tablespoons flour
- 1/2 teaspoon salt
- 1/4 teaspoon fresh ground pepper
- 4 teaspoons butter
- 4 teaspoons minced shallots, thinly sliced
- 3/4 pound fresh mushrooms
- 1/2 cup dry white wine
- 1 tablespoon paprika
- 2 cups sour cream, room temperature
- 1-1/2 teaspoons Worcestershire sauce
- 1/2 teaspoon beef bouillon powder

Slice chicken into julienne strips about 3 inches by 1/4 inch. Combine flour, salt and pepper in a bag. Add chicken and shake to coat. In a skillet, saute chicken in butter over medium high heat just until golden and tender. Remove to a serving dish and keep warm. Add shallots, mushrooms and wine to the skillet. Cook, stirring, until liquid disappears. Reduce heat to low. Stir in paprika, sour cream, Worcestershire, and beef bouillon powder. Season to taste with salt and pepper. Heat sauce and pour over chicken.

Serves 4

Michelle K. Hohnke

Chicken Tetrazzini I

- 1/4 pound margarine
- 1/2 cup flour
- 1 pint milk
- 1/2 pound Old English cheese
- 1 can cream of mushroom soup
- 3-4 stalks celery, chopped
- 1 medium onion, chopped
- chicken broth
- 8 ounces spaghetti, cooked
- 4 chicken breasts, cooked and cut into bite size pieces

Make white sauce with margarine, flour and milk. Add cheese and soup blending well. Saute onions and celery in chicken broth. Mix spaghetti, chicken, celery, onions, and cream sauce together. If too thick add a little chicken broth. Place in buttered 9x13 casserole. Top with bread crumbs and bake 30-45 minutes at 350 degrees. Best if made a day ahead of time.

Serves 8

Jeanne Dean

Chicken Tetrazzini II

1-1/2 cups or more cooked chicken cut into small pieces
1 cup sour cream
1 can cream of chicken or mushroom soup
mushrooms, optional
slivered almonds, optional
1/4 stick butter or margarine
small box spaghetti noodles, cooked and drained
Cheddar, Jack or other cheese, grated

Mix all ingredients together reserving half of the cheese. Place in casserole dish. Sprinkle with remaining cheese and dot with butter. Bake at 350 degrees for 30-40 minutes or freeze for later use. This is definitely not a low fat recipe!

Serves 6-8

Liza Wright

Cordon Bleu

2 thin slices of very tender veal or pork
salt
pepper
1 slice ham or Polish beef
1 slice Swiss cheese
flour
1 egg, beaten, or milk
bread crumbs
oil

Salt and pepper the slices of meat. Put ham and cheese together and place between the two pieces of meat. Use toothpicks to hold sides together. Coat the meat first in flour, then in egg (or milk) and then into the bread crumbs. Fry in a pan with very hot oil for about 6 minutes on each side. This recipe is for one serving, so multiply by the number you are serving. ENJOY!

Serves: 1

Marilyn Healy

Cajun Pork Chops

6 pork chops
cooking oil
3 tablespoons paprika
1/2 teaspoon red pepper (or more, to taste)
1 tablespoon garlic powder
2 teaspoons oregano
1/2 teaspoon salt
1/2 teaspoon white pepper
1/2 teaspoon cumin
1/4 teaspoon nutmeg

Rub chops all over with oil. Combine all seasonings and rub well over all pork surfaces. Place meat in shallow pan and bake in 350 degree oven 40 to 45 minutes.

Jane McFaddin

Pork Chops A La Baudin

6 pork chops
2 tablespoons shortening
1-1/2 teaspoon salt
1/4 teaspoon pepper
1 cup raw rice
3-1/2 cups chicken bouillon
1/4 teaspoon thyme
1/2 green pepper, diced
1/2 cup onion, diced

Brown chops in shortening and remove from skillet. Season with salt and pepper. Brown rice in drippings, stirring constantly. Add remaining ingredients and pour into 3 quart casserole, placing pork chops on top. Cover and bake at 350 degrees for 1 hour.

Serves 6

Ann McFadin

Smothered Pork Chops

6 center cut pork chops
1 teaspoon salt
1/4 teaspoon white pepper
1/4 cup pancake mix
2 tablespoons vegetable shortening
3 medium onions, peeled and sliced
1 teaspoon salt
1/4 teaspoon white pepper
1 tablespoon sugar
1/4 cup all purpose flour
2 cups boiling water

Wipe pork chops clean and sprinkle with 1 teaspoon salt and 1/4 teaspoon white pepper; coat with pancake mix. Heat shortening in large skillet; brown chops well on both sides. Remove from skillet to shallow roasting pan. Saute onions with remaining salt and pepper and sugar in same skillet until lightly browned. Stir in flour and cook until well blended. Gradually add boiling water and cook over medium heat, stirring constantly, until sauce thickens and boils. Pour over chops. Cover roasting pan with aluminum foil. Bake in a 350 degree oven for about 1 hour and 20 minutes. Remove chops from pan and keep them warm. Strain gravy through sieve, pressing onions through with a wooden spoon. Skim fat from surface if necessary. Serve chops with generous portions of gravy. Good with mashed potatoes.

Serves 6.

Lou Bruno

If you break an egg on the floor, sprinkle it heavily with salt and leave it alone for 5-10 minutes. Sweep the dried egg into a dust pan.

Pork Chops and Rice

- **4 thick loin pork chops**
- **oil for browning**
- **1 cup raw rice**
- **4 thick slices onion**
- **4 thick slices green pepper (seeded)**
- **4 thick slices tomato**
- **2-1/2 cups beef bouillon**
- **1/2 teaspoon marjoram**
- **1/4 teaspoon thyme**
- **salt and pepper to taste**

Saute chops on both sides in oil. Place chops in shallow buttered pan and spread rice over them. On each chop place 1 slice onion, 1 slice green pepper and 1 slice tomato. Pour bouillon over all and sprinkle with marjoram, thyme, salt and pepper. Cover and bake at 325 degrees for about 50 minutes. Serve with salad and hot rolls.

Serves 4

Marie Sullivan

Dianne's Stuffed Pork Chops

- **2 (1 inch) pork chops**
- **1 package Shake & Bake (pork)**
- **2 slices Swiss cheese**
- **2 slices imported ham**

Cut pocket in pork chops. Cover with shake & bake and bake in oven at 425 degrees for 45 minutes to 1 hour. When done, stuff each pork chop with 1 slice of ham and cheese. Return to oven and cook until cheese is melted. Great served with twice baked potatoes.

Dianne Ibenthal

Spareribs Worcestershire

- **3 pounds spareribs, cut into serving pieces**
- **6 tablespoons Worcestershire, divided**
- **1/2 cup orange marmalade**
- **3 tablespoons chopped onion**
- **1-1/2 teaspoon salt**

Brush 3 tablespoons of Worcestershire sauce over both sides of ribs. Bake on rack in pan at 400 degrees for 45 minutes, turning occasionally. Pour off drippings. Reduce heat to 350 degrees. Combine rest of ingredients, mix well. Brush sauce over ribs. Bake 20-30 minutes, basting until nicely glazed.

Susan Bick-Binse

Ham and Broccoli

4 cups fresh broccoli
2 cups cooked, diced ham
2 tablespoons butter
2 tablespoons flour
1/2 teaspoon salt
1-1/2 cups milk
1/4 cup shredded cheese
paprika
3 slices bread

Cook broccoli in salt water until tender. Put into a buttered baking dish and sprinkle ham over top. Melt butter, stir in flour and salt and gradually add milk. Continue stirring until sauce thickens and comes to a boil. Pour over ham and broccoli and sprinkle cheese and paprika over top. Cut bread into cubes and sprinkle over all. Bake at 375 degrees for 20 minutes.

Serves 4

W. F. Hampton

Ham N' Potatoes

1-2 inch slice of ham, center cut
3 medium Irish potatoes
1 cup milk
1 teaspoon prepared mustard

Place ham in large shallow baking pan. Slice potatoes in rounds, place around ham. Stir milk and mustard together and pour over ham and potatoes. Bake in 350 degree oven until potatoes are done. Serve with tossed salad for complete meal.

Serves 6

Beth Evers

No Mess Sausage

1 pound loose pork sausage (of course, this Texas gal uses HOT)
1-1/2 cups dry bread crumbs
3/4 cup milk
1 beaten egg

Mix ingredients well and pack into 12 muffin tins. Bake at 350 degrees for 20 minutes. Serve with grits, biscuits, English muffins or eggs. They are especially great with coddled eggs.

Thommye Stewart

Eggs separate most easily if they are very cold. Whites, however, should be beaten at room temperature.

Smoked Sausage and Cabbage

- **1 package smoked sausage links**
- **3-4 small potatoes**
- **3-4 carrots**
- **1 onion**
- **1 medium head of cabbage**

Cut sausage, potatoes and carrots into smaller pieces. Peel and quarter onion. Core cabbage and cut into wedges. Place everything but cabbage in boiling water. Cover and cook until potatoes and carrots are tender. Add cabbage and cook 10-15 minutes more. Season to taste. Great with corn-bread.

Serves 4

Liza Wright

Veal Parmigiana

- **flour**
- **1 teaspoon salt**
- **1/4 teaspoon pepper**
- **2 tablespoons grated Parmesan cheese**
- **2 eggs, well beaten**
- **1 pound thinly cut veal cutlets**
- **bread crumbs, Italian style**
- **1 (1 pound) can peeled whole tomatoes**
- **3 tablespoons tomato paste**
- **1 bay leaf**
- **olive oil (plenty)**
- **2 cloves garlic, minced**
- **1/2 pound mozzarella cheese, sliced thin**

Mix flour with salt and pepper. Set aside. Beat 2 tablespoons Parmesan cheese into beaten eggs. Dip cutlets first into flour, coating well, then into egg mixture and last into bread crumbs. Place breaded cutlets on a large platter and separate layers of cutlets with waxed paper. Refrigerate them for a couple of hours. To make sauce press tomatoes through a sieve into a skillet and add tomato paste; stir over high heat until tomatoes and paste are combined. Add bay leaf, lower heat and simmer for 20 minutes. If you prefer, you can use a jar of ready made sauce. To cook cutlets put about 2 tablespoons olive oil into a skillet, add minced garlic and saute until slightly browned. Add cutlets and fry on both sides until golden brown. Add more olive oil as needed. After cutlets are done place them in a baking dish and sprinkle them with Parmesan cheese and douse them with tomato sauce. Cover each cutlet with mozzarella cheese and sprinkle with more Parmesan. Bake at 350 degrees until cheese is melted and bubbly, about 20 to 30 minutes. This recipe may look and sound hard to make, but it isn't!

Lou Bruno

Sausage Casserole

- 2 pounds Polish link sausage
- 4 potatoes, sliced
- 1 onion, sliced
- 1 green pepper, sliced into rings
- 1/4 teaspoon salt
- 1/4 teaspoon pepper
- 1/2 teaspoon garlic powder

Brown sausage in skillet. Put in a baking dish and prick with a fork. Arrange potatoes, onions, and green pepper around sausage. Season with salt, pepper and garlic powder. Cover with foil. Bake at 350 degrees for 1 to 1-1/2 hours. Great cool weather or rainy day dish.

Serves 4

Dora Hughes

Breaded Veal Scallopini

- 8 veal scallopini (1-1/4 pounds)
- 2 eggs, lightly beaten
- 3 tablespoons cold water
- 2 teaspoons vegetable oil
- salt to taste, if desired
- freshly ground pepper to taste
- 1/2 cup flour
- 2-1/2 cups fine fresh bread crumbs
- 8 tablespoons vegetable oil
- 4 tablespoons butter
- 4 thin seeded lemon slices
- 4 small sprigs of fresh parsley

Pound each scallopini between sheets of clear plastic to flatten. Combine the eggs, water and 2 tablespoons of oil in a flat dish. Put flour mixed with some salt, pepper and bread crumbs in a separate flat dish. Reserve some bread crumbs on the side. Dip the scallopini, one at a time in the flour to coat. Shake off the excess. Then dip in the mixture and finally in the bread crumbs. Add extra bread crumbs and press in with flat side of heavy knife or spatula. Heat 2 tablespoons oil in heavy skillet and when quite hot add 2 scallopini cooking 2 minutes and turning over. Repeat this process until all scallopini are cooked. You will have to clean skillet several times in between adding oil after each cleaning. Keep cooked scallopini in oven as you proceed. Finally, heat 4 tablespoons butter and swirl in a skillet until it foams and starts to turn brown. Pour the butter over the scallopini. Garnish with lemon slices and parsley.

Serves 4

Bob Burrill

Veal Picatta

- 1-1/2 pounds veal round cut 1/4 to 1/2 inch thick
- salt and pepper to taste
- flour
- 3 tablespoons butter
- 1 tablespoon olive oil
- 2 cloves garlic, minced
- 1/2 pound fresh mushrooms, sliced
- 2 tablespoons lemon juice
- 1/2 cup dry white wine
- 2 teaspoons capers plus 1 teaspoon caper juice
- 3 tablespoons minced parsley
- 1/2 lemon, thinly sliced

Sprinkle veal (which has been cut into strips) with salt and pepper and dust with flour. Heat butter and olive oil in large skillet. Add veal and brown on both sides. Remove veal from skillet. Add garlic and mushrooms to pan and cook 1 to 2 minutes. Return veal to pan. Add lemon juice and white wine; cover and simmer for 20 minutes or until veal is tender. Add capers and caper juice. Remove to warm platter and sprinkle with parsley. Garnish with lemon slices. Serves approximately four.

Estelle Kastleman

Shiekh Family Wiener Schnitzel

- 8 veal scalloppine or 8 boneless thin cut pork chops
- 2 eggs
- 1 teaspoon salt, or to taste
- 3/4 teaspoon black pepper, or to taste
- 3/4 teaspoon nutmeg, or to taste
- 1 cup all purpose flour
- 1-1/2 cups cornflake crumbs
- 1 cup vegetable or peanut oil
- 2 tablespoons butter

Rinse and pat dry veal or pork. If using pork, pound each chop with a meat mallet to 1/4 to 1/3 thickness. In a shallow bowl, combine eggs, salt, pepper and nutmeg. Mix well. Put the flour and cornflake crumbs onto 2 separate pieces of wax paper or into 2 separate shallow dishes. Dip the scalloppine, one at a time, into the flour, shaking off any excess, then into the beaten egg mixture, letting any excess drip off. Then, cover the scalloppine thoroughly with the cornflake crumbs. Set aside. (Can be made ahead and refrigerated at this point). Heat oil and butter in electric skillet. Fry the meat, one side at a time, until well browned and cooked through.

Shirin Shiekh Blackwell

To keep raw fish fresh and odorless, rinse with fresh lemon juice and water, dry thoroughly, wrap in plastic wrap or air-tight bags and refrigerate.

Beef Burgundy

- 1 tablespoon salad oil
- 1 pound stew beef, cubed
- 1 tablespoon flour
- 1/2 teaspoon thyme
- 1 bouillon cube
- 1 cup water
- 1 cup burgundy
- 1 (3 ounces) can mushrooms
- 1/4 sliced onion

In skillet, brown meat in oil. When browned, add flour and thyme. Mix well. Put into a 3 quart casserole along with remaining ingredients. Bake for 2 hours at 350 degrees. Can be made in advance and either refrigerated or frozen. Serve over mashed potatoes or rice.

Serves: 4

Dianne Ibenthal

Beef Stew a la George

- 2 pounds top sirloin, cubed
- 2 cans beef broth
- 8 medium white onions, diced
- water as needed
- 4 large carrots, sliced
- 4 large potatoes, cubed
- 1 pound bacon, fried and crumbled
- 1 pint sour cream

Brown meat. Add broth and onions. Cook over medium heat for 1 hour, adding water, if necessary. Add carrots and potatoes and cook until tender. Add crumbled bacon and cook additional 15 minutes. Ten minutes before serving, add sour cream.

Serves 8

George Rimmey

Easy Beef Stew

- 3 pounds beef chuck roast cut in 1 inch cubes
- 1 can cream of mushroom soup
- 1 can condensed onion soup
- 1 cup red wine
- 1/2 cup fresh mushrooms sliced or 1 jar sliced mushrooms
- boiled noodles or steamed rice

Place beef in oven proof casserole with cans of undiluted soups. Add wine and mushrooms. Cover and bake 3 hours at 325 degrees. Serve over boiled noodles or steamed rice.

Helen Harbeson

Laredo Beef with Chili Dumplings

- 2 pounds lean boneless beef chuck
- 1/4 cup flour
- 2 teaspoons salt
- 1 teaspoon chili powder
- 1/2 teaspoon ground cumin
- 1/4 teaspoon pepper
- 2 tablespoons oil
- 1 large onion, chopped
- 1 (12 to 16 ounces) can whole-kernel corn
- 1 (1 pound) can red kidney beans
- 1 beef bouillon cube

Chili Dumplings:

- 1 tablespoon butter or margarine
- 1 teaspoon chili powder
- 3/4 cup milk
- 2 cups biscuit mix

Trim all fat from beef and cut into 1 inch cubes. Shake meat with flour, salt, chili powder, cumin and pepper in a paper bag to coat well. Add beef cubes to oil, a few at a time, and brown. Stir in onion and saute until soft. Drain liquids from corn and beans into a large measuring container; add water, if needed, to make 3 cups. Stir into beef mixture with beef bouillon cube and cover. Heat to boiling; lower heat and simmer for 2 hours, or until beef is tender. Stir in corn and beans; heat to boiling again. While vegetables heat, make chili dumplings. Heat 1 tablespoon butter with chili powder in a small saucepan until bubbly. In a large bowl add milk and chili-butter mix all at once and stir with a fork until evenly moist. Drop batter by tablespoonfuls on top of boiling stew to make 12 mounds. Cook, uncovered, 10 minutes. Cover. Cook 10 minutes longer or until dumplings are fluffy-light.

Ruth Crowe

Sherried Beef

- 1-1/2 pounds stewing beef, cut into bite sized pieces
- 1/2 cup sherry wine (can use 1/4 cup wine and 1/4 cup water if desired)
- 1 can cream of mushroom soup
- 1/2 cup onion soup mix

Combine all ingredients in a casserole. Cover and bake for 3 hours at 325 degrees. This is very good over noodles.

Ruth Crowe

Braciole (Stuffed Steak, Italian Style)

- 1 cup bread crumbs
- 1 teaspoon coarse black pepper
- 2 tablespoons minced onion minced garlic, to taste
- 1 teaspoon oregano
- 3 tablespoons minced parsley
- 6 tablespoons grated Parmesan cheese (or Romano)
- 2 pounds meat, top round or flank steak cut into 8 to 10 pieces that are 6x4 inches (Steak should be paper thin before cutting into pieces.)
- olive oil for frying
- minced garlic and onion for frying

Mix together the crumbs, pepper, onion, garlic, oregano, parsley and cheese. Spread about 2 tablespoons in center of each 6x4 inch piece of steak. Roll up or fold each piece and tie with string or skewer. Lightly brown braciole in olive oil with garlic and onions. Add one quart of prepared tomato meat sauce. Cover and simmer for 1 hour. Serve over macaroni, noodles, etc.

Serves 8 to 10

Lou Bruno

Incredible Pot Roast

- 3-4 pound chuck roast
- A-1 Sauce
- 2 cans Cream of Mushroom Soup
- 1 package Lipton Onion Soup Mix

Line 9x13 pan with foil. Place large sheet of heavy duty foil in pan. Place roast on foil. Rub roast with A-1 sauce. Pour on both cans Cream of Mushroom soup. Sprinkle with Lipton Onion Soup mix. Seal meat **tightly** in foil, so that no juices escape. Bake in 350 degree oven for four hours. It's delicious, tender and the gravy is asolutely scrumptious. One of our all-time favorites!

Bet Lindgren

Chinese Pepper Steak

- 1/4 cup soy sauce
- 1 tablespoon sugar
- 1 pound sirloin, cut in thin diagonal slices
- 1/4 cup olive oil
- 1 clove garlic, thinly sliced
- 2 large tomatoes, cut in 1-inch cubes
- 2 large green peppers, cubed
- 1 tablespoon cornstarch
- 1 cup water

Combine soy sauce and sugar. Pour over meat and marinate 1/2 hour. Heat oil in wok, add garlic and cook 3 minutes. Discard garlic. Add meat and marinate and saute 5 minutes. Add tomatoes and peppers. Blend cornstarch with water. Add to wok. Cook covered for 10 minutes.

Serves 4

Linda Young

Russian Steak

2 pounds round top steak (2-3 inches thick)
1/3 cup Kraft French dressing (Catalina style)
1 cup ketchup
1 tablespoon garlic powder
2 tablespoons Worcestershire sauce
1/2 cup soy sauce

Mix all above ingredients together except steak. Pierce steak with a fork and pour mixture over. Marinate overnight. Broil each side 10 to 15 minutes or until desired doneness.

Serves: 6-8

Sandy Schmelzer

Spicy Steak

1-1/2 pounds round steak, cut into 1x3 inch strips
1/2 cup all purpose flour
1 teaspoon salt
1/8 to 1/4 teaspoon black pepper
1/2 cup oil
1 tablespoon Worcestershire sauce
2 cups finely chopped onion
2 cups finely chopped fresh tomatoes (or 1 medium size can stewed tomatoes)
1 bell pepper, finely chopped

Shake flour, salt and pepper in plastic bag to mix. Drop steak pieces into flour mixture and shake to coat. In a skillet heat oil to high and brown meat on both sides. Drain on paper towels. Place the browned steak in a baking dish. Combine all other ingredients and pour over steak. Bake at 350 degrees for 1 hour (a little water can be added).

Helen Lowstetter

Thommye's Lazy Recipes

To substitute for cornbread in dressing, use a large sack of Fritos, mashed. Roast (any size) preheat oven to 375 degrees. Place roast in oven for 1 hour cooking time. Turn oven off. DO NOT OPEN OVEN DOOR. Forty minutes before serving, turn oven back on.

Filet of beef, 2-1/2 to 3 pounds. Place in preheated 425 degree oven 30 to 35 minutes for medium rare.

Eye of round roast (at room temperature). Sprinkle with coarse pepper and salt. Preheat oven to 500 degrees. Bake 5 minutes per pound. Turn oven off. DO NOT OPEN FOR 2 HOURS.

Thommye Stewart

Steak Burgundy

1-2 pounds flank steak
4 cups soft bread crumbs
1/2 cup melted butter or margarine, divided use
1 small onion, minced
1 teaspoon poultry seasoning
salt and pepper to taste
1/4 cup water
flour, seasoned to taste
1 cup Burgundy wine
1 can cream of mushroom soup

Score the flank steak in diagonal lines, using a very sharp knife. Prepare stuffing by mixing bread crumbs, 1/3 cup melted butter, onion, poultry seasoning, salt, pepper and water. Spread stuffing evenly over the steak; roll up steak with stuffing inside, rolling from one wide edge to the other. Tuck ends in; fasten with toothpicks. Cut roll in two pieces and dust with seasoned flour. Heat remaining melted butter in large, heavy skillet and brown the steak rolls. Add wine, cover, and simmer 1-1/2 hours, or until meat is tender, turning roll occasionally. Remove toothpicks, slice steak rolls and place on hot platter. Add mushroom soup to drippings in pan; blend well and bring to a boil; put in a warm gravy bowl and serve with steak.

Serves 6

Ruth Crowe

Easy Oven-Baked Brisket

beef brisket, any size
meat tenderizer
1 package onion soup mix
2 cups hot water

Tenderize brisket according to directions on tenderizer packet. Dissolve onion soup mix in water. Put brisket, fat side up, in roasting pan. Pour onion soup mixture into pan. Bake, uncovered, in 350 degree oven until browned, about 30 minutes. Reduce heat to 300 degrees and cover pan. Bake until tender, about 45 minutes per pound.

Ruth Tanner

Chinese Pot Roast

1 pot roast
2 cups water
1/3 cup soy sauce
2 tablespoons wine
4 teaspoons sugar
1 slice fresh ginger
4 potatoes, cut into chunks
4 carrots sliced
1 large onion, sliced

Brown roast on both sides in large pan. Add water, soy sauce, wine, sugar and ginger. Bring to a boil, lower heat, cover and simmer for 3 hours. Add potatoes, carrots and onions during last hour.

Nathan Huang

Quick and Easy Roast

4 pound chuck or rump roast, FROZEN
1/2 cup brandy
1 package unflavored gelatin
1 cup red wine
2 packages Lipton dry onion soup
potatoes
carrots
boiling onions
mushrooms, optional
peas (frozen), optional

For six to eight people start with a solidly frozen 4 pound chuck or rump roast, preferably with 1/2 inch overcoat of fat on at least one side. Wipe roast with a damp cloth. Lay a double thickness of extra-wide heavy duty aluminum foil in a shallow pan; place roast in the middle. In a small saucepan slightly warm brandy. Set spirit afire and pour, blazing, over the frozen meat. It will burn and impart an interesting flavor. Stir gelatin into the cup of red wine and pour over meat. Sprinkle roast with onion soup mix, covering all surfaces. Fold foil in a "drugstore wrap" to form a snug package, and place in a very slow oven, 250 degrees, for about 8 hours. About 2 hours before end of roasting cycle, par-boil potatoes, carrots and onions and place around meat. If mushrooms and frozen peas are used they should be added in the last hour of baking. The meat will be brown and tender, the gravy dark, rich and full bodied. At serving time unwrap and transfer meat to a large, deep platter.

Regina Werner

Black Eye Pea Casserole

1 medium onion, diced
1 tablespoon margarine
1 pound ground beef
2 cans blackeye peas
2 cups cooked rice
1 (16 ounce) can tomatoes and green chilies, drained
1 cup extra sharp Cheddar cheese, grated

Heat oven to 350 degrees. In a medium skillet saute the onions in margarine. Stir in beef and brown. In a 2 quart casserole, put peas, rice, and tomatoes. Stir in ground beef. Top with cheese and bake 20 minutes until cheese is bubbly.

Marie Brown

Pasta salads are at their best when served at room temperature, or very soon after being assembled.

Burrito Bake

- 1 can refried beans
- 1 cup Bisquick
- 1/4 cup water
- 1 pound ground beef
- 1 small jar Pace Picante Sauce
- 1 tomato, chopped
- 1 avocado, sliced
- 1 to 2 cups shredded Cheddar cheese
- sour cream

Combine refried beans, Bisquick and water and spread on a greased pie pan. Brown meat and spread on bean mixture; layer picante, tomatoes, avocado and cheese on top of meat. Bake at 350 degrees for 30 minutes. Remove from oven and spread sour cream on top.

Marie Sullivan

Cabbage Rolls

- 1 large head cabbage (18 leaves)
- boiling water
- 1-1/2 pounds ground beef
- 2 eggs
- 1 onion, finely chopped
- salt
- garlic seasoning
- pepper
- 1 (8 ounce) can tomato sauce
- 1/4 cup cider vinegar
- 1/2 cup dark brown sugar
- 2 cups beer

Core cabbage and carefully remove large outer leaves. Place leaves in pan and pour on boiling water to cover. Let stand 5 minutes or until leaves are flexible and easily rolled. Mix meat, eggs, onions and seasonings. Drain leaves and place a ball of meat mixture on each leaf. Roll leaf around meat and place in large skillet, seam down. Mix remaining ingredients and pour over cabbage rolls. Add more beer, if necessary, so rolls will be covered with liquid. Cover and simmer slowly about 1 hour. Serve with rice.

Vi Stolz

Cabbage Stew

- 2 pounds lean ground beef
- 1 tablespoon olive oil
- 2 medium onions, chopped
- 6-8 garlic cloves, chopped
- 1 small cabbage, chopped
- 2 (15 ounce) cans crushed tomatoes
- 1 can Rotel tomatoes, crushed
- 1 (16 ounce) can tomato sauce
- salt and pepper to taste
- water

Brown beef in olive oil. Add onions and garlic saute lightly. Add cabbage, cover and let steam 15 minutes on low heat. Add rest of ingredients and water as required. Bring to a boil. Reduce heat; cover and simmer for 1-1/2 hours. Serve with cornbread.

Serves 8-10

Kenneth Munn

Darroh's Broccoli Beef Casserole

1 (10 ounce) package frozen chopped broccoli
1-1/2 pounds ground chuck or beef
1 (10-3/4 ounce) can cream of mushroom soup
1 (6 ounce) roll garlic cheese, cubed
salt and pepper to taste
round buttery crackers, such as Ritz, crushed
1 teaspoon margarine, melted

Cook broccoli according to package directions. Brown meat and set aside while broccoli cooks. Mix drained broccoli, meat, soup, cheese, salt and pepper. Pour into a 2 quart casserole. Toss crackers with margarine and place on top of casserole. Bake 350 degrees for 20-25 minutes or until top is lightly browned.

Serves 6-8

Diana Horowitz

Debbie's Quiche

1-1/2 pounds ground chuck beef
1/2 onion, chopped
1 tablespoon cornstarch
1/2 cup milk
2 cups shredded Cheddar cheese
1 cup shredded Swiss or mozzarella cheese
2 eggs, beaten
1/2 cup mayonnaise
1 deep dish 8 or 9 inch prepared pie crust

Brown meat with onion and drain off fat. Dissolve cornstarch in milk. In bowl combine remaining ingredients; adding milk and meat. Pour into unbaked pie crust. Bake 350 degrees for 35-40 minutes, or until brown.

Serves 6-8

Diana Horowitz

Hidden Onions

1-1/2 pounds chopped or ground meat
2 tablespoons salad oil
3-4 large onions, sliced thin
1 can green beans
1 can cream of tomato soup
Parmesan cheese

Brown meat in oil and drain grease. In a casserole put a layer of sliced onion, beans and browned meat. Repeat layers, ending with meat on top. Pour tomato soup along sides of casserole so the soup reaches bottom. Top with Parmesan cheese and bake in moderate oven, about 350 degrees, for 1 hour. Serve with rice or spaghetti shells or eat plain.

Lou Bruno

Hamburger Yum Yum

1 pound hamburger meat
1 cup onion, coarsely chopped
1 cup chopped celery
1/2 cup green pepper, chopped
butter
seasonings of choice
1 can cream of mushroom soup, diluted with 1/2 can water
1 (3 ounce) can chow mein noodles

Brown meat until crisp. In separate pan saute onions, celery and green pepper in butter until onion is pale gold. In a casserole, combine meat with vegetables. Season to taste. Rinse out both pans with a little water to get out all juices, and pour over casserole mixture. Add diluted soup and stir together. Cover and bake in moderate oven (350 degrees) 45 minutes. Spread noodles on top and allow to heat thoroughly.

Serves 6

Les Lawrence

Carole McGarry's Mexican Lasagna

1 pound ground beef
1 package dry taco mix
1 (16 ounce) can stewed tomatoes
1 (10 ounce) can enchilada sauce
salt and pepper, to taste
1/2 cup ripe olives, sliced
1 egg, slightly beaten
4 ounces Cheddar cheese, grated and divided in half
8 corn tortillas, cut in quarters
8 ounces creamed cottage cheese

In a large skillet, brown meat, then add taco mix, tomatoes, enchilada sauce, salt, pepper, and black olives. Cover and simmer for 20 minutes. Combine eggs, 1/2 of the cheese and all of the cottage cheese. In a 13x9x2 inch pan layer meat, tortillas and cheese mixture. Top with remaining Cheddar cheese. Heat 5 minutes in a preheated 450 degree oven. Let stand 5 minutes. Cut into squares.

Serves 6

Leah Whitty

Dried herbs in your pantry? Use restraint when using dried herbs. They are much more potent than fresh herbs and a little too much can render a dish bitter.

Meat and Potato Pie

1 pound ground beef
1/2 can cream of mushroom soup
1/4 cup chopped onion
1 egg
1/4 cup dry bread crumbs
2 tablespoons parsley
salt and pepper to taste
2 cups mashed potatoes
American cheese

Mix first 7 ingredients well. Press firmly in a 9 inch pie plate. Bake at 350 degrees for 25 minutes. Spoon off fat, and add mashed potatoes and top with cheese. Bake for an additional 10 minutes.

Serves: 4

Dianne Ibenthal

Delicious Meatloaf

1 pound ground beef
salt and pepper to taste
1 teaspoon garlic powder
1 egg, beaten
1 cup cracker crumbs
1 can tomato sauce
1 teaspoon flour
2 tablespoons water

Combine all ingredients, mixing well. Form a loaf, by hand. Place meat in a shallow pan. Bake at 350 degrees until well done, about 1 hour.

Patricia Tobe

Meat Loaf

1-1/2 pounds beef or turkey, ground
1 cup bread crumbs or 1/2 cup rice
1 large egg, beaten
1 medium onion, chopped
1-1/2 teaspoons salt
1/4 teaspoon pepper
1 small can tomato sauce
2 teaspoons vinegar
2 teaspoons mustard
1 cup water
2 tablespoons brown sugar

Preheat oven to 350 degrees. Lightly mix together meat, bread crumbs or rice, egg, onion, salt, pepper and 1/2 can tomato sauce. Form a loaf. Place in a shallow pan and start to cook. While it starts to bake, make a sweet, tart sauce by combining the remaining tomato sauce, vinegar, mustard, water, and brown sugar. Pour sauce over meat loaf and continue baking for 1 to 1-1/2 hours.

Lynn Miller

Meat Loaf (Spicy)

- **10 Saltine crackers, crushed**
- **2 eggs, beaten**
- **1 medium onion, chopped**
- **1 small bell pepper, chopped**
- **2 carrots, grated**
- **1 (10 ounce) can Rotel tomatoes with green chilies**
- **1-1/2 pounds ground beef**
- **ketchup**

Add cracker crumbs to beaten eggs. Combine onion, pepper and carrots and add to egg mixture. Add can of Rotel tomatoes. Mix well with ground beef. Put mixture in loaf pan and top with ketchup. Bake in 350 degree oven for 1 hour. Remove from oven and decant collected grease. Return to oven and broil for 5 minutes.

Serves 4

Scoot Harrison

Mini Meat Loaf

- **1 pound ground chuck**
- **1/2 onion, chopped**
- **1 teaspoon salt**
- **1/2 cup bread crumbs**
- **1 can Vegetarian vegetable soup**
- **1/2 teaspoon pepper**

Preheat oven to 450 degrees. Mix all ingredients together. Spoon into 12 muffin tins. Bake uncovered for 15-20 minutes.

Serves 6

Cher Longoria

Quick and Easy Meat Loaf

- **2 pounds lean ground beef**
- **1/2 teaspoon salt**
- **1/2 teaspoon oregano**
- **1/2 teaspoon bouquet garni (or marjoram and/or other spice of choice)**
- **pepper to taste**
- **1/3 medium onion, chopped**
- **fresh parsley, chopped**
- **1/4 green pepper, chopped (or pimento)**
- **1 can cream of mushroom soup**
- **3 cups Bran flakes**
- **chili sauce or ketchup**

In large mixing bowl blend well all ingredients except bran flakes and chili sauce. Fold in bran flakes until well mixed. Pack mixture **very firmly** into an ungreased loaf pan, using the palm of your hand. The firmer you pack it the easier it will be to cut. Coat top of loaf with chili sauce or ketchup and press down with a wide fork. Bake for one hour at 350 degrees.

Serves 12

A. Marion Webster

Susan's Original Meatloaf

- **2** pounds ground beef
- **3/4** cup Pepperidge Farm dry bread crumbs
- **3/4** cup canned applesauce
- **6** tablespoons catsup
- **3/4** teaspoon salt
- **1/4** teaspoon ground sage
- **1** slightly beaten egg
- **2** tablespoons finely chopped onion
- dash of pepper
- **2-3** strips of bacon
- Meatloaf Sauce, optional (recipe follows)

Mix ground beef lightly with next 8 ingredients until well blended. Shape into loaf and place in a shallow baking pan, with bacon strips on top. Place a meat thermometer in the center of the meat and bake at 350 degrees until well done. You may want to remove some of the hot meat juices and drippings collecting at the sides of the pan while cooking.

Susan's Special Meatloaf Sauce:

- **1** (15 ounce) can tomato sauce
- **1/2** cup canned tomatoes cut in small pieces and partially drained
- **1/3** cup brown sugar
- **1/4** teaspoon salt
- dash of cinnamon
- pepper to taste
- **1** medium onion, finely chopped
- **1/4** cup vinegar

Combine all ingredients in saucepan. Boil slowly until onions are done. Pour over the meat loaf or serve as an option on the side.

Susan Bick-Binse

Now That's Chili!!

- **1** pound ground beef
- **1** clove garlic, minced
- **1** large onion, finely chopped (about 1 cup)
- **1** medium green pepper, finely chopped (about 2/3 cup)
- **4** tablespoons chili powder
- **1** tablespoon cider vinegar
- **1/4** teaspoon allspice
- **1/4** teaspoon coriander
- **1** teaspoon cumin
- **1/2** teaspoon salt, or to taste
- **1/2** cup water
- **2** cups canned crushed tomatoes
- **1** (16 ounce) can red kidney beans with liquid

Cook beef, garlic, onion and green pepper in a heavy skillet over medium high heat, stirring frequently to break up meat. Cook until onion is soft and meat has lost its pink color. Add remaining ingredients. Bring to a boil. Cover and reduce heat. Simmer the chili for 45 minutes, stirring frequently. Makes about seven 7-1/2 ounce servings. Note: If you use very lean beef in addition to pouring off all the fat, and use an oil spray to brown the meat, the fat grams and calories are very low in this recipe. It is a favorite in my household.

Stella Andersen

Pastitsio
(Greek casserole of ground beef and macaroni)

1 medium onion, chopped
1 clove garlic, minced
2 tablespoons olive oil
1-1/2 pounds lean ground beef
1-1/2 teaspoons salt, divided use
2 dashes cinnamon
1 (8 ounce) can tomato sauce
5 tablespoons margarine, divided use
1/4 cup flour
2 cups skim milk
dash of white pepper
nutmeg (a pinch)
1/3 cup grated Parmesan cheese
1 (8 ounce) package small elbow macaroni
2 eggs
2 cups coarsely shredded Cheddar cheese

Saute onion and garlic in olive oil until soft. Crumble in the beef and add 1 teaspoon salt. Cook, stirring, until meat loses its red color. Pour off fat. Stir in cinnamon and tomato sauce and set aside. In a saucepan melt 3 tablespoons margarine and stir in flour. Add milk and cook, stirring until thickened. Add 1/2 teaspoon salt, pepper, nutmeg and Parmesan cheese. Set aside. Cook macaroni in boiling salted water 10 to 12 minutes or until tender. Drain well and put back in pot. Add eggs and 2 tablespoons margarine. Beat briskly with wooden spoon until well mixed. Butter a shallow 2-1/2 quart baking dish and layer ingredients as follows: put half the macaroni in dish, all the meat, half the Cheddar cheese, remaining macaroni, then the white sauce (stir again before pouring). Shake dish gently to settle white sauce. Sprinkle on Cheddar, dot with margarine and sprinkle with nutmeg. Bake in preheated 375 degree oven for 1 hour; or cover and refrigerate until needed, then bake, uncovered, 1 hour and 15 minutes.

Serves 6 to 8

Ruth Crowe

Pizza In A Burger

1-1/2 pounds ground beef
1/3 cup grated Parmesan cheese
1/4 cup finely chopped onion
1/4 cup chopped pitted ripe olives
1 teaspoon salt
1 teaspoon dried oregano, crushed
1 (6 ounce) can tomato paste
dash of pepper
4 slices mozzarella cheese, cut in strips
8 cherry tomatoes, halved
8 slices French bread, toasted

Combine first 7 ingredients and dash of pepper; shape into 8 oval patties. Broil over medium coals 5 to 6 minutes. Turn; top each with cheese and tomatoes. Broil 5 minutes or to desired doneness. Serve on toasted French bread slices.

Elva Lopez

"Pewter Mug" Sauerkraut Balls

Cream Sauce:
- **1 cup butter or margarine**
- **1/3 cup chopped onion (1 small onion)**
- **1 cup all purpose flour**
- **1-1/2 cups milk**

Meatballs:
- **2 pounds ground chuck**
- **1 tablespoon drained horseradish**
- **1 tablespoon Worcestershire sauce**
- **1-1/2 teaspoons prepared mustard**
- **1 teaspoon salt**
- **1/8 teaspoon pepper**
- **1-2 drops hot pepper sauce**
- **1 (1 pound) can sauerkraut, drained and very finely chopped**

Coating:
- **1 cup all purpose flour**
- **1 egg**
- **1 cup milk**
- **2 cups dry, unseasoned bread crumbs**

Make cream sauce by melting 1 cup butter or margarine in a large saucepan. Saute 1/3 cup chopped onion for 3 minutes. Stir in 1 cup all purpose flour. Cook 1 minute. Blend in 1-1/2 cups milk, stirring well to keep smooth. Bring to a boil, cook 1 minute, remove from heat and cool slightly.

To make meatballs: Saute in a large skillet 2 pounds ground chuck. Cook in own fat until all pink color disappears. Stir in 1 tablespoon drained horseradish, 1 tablespoon Worcestershire sauce, 1-1/2 teaspoons prepared mustard, 1 teaspoon salt, 1/8 teaspoon pepper and 1-2 drops hot pepper sauce. Cook 2 minutes longer. Stir into prepared sauce together with sauerkraut, drained and very finely chopped. Cover and chill mixture in refrigerator at least 4 hours or overnight. Shape meatballs by using a large tablespoon of mixture for each one. Roll into 1 cup flour. Then dip into a mixture made by beating 1 egg with 1 cup milk. Coat in a little of dry bread crumbs. To cook: Heat at least 2 inches oil in a large saucepan or electric skillet to 375 degrees. Fry meatballs a few at a time until deep golden, approximately 3-4 minutes. Drain on paper towels. Keep warm. Makes about 4 dozen.

Serves 6

Marilyn Healy

Quick and Easy Beef Stroganoff

- **1 pound ground beef**
- **1 teaspoon garlic salt**
- **1 onion, chopped**
- **1 can cream of mushroom soup**
- **1-1/2 to 2 cups sour cream**
- **8 ounces egg noodles**

Brown beef with garlic salt and onion. Drain well. Add soup and sour cream. Simmer for 10 minutes. Prepare noodles as directed. Pour meat sauce over warm noodles.

Liza Wright

Poor Man Steak

2 pounds ground chuck
1 cup cracker crumbs
1 cup milk
1 teaspoon salt
1/4 teaspoon pepper
1 onion, chopped
flour
oil
1 can cream of mushroom soup
1-1/4 cups water

Mix first 6 ingredients together, combining well. Put into large piece of foil, cover and keep in refrigerator overnight. When ready to prepare, form patties, coat with flour and brown with oil in a skillet. Place patties in roasting pan, and pour in mushroom soup and water. Bake at 300 degrees for 1-1/2 hours.

Serves: 4

W. F. Hampton

"Porcupines"

1/2 pound ground beef
1/4 cup uncooked rice
1/4 cup milk (or water)
2 tablespoons chopped onion
1/2 teaspoon salt (may be omitted)
1/4 teaspoon celery salt
1/8 teaspoon garlic salt
dash pepper
1 tablespoon olive oil
1 (8 ounce) can tomato sauce
1/2 cup water
1-1/2 teaspoons Worcestershire sauce

Mix ground beef, rice, milk, onion and seasonings and form into 4 balls. Fry, in olive oil, turning frequently, until light brown but not crusty. Add tomato sauce, water and Worcestershire to skillet, mixing well. Cover and simmer 45 minutes over low heat. Add additional water if liquid cooks down too much.

Serves 2

Kaye Murray

Marjorie's Shepherd's Pie

1 pound ground beef
1 onion, chopped
1 heaping tablespoon flour
seasonings to taste
cold water
5 large potatoes
butter
milk

Brown the meat in a large skillet with the chopped onion. Add the flour and seasonings. When browned, add cold water to cover meat. Stir until gravy thickens. Pour into casserole. Next, boil and mash potatoes, using butter and milk to make them fluffy. Place potatoes on top of meat and dot with butter. Brown for 15-20 minutes in 375-400 degree oven.

Serves 4-6

Marjorie Evans

Rebecca's Hamburger Noodle Bake

- 3 teaspoons butter
- 1 pound lean hamburger meat
- 2 cloves garlic, minced
- 1 teaspoon sugar
- 2 (8 ounce) cans tomato sauce
- 3 scallions, finely chopped
- salt and pepper to taste
- 1 (3 ounce) package cream cheese
- 1 cup sour cream
- 1 small package noodles, cooked according to package directions
- 1/2 cup grated cheese

Brown meat in butter. Combine garlic, sugar, tomato sauce and scallions with meat and cook for 20 minutes on stove. Add salt and pepper. In a separate bowl blend cream cheese and sour cream. In baking dish, pour cooked, drained noodles to form first layer. Add cream cheese and sour cream mixture for second layer. Top layer is the hamburger mixture. Sprinkle top with grated cheese and bake in a 350 oven for 20 minutes.

John Gardner

Kathy's Shepherd's Pie

- 1 onion, minced
- 5 tablespoons butter
- 4 cups ground leftover cooked roast beef
- 2 cups gravy, leftover or canned
- 1 teaspoon Worcestershire sauce
- 1/2 teaspoon Tabasco sauce
- 2 teaspoons salt
- 8 medium potatoes, peeled
- 1/4 teaspoon pepper
- 1/3 cup hot milk or light cream
- 1 egg, slightly beaten

Saute onion in 1 tablespoon butter until soft but not brown; remove from heat and mix in meat, gravy, Worcestershire sauce, Tabasco sauce and 1 teaspoon salt. Make mashed potatoes with hot cooked potatoes, remaining butter, salt, pepper and hot milk. Beat until fluffy. Place meat mixture in bottom of 1-1/2 quart baking dish; top with mashed potatoes. Score potatoes with a fork to make a pattern. Brush with beaten eggs; bake in 425 degree oven for 15-20 minutes or until slightly brown.

Serves 6

Kathy O'Brien

Experts call pasta the perfect food. Pasta is low in calories and an excellent source of complex carbohydrates and fiber, also a good source of B-vitamins.

Spaghetti Pie

- 1 (8 ounce) package spaghetti, broken into 2 inch pieces
- 2 tablespoons butter, softened
- 1/2 cup grated Parmesan cheese
- 1/2 teaspoon salt
- 1/4 teaspoon pepper
- 1 egg, well beaten
- 1-1/2 pounds ground chuck
- 1 medium onion, chopped
- 1 green pepper, chopped
- 2 cloves garlic, minced
- 1 quart spaghetti sauce
- 1 teaspoon sugar
- 1/2 teaspoon oregano
- 1 pound cottage cheese
- mozzarella cheese

Cook spaghetti according to package directions; drain. In large bowl, mix butter, Parmesan cheese, salt, pepper and egg. Add spaghetti and toss to coat well. Spread evenly in 9x13 inch pan. Brown meat in large saucepan, adding onion, green pepper and garlic just as meat begins to cook. When the meat is browned, drain off fat. Stir in spaghetti sauce, sugar and oregano. Spread cottage cheese over spaghetti layer and top with meat mixture. Bake 30 minutes at 350 degrees. Sprinkle with mozzarella cheese and bake for ten minutes more. Let stand for 15 minutes before serving.

Serves 8 to 10

Bob Burrill

Spaghetti with Meat Sauce

- 2 pounds ground beef
- 1 green pepper, finely chopped
- 1 medium onion, finely chopped
- 2 (15 ounce) cans tomato sauce
- 2 (12 ounce) cans tomato paste
- 1 (7.5 ounce) can pitted ripe olives, drained and sliced
- 2 (1.5 ounce) envelopes Italian spaghetti sauce mixed with mushrooms
- 3 cups water
- 1 tablespoon sugar
- 1 teaspoon crushed oregano leaves
- 2 cloves garlic, crushed
- 1 bay leaf, crumbled
- 16 ounces Italian style spaghetti
- Parmesan cheese

Cook and stir ground beef, onion and pepper until meat is brown and onion is tender. Stir in remaining ingredients except spaghetti and Parmesan cheese. Simmer uncovered 1-1/2 hours, stirring occasionally. Place in covered container and refrigerate overnight. Cook spaghetti as directed on package. Heat sauce and serve over hot cooked spaghetti and sprinkle with Parmesan cheese. I serve it immediately, if necessary; however, it is better the 2nd day. Enjoy it.

Serves 8

Anne Clark

Stuffed Green Peppers

3 large green peppers
1 cup water
1/2 teaspoon salt
1/2 pound ground beef
1 cup dry bread crumbs or cracker crumbs
1 tablespoon chopped onion
1 teaspoon salt
1/4 teaspoon pepper
1 (8 ounce) can tomato sauce

Preheat oven to 350 degrees. Cut thin slice from stem end of each pepper. Remove all seeds and membranes. Wash inside and outside. Heat water and salt to boiling. Add peppers, cook 5 minutes and drain. Mix together remaining ingredients. Lightly stuff each pepper with 1/3 of the meat mixture. Stand peppers upright in ungreased baking dish, 8x8x2 inch. Cover and bake 45 minutes. Uncover and bake 15 minutes longer.

Serves 2-3

Patricia Tobe

Swedish Meatballs I

2 pounds ground meat (1 pound chuck, 1/2 pound veal, 1/2 pound pork)
2 cups cream
1-1/3 cups dry bread crumbs
2 eggs
1/4 teaspoon allspice
1/4 teaspoon nutmeg
2 teaspoons salt

Have butcher grind meat together. Combine cream and bread crumbs, add other seasonings and add to meat. Mix several hours in advance. Refrigerate to make it easier to work with. Wet hands and spray plate with Pam. Make into balls and brown slightly in butter. Shake pan while frying (put drippings into separate container). Pour a little water in bottom of ovenproof dish, add browned meatballs and steam in oven, 300 degrees for 2 hours or simmer in pan on top of stove with drippings for 15 minutes.

Dora Hughes

Swedish Meat Balls II

1 pound hamburger meat
1 egg
2 tablespoons grated onion
1/3 cup milk
1/2 cup bread crumbs
1 teaspoon salt
1/8 teaspoon nutmeg
1 can beef consomme, diluted with 1/2 can water

Mix all ingredients, except consomme, and shape into meatballs about 1 inch in diameter; brown over medium heat. Lower heat and add consomme; simmer for approximately 30 minutes. Make gravy with liquid. Serve meatballs and gravy over rice, noodles, or chow mein noodles.

Serves 6

Les Lawrence

Tomato Sauce with Meatballs

1 small onion
1 clove garlic, chopped
2 (15 ounce) cans tomato puree
2 (8 ounce) cans tomato paste
1 (28 ounce) can Italian tomatoes
1/2 teaspoon sugar or piece of carrot
1 tablespoon Parmesan
1 tablespoon garlic powder
1 tablespoon oregano
1-2 bay leaves
1 tablespoon parsley
1 tablespoon basil
2 (15 ounce) cans water
salt and pepper, to taste
Meatballs (recipe follows), optional

Put some oil in the bottom of pan. Heat it. Put in onions and garlic; brown, but do not burn. Add puree, paste, and tomatoes. Mix well. Bring to a simmer. Add rest of the ingredients and cook for 3-4 hours. You can also add mushrooms or chopped bell pepper to sauce. I brown a little pepperoni with my sauce and it tastes great!

Lou Bruno's Meatballs:

2 pounds ground beef
1 pound ground pork
2 eggs
1 clove garlic, chopped
1 small onion, chopped
black pepper and salt, to taste
1 tablespoon parsley
1/2 teaspoon basil
1/2 teaspoon oregano
1/4 cup Parmesan cheese
1/4 cup seasoned Italian bread crumbs

Mix all ingredients together and shape into meatballs. Brown well. Put in sauce and cook for 3-4 hours. Stir quite often. Cook to desired thickness. Add a little water to sauce if too thick.

Lou Bruno

Tostada Supreme

safflower oil
4 flour tortillas
1 pound ground beef
salt and pepper, to taste
1 (16 ounce) can refried beans
grated sharp Cheddar cheese
1/2 head iceberg lettuce, shredded
2 tomatoes, chopped
4-5 green onions, chopped
guacamole and/or sour cream, if desired

Fry tortillas in skillet with safflower oil until crisp. Set aside. Cook ground beef in same skillet until done; season to taste. Add refried beans to meat and set aside. When ready to serve, put meat and bean mixture on top of tortilla; add grated cheese on top. Place on cookie sheet and warm in a 250 degree oven. Remove from oven and top with remaining ingredients.

Tim Lassiter

DESSERTS

Almond Crescent Cookies

- 3/4 cup confectioners sugar, sifted
- 1 cup butter, softened
- 2 teaspoons vanilla
- 1 teaspoon cinnamon
- 1 cup ground blanched almonds
- 2-1/2 cups flour
- confectioners sugar (to be used for dusting cookies after they are baked)

Gradually add sugar to butter, creaming well. Add remaining ingredients, mixing until thoroughly combined. Chill dough at least 1 or 2 hours. Roll out dough and cut or form into desired shapes. Bake on a greased cookie sheet at 350 degrees for 15 minutes. Cool and dust with powdered sugar.

Selma Leff

Breakfast Cookies

- 1/4 cup whole wheat flour
- 1/2 cup all purpose flour
- 1/2 teaspoon baking soda
- 1/2 teaspoon salt
- 3/4 cup butter or margarine, softened
- 1 cup brown sugar, firmly packed
- 1/2 cup granulated sugar
- 1 egg, lightly beaten
- 1 teaspoon water or orange juice
- 1 teaspoon vanilla
- 6 ounces semi-sweet chocolate chips (or carob)
- 1/2 cup flaked coconut
- 2 tablespoons wheat germ
- 1/2 cup chopped nuts
- 2-1/2 cups oatmeal

Optional:

- 1/2 cup peanut butter
- 1/2 cup raisins
- 1/2 cup sunflower seeds

In large bowl mix flours, baking soda and salt. In separate bowl, cream butter and sugars. Add lightly beaten egg, water and vanilla. Stir flour mixture into liquid mixture. Fold in chocolate chips, coconut, wheat germ, nuts and oatmeal (and optional items if desired). Drop by well rounded teaspoons onto greased cookie sheet. Bake 12-15 minutes at 350 degrees. Makes 4-1/2 dozen cookies.

Glen Claypool

"Love and eggs are best when they are fresh."
— Russian Proverb

Buttery Tea Balls

1/2 pound unsalted butter at room temperature
4 cups confectioners sugar
1 teaspoon vanilla
2-1/4 cups all purpose flour
1/4 teaspoon salt
3/4 cup finely chopped pecans or walnuts

Preheat oven to 350 degrees. In a large bowl, mix butter with 1/2 cup sugar, vanilla, flour, salt, and nuts until a dough is formed. Roll the dough into 1 inch balls in the palm of your hand. Place on ungreased baking sheet and bake 10-12 minutes or until bottoms are slightly browned. Place remaining sugar in shallow dish. Roll balls in it while still hot. Let cool and roll again.

Yields 4 dozen

Jeanne Dean

Caramel Squares

1 cup brown sugar
3/4 stick butter or margarine
1 cup all-purpose flour
1 teaspoon baking powder
1 egg, beaten
1 teaspoon vanilla
1 cup chopped pecans

Melt sugar with butter in saucepan. Cool. Add flour, baking powder, egg and vanilla. Stir in nuts. Spread in a 8 or 9 inch square pan. Bake at 325 degrees for 20-30 minutes. Cool before cutting into squares.

Jan Purzer Wallace

Carmelitas Cookies

32 light caramels
1/4 cup evaporated milk
1 roll (refrigerated) Pillsbury chocolate chip cookies
1 (6 ounce) package semisweet chocolate chips
1 cup chopped pecans

Melt caramels with milk in top of double boiler. Slice chocolate chip cookies 1/4 inch thick and press together in bottom of greased 8 or 9 inch square pan. Bake 20-25 minutes at 375 degrees until browned. Spread caramel mixture on top of dough and sprinkle with chocolate chips and pecans. Refrigerate 2 hours and cut cookies into squares.

Selma Leff

Chocolate Chip Cookie Bars

- 1 cup butter, softened
- 3/4 cup granulated sugar
- 3/4 cup brown sugar, firmly packed
- 1 teaspoon vanilla
- 1 teaspoon water
- 2 eggs
- 1 cup oatmeal
- 2-1/4 cups flour
- 1 teaspoon baking soda
- 2 cups chocolate chips
- 1 cup chopped nuts (optional)

Cream butter and sugars; add vanilla and water and beat until creamy; beat in eggs. Mix in oatmeal, flour and soda. Stir in chocolate chips and nuts. Spread in greased jelly-roll pan (12x15 inch). Bake at 375 degrees for 20 minutes. Cool slightly; cut into 60 squares. Store in air tight container between layers of paper towels. Hint: A slice of bread left on the top layer of paper towel will keep bars fresh for a longer time!

Catherine Arlinghaus

Christmas Cookies

- 1/2 pound red candied cherries (whole)
- 1/2 pound green candied cherries (whole)
- 1/2 pound candied pineapple, chopped
- 3 cups pecans, chopped
- 1 cup flour
- 1 can sweetened condensed milk

Mix fruit and nuts. Add flour and then condensed milk. Drop by spoonful on greased baking sheet. Bake at 350 degrees about 15 minutes. Makes about 6 dozen. They are delicious!

Dorothy Teel

Cocoons

- 1/2 pound butter
- 2 cups flour
- 2 tablespoons powdered sugar
- 1/2 teaspoon vanilla
- 1-1/2 cups ground nuts
- powdered sugar

Put all ingredients into a bowl and knead until well mixed. Take off small pieces of dough, the size of a pecan or walnut, and shape in the palms of hands like almonds. Place shaped cookies onto an ungreased cookie sheet and bake in a moderate oven, about 325 degrees, approximately 30 minutes or until light brown. While hot, roll in powdered sugar.

Sophia Papas

Lemon Love Notes

- 1 cup (two sticks) margarine, softened
- 2 cups flour
- 3/4 cup powdered sugar
- 4 eggs
- 2 cups sugar
- 8 or 9 tablespoons fresh lemon juice
- 4 tablespoons flour
- 1 teaspoon baking powder

Combine margarine, 2 cups flour and powdered sugar and press into 9x13 inch greased pan. Bake at 350 degrees for 20 minutes. Beat eggs; add sugar, lemon juice, 4 tablespoons flour and 1 teaspoon baking powder. Pour over baked crust and bake 25 minutes longer. Cool in pan and while still warm sprinkle with powdered sugar. Cut into two inch squares.

Yields 30 squares

Dorothy Teel

Chewy Oatmeal Cookies

- 1 cup brown sugar
- 1 cup granulated sugar
- 2 eggs
- 2 sticks margarine, softened
- 1/2 teaspoon baking soda
- 1 cup flour
- 1 teaspoon vanilla
- 4 cups oatmeal
- 1 cup raisins
- 1 cup dates
- 1 cup chopped pecans
- 1 cup coconut

Beat sugars and eggs together; add margarine. Add soda to flour and add to egg mixture; add vanilla and blend well. Add oatmeal. Raisins and dates should be ground together in a food processor or blender and then added to oatmeal mixture. Stir in nuts and coconut. Drop by teaspoonfuls onto greased cookie sheets and bake in 350 degree oven for 10 minutes or until brown. Makes at least 8-10 dozen and they are delicious!

Selma Leff

Chocolate Oatmeal Cookies

- 2 cups sugar
- 1/2 cup cocoa
- 1/2 cup milk
- 1 stick margarine
- 1 teaspoon vanilla
- 3 cups "minute" oatmeal
- 1 cup chopped pecans

Bring sugar, cocoa, milk and margarine to a boil over a low fire. When mixture boils, add the vanilla, oatmeal and pecans and mix well. Spoon on waxed paper and let cool. The nice part about these cookies is that you don't have to have an oven!

Louise Breedlove

Honey-Oatmeal Cookies

1-1/4 cups sugar
1/2 cup shortening
2 eggs
1/3 cup honey
1-3/4 cups all-purpose flour
1 teaspoon baking soda
1 teaspoon salt
2 cups quick-cooking or regular oats
1 cup raisins
1/3 cup chopped nuts

Heat oven to 375 degrees. Mix sugar, shortening, eggs and honey and combine well. Stir in remaining ingredients. Drop dough by rounded teaspoonfuls about 2 inches apart onto ungreased cookie sheet. Bake until brown, 8 to 10 minutes. Immediately remove from cookie sheet to cool.

Anita Chin

Lemon Drops

1 package Duncan Hines lemon supreme, moist deluxe cake mix
1 lemon, use 1 tablespoon of juice
1 egg
1 (4 ounce) small carton Cool Whip

Combine all ingredients and mix well. Drop 1/2 tablespoon of dough on greased cookie sheet. Bake at 350 degrees 8 or 10 minutes (no more). They will be just a tiny bit brown and soft. Makes about 40 cookies.

Tibby Lloyd

Oatmeal Cookies

1 stick margarine
1/2 cup milk
2 cups sugar
2-1/2 cups quick 3 minute oats
4 tablespoons cocoa
4 tablespoons vanilla
1/2 cup nuts

Combine first 3 ingredients and heat to a boil, about 4 minutes. Remove from heat. Add the next 4 ingredients and mix well. Drop by teaspoonfuls onto wax paper.

Michael Kunc

To lower cholesterol in baked goods, substitute two egg whites for one whole egg.

Grandma Steven's Orange Cookies

Cookie:
3/4 cup sugar
1/2 cup shortening
1 egg
1/2 cup sour milk or 1-1/2 teaspoons vinegar plus enough milk to measure 1/2 cup
1-1/2 cups flour
1/2 teaspoon baking soda
1 teaspoon baking powder
juice and grated rind of 1/2 orange

Icing:
1 cup powdered sugar
2 tablespoons melted butter
juice and grated rind of 1/2 orange

For cookies, cream sugar and shortening. Add egg and milk. Combine flour, soda, and powder and add to mixture. Stir in orange juice and grated rind. Bake on greased cookie sheet at 400 degrees for 8 minutes. Remove from sheet, cool and ice with combined icing ingredients.

Serves 3-4 dozen

Catherine P. Arlinghaus

Peanut Butter Granola Cookies

1/2 cup cocoa
2 cups sugar
1/2 cup milk
1 stick margarine, softened
1/2 cup peanut butter
1 teaspoon vanilla
1/2 teaspoon salt
3 cups granola

Stir cocoa, sugar and milk together in saucepan. Slowly bring to a boil. Remove from heat and add margarine, peanut butter, vanilla, and salt. Stir in granola. Drop by teaspoonfuls onto wax paper and chill. Easy and delicious.

Serves 3 dozen

Liza Wright

Granny's Kolachy

1 (3 ounce) package cream cheese, softened
1 stick margarine, softened
1 cup flour
1 teaspoon sugar
1 can apricot filling
1 (7 ounce) package coconut

Blend cream cheese and margarine and knead until soft; gradually add sugar. Roll into a ball and wrap in waxed paper or plastic and refrigerate at least 24 hours. Roll dough out 1/4 inch thick on floured board and cut into 1-1/2 inch rounds. Place on cookie sheet. Make indentation and fill with apricot filling. Sprinkle with coconut and bake at 375 degrees for 10 minutes or until brown.

Kathy O'Brien

Pecan Dainties

1 cup butter, softened
1/2 cup sugar
2 cups sifted all purpose flour
1 teaspoon vanilla extract
1 tablespoon water
2 cups pecans, ground
pecan halves

Cream butter and sugar until light; add remaining ingredients except pecan halves. Mix well and chill until firm. Shape into 3/4 inch balls. Arrange on ungreased cookie sheets and top with a pecan half. Bake in preheated 325 degree oven for 20 minutes. Makes 6 to 8 dozen.

Bobbie Davis

Potato Chip Cookies I

1 cup butter, softened
1/2 cup sugar
1 teaspoon vanilla
1-3/4 cups flour
1/2 cup crushed potato chips
1/2 cup chopped pecans

Cream butter, sugar and vanilla. Add flour, chips and pecans. Form balls about 1 inch in diameter. Place on cookie sheet, press down with bottom of small glass and bake in 350 degree oven for 12-14 minutes.

Jane Frank

Potato Chip Cookies II

1 cup butter, softened
1 cup sugar
1 teaspoon vanilla
3-1/4 cups flour
1-1/2 cups crushed potato chips
powdered sugar

Cream butter and sugar; add vanilla. Stir in flour, then potato chips. Roll into walnut sized balls and flatten on ungreased cookie sheet with a fork. Bake at 300 degrees for 20 minutes. Remove to a paper towel and sprinkle with powdered sugar.

Yield: 5 dozen

Catherine Arlinghaus

Cut a meringue pie easily by coating both sides of knife lightly with butter.

Cheddar Shortbread

- **1 cup butter or margarine, softened**
- **3/4 cup grated sharp Cheddar cheese, room temperature**
- **1 teaspoon Worcestershire sauce**
- **1/8 teaspoon cayenne**
- **2 cups flour**
- **poppy, sesame or caraway seeds (optional)**

Lightly butter two baking sheets. Heat oven to 350 degrees. Beat butter with the cheese until smooth. Beat in seasonings, then flour. Turn dough out onto a lightly floured board and knead for a minute or two until well blended. Roll out dough to 1/2 inch thickness. Cut into small shapes with cookie cutters. Transfer cookies to baking sheets, sprinkle with seeds, if desired, and bake about 10 minutes until lightly browned around the edges. Cool 10 minutes before serving. Makes 3 dozen cookies.

Ruth Crowe

Sugar Cookies

- **1 cup butter, softened**
- **1 cup oil**
- **1 cup powdered sugar**
- **1 cup white sugar**
- **2 eggs**
- **2 teaspoons vanilla**
- **1 teaspoon salt**
- **5 cups flour**
- **1 teaspoon cream of tartar**
- **1 teaspoon baking soda**

Beat first seven ingredients together. Pre-measure the flour, then sift with cream of tartar and baking soda. Blend with creamed ingredients. Chill thoroughly in the refrigerator. Make small balls and flatten with the bottom of a glass dipped in sugar. Bake on ungreased cookie sheet at 350 degrees to a light tanning of edges and bottom of cookies, 10 to 12 minutes.

Glen Claypool

Texas Gold Bars

- **1 box yellow cake mix without pudding added**
- **1 egg, slightly beaten**
- **1 stick margarine, melted**

Topping:

- **1 tablespoon vanilla**
- **1 (8 ounce) cream cheese, softened**
- **1 box powdered sugar**
- **2 eggs, slightly beaten**

Combine mix, egg and margarine and press into a 9x13 pan. Use Pyrex not metal pan. Mix topping ingredients and pour over top of cake mixture. Bake in 300 degree oven for 50 minutes. Cut into bars when cool.

Margo Cannom

Almond Hershey Pie

11 single graham crackers crushed
5 tablespoons melted margarine
1 large almond Hershey bar
1 (10 ounce) carton of refrigerated topping, room temperature

Combine first two ingredients and press into 9 inch pie pan. Melt almond Hershey bar in top of double boiler over hot, but not boiling water. Combine melted chocolate with topping. Fold chocolate mixture in carefully and slowly so mixture will stay light and airy. Then put it in the crumb crust. A pastry crust can be used also.

Serves 6-8

Virginia Horton

Apple Pie

2 pie crusts
6-8 large tart apples, sliced
4-6 crushed graham crackers or vanilla wafers
1 tablespoon lemon juice
1 teaspoon vanilla
3/4 cup granulated sugar
1/4 cup brown sugar
1 tablespoon butter or margarine

Line a large pie pan with one crust. Combine apples with all ingredients and place in pie crust. Cover with remaining crust and prick with fork in several places. Bake at 400 degrees for 50 minutes or until done.

Selma Leff

No Crust Apple Pie

6 cooking apples, peeled, cored and cut into eighths
1/2 cup sugar
1/2 cup water
1 teaspoon ground cinnamon
1/2 teaspoon allspice
1/2 cup flour
1/4 firmly packed brown sugar
1/2 teaspoon baking powder
1/4 teaspoon salt
3 tablespoons butter or margarine

Combine first 5 ingredients in large saucepan; bring to a boil, cover, reduce heat, and simmer 8-10 minutes or until apples are almost tender. Spoon into a deep dish 9 inch pie plate. Combine flour, brown sugar, baking powder and salt; cut in butter with a pastry blender until mixture resembles coarse meal. Crumble mixture over apples. Bake 350 degrees for 30 minutes or until top is browned.

Serves 4

Mary Belle Woody

Sugar Free Apple Pie

- 1 (6 ounce) can apple juice concentrate
- 1 tablespoon margarine or butter
- 2 tablespoons cornstarch
- 1 teaspoon cinnamon
- 1/4 teaspoon nutmeg
- 6 large Granny Smith or Golden Delicious apples, peeled and thinly sliced
- 2 (9 or 9-1/2 inch) pie crusts

Mix first 5 ingredients and heat until cornstarch is clear. Pour over sliced apples and mix until apples are coated. Pour into 9 or 9-1/2 inch pie shell and top with second crust. Bake at 425 degrees for 30 minutes. Reduce heat to 350 degrees and bake an additional 30 minutes.

Alberta Bain

Swedish Apple Pie

- 4-5 apples, sliced
- 1 teaspoon cinnamon
- 3 tablespoons sugar
- 1 cup sugar
- 3/4 cup melted margarine
- 1/2 cup chopped nuts
- 1 cup flour
- 1 egg, beaten
- salt

Grease a 9 inch pie pan with margarine. Fill pan 2/3 full of sliced apples. Combine cinnamon and 3 tablespoons of sugar. Sprinkle over apples. In a separate bowl mix 1 cup sugar, margarine, nuts, flour, egg and salt; spread over apples. Bake at 350 degrees for 65 minutes.

Serves 6-8

Vi Stolz

Buttermilk Pie

- 2 sticks margarine
- 3-3/4 cups sugar
- 1/2 cup flour
- 6 whole eggs
- 1 cup buttermilk
- 1 teaspoon salt
- 2 teaspoons vanilla
- 2 (9 inch) unbaked pie crusts

Melt margarine and combine with sugar and flour. Add eggs, buttermilk, salt and vanilla. Mix at slow speed. Divide mixture into two (9 inch) unbaked pie crusts. Bake at 350 degrees about 40 minutes.

Yields 2 pies

Clara Dawson

Cherry Pie

Crust:
2 cups flour
1/2 teaspoon salt
1/2 cup oil
1/4 cup milk

Pie Filling:
1 can Comstock Cherry Pie filling
1 cup sugar
1/2 cup flour
1/4 teaspoon almond extract
1/2 stick butter or margarine

Crust: Sift dry ingredients; add liquids and stir. Roll between wax paper, one half the dough at a time. Line pie pan with one crust. Filling: Combine first 4 ingredients in a bowl and pour into pie pan. Slice butter or margarine on top of filling. Arrange top crust on pie. Bake 450 degrees for 15 minutes; lower temperature to 350 degrees for approximately 20-30 minutes.

Serves 8

Dixie Talley

Randy Blackwell's Key Lime Pie

1-1/2 cups graham cracker crumbs
1/4 cup (heaping) almonds, ground
1/2 cup butter, melted
5 egg yolks
1 (14 ounce) can sweetened condensed milk
8-12 tablespoons key lime juice (Nellie & Joe's Key Lime Juice works well)
1 teaspoon vanilla
3 tablespoons powdered sugar
1/2 cup whipping cream
4 ounces Neufchatel, softened

Mix graham cracker crumbs and almonds with butter. Press into a buttered 10 inch pie plate. Bake 10 minutes at 325 degrees, until golden. Cool. Increase oven temperature to 350 degrees. Put the egg yolks in a large bowl and gently beat them with a whisk, just breaking them and mixing them well. Slowly stir in the sweetened condensed milk. Mixing well, stir in the key lime juice. The filling should be tart — taste and add more juice, if desired. Pour filling into pie plate. Bake for 12-15 minutes, until set. Remove and cool to room temperature. In a small mixing bowl, beat vanilla, sugar and cream until very soft peaks form. Add the Neufchatel and beat until of spreading consistency. Spread on pie and chill. Note: This can also be made in a 9x9 inch square pan.

Shirin Shiekh Blackwell

Edna's Kahlua Pie

Coconut Crust:
1-1/3 cups coconut
2 tablespoons melted butter

Filling:
1 (8 ounce) Hershey almond bar
2 or 3 tablespoons Kahlua
12 ounces Cool Whip

Press coconut and melted butter into a 9 inch pie plate. Brown at 300 degrees about 15 minutes. Melt Hershey bar. Combine melted chocolate with Kahlua and Cool Whip. Spoon filling into crust. Freeze. Store leftovers in freezer.

Serves 6-8

Linda Young

Meringue Crust Lemon Pie

Crust:
4 egg whites, reserve yolks
1/4 teaspoon cream of tartar
1/4 cup sugar

Beat egg whites until stiff and slowly add cream of tartar and sugar. Spread in pie plate and push up sides. Bake 1 hour at 275 degrees. Cool before filling.

Filling:
4 egg yolks
1/2 cup sugar
3 tablespoons lemon juice
1 tablespoon lemon rind
1/8 teaspoon salt
1 cup whipped cream

Mix first 5 ingredients and cook until thick, stirring frequently. Cool. Fold filling into one cup whipped cream. Spread filling into crust and chill. This pie can be frozen. It is rich but absolutely scrumptious, perfect for special company!

Serves 6-8

Susan Scott

Sour Cream Lemon Pie

1 cup sugar
3-1/2 tablespoons cornstarch
1 tablespoon grated lemon rind
1/2 cup fresh lemon juice
3 egg yolks, slightly beaten
1 cup milk
1/4 cup butter
1 cup cultured sour cream
1 (9 inch) baked pie shell
1 cup heavy whipping cream, whipped
lemon twists for garnish

Combine sugar, cornstarch, lemon rind, juice, egg yolks and milk in heavy saucepan. Cook over medium heat until thick. Stir in butter, and cool mixture to room temperature. Stir in sour cream and pour filling into pie shell. Cover with whipped cream and garnish with lemon twists. Store in refrigerator until ready to serve.

Lea Jones

Mississippi Mud Pie

2 cups sugar
2 sticks margarine, softened
3 eggs
1-1/4 cups all purpose flour
1/2 cup cocoa
dash of salt
1 teaspoon vanilla
1-1/2 cups pecans
3/4 bag miniature marshmallows
Icing

Cream sugar, margarine and eggs. Add the flour, cocoa, salt, vanilla and pecans and mix well. Bake in sheath pan at 350 degrees for 35 minutes. Place 3/4 bag of miniature marshmallows on top. Put back in oven to melt. Cool and top with icing.

Icing:

1 box powdered sugar
1/2 cup cocoa
1/2 stick margarine, softened
1/2 cup evaporated milk

Combine all ingredients until of spreading consistency.

Marie Brown

Mistake Pie
(For coconut lovers)

3 eggs, beaten
1-1/2 cups sugar
1/2 cup butter or margarine, melted
4 teaspoons lemon juice
1 teaspoon vanilla
2-1/2 cups flaked coconut
1 (9 inch) unbaked pie shell
whipped cream or Cool Whip
toasted coconut

Thoroughly combine eggs, sugar, butter, lemon juice and vanilla; stir in coconut. Pour filling into unbaked pie shell. Bake in moderate oven, 350 degrees, for 40 to 45 minutes, or until knife midway to center comes out clean. Cool before serving. If desired, garnish with whipped cream or dessert topping and toasted coconut.

Ruth Crowe

Peanut Butter Pie

2 (8 ounce) packages Philadelphia cream cheese
1 (1 pound) box powdered sugar

Cream the above and add:

12 ounces crunchy peanut butter
2 large containers Cool Whip
2 large pie crusts (graham cracker crusts may be used)

Mix well, then put into pie crust. Set in refrigerator and cool for approximately six hours before serving. Makes 2 large pies.

Dorothy Teel

Debbie's Pecan Delight Pie

3 egg whites
1 cup sugar
1 teaspoon baking powder
22 Ritz crackers, crushed
1 cup pecans, chopped
1 teaspoon vanilla
Cool Whip or vanilla ice cream

Beat egg whites until stiff. Fold in sugar. Add crackers, pecans, and vanilla. Put in buttered (8 or 9 inch) pie plate. Bake 350 degrees about 30 minutes. Test with toothpick. Serve with Cool Whip or vanilla ice cream.

Serves 6-8

Diana Horowitz

Perry's Caramel Pecan Pie

1 ready made pie crust
1 egg white
3 egg yolks
3/4 cup light brown sugar
3/4 cup white sugar
1-1/4 cups pecans
pinch of salt
3 tablespoons melted butter
1 tablespoon flour
1 small can evaporated milk

After piercing crust with fork in several places, coat crust with the egg white; place crust in oven and bake for 3 to 4 minutes to seal the crust. Mix remaining ingredients together, pour into crust and bake, covered, at 350 degrees for approximately 1 hour or until knife comes out relatively clean.

Serves 8

J. F. DeCell

Rum Pie

6 egg yolks
7/8 cup sugar
1 package Knox gelatin
1/2 cup cold water
1/2 cup white rum
1-1/2 pints whipping cream, whipped (or large carton whipped topping)
2 graham cracker crusts
semi-sweet chocolate, shaved
toasted almonds

Beat egg yolks until light, gradually adding sugar. Set aside. In saucepan soak gelatin in cold water. Place over low heat and stir until gelatin dissolves. Pour over egg mixture, beating constantly. Add 1/2 cup rum, or more if desired. Cool. Fold in beaten whipped cream. Refrigerate until set. Mound into 2 graham cracker crusts and top each with shaven chocolate and almonds. Refrigerate before serving.

Yields 2 pies

Pat Gruenert

Strawberry Pie

1 (3 ounce) package strawberry jello
1-1/2 cups sugar
1-1/2 cups water
1/4 cup cornstarch
1 pie shell, baked
1 quart fresh strawberries

Boil jello, sugar, water and cornstarch in saucepan until mixture is clear. Cool. Place strawberries in baked pie shell and pour jello mixture over them. Refrigerate.

Lou Bruno

Almond Fruit Tart with Raspberry Sauce

3-1/2 ounces (7/8 cup) whole blanched almonds
1/2 cup sugar
2 eggs
7 tablespoons butter, cut in chunks
1/8 teaspoon salt
1/3 cup seedless raspberry preserves
2-3 cups fresh fruit of your choice, i.e. peaches, mangoes, grapes, pears or strawberries
1/3 cup apricot jam
3 tablespoons lemon juice

Place almonds in a food processor and blend until minced. Add sugar and eggs and process for 1 minute. Add butter and salt and process 1 minute longer. Spread batter in a 9 inch round cake pan lined with parchment paper or in a tart pan that has removable sides. Bake for 20-25 minutes at 350 degrees until quite brown. Cool on wire rack; unmold onto a platter. Spread raspberry preserves on tart and distribute fruit in a decorative way on top of this. Melt apricot jam mixed with lemon juice and drizzle over the fruit. Refrigerate.

Selma Leff

Good and Easy Fruit Cobbler

1 stick butter or margarine
1 cup flour
1 cup sugar
2 teaspoons baking powder
2/3 cup milk
3 cups fruit

Melt butter or margarine in baking dish in oven while preheating to 350 degrees. Mix together flour, sugar, baking powder and milk. Pour this mixture into baking dish with melted margarine. Add fruit, spreading evenly over other mixture. Bake at 350 degrees 1 hour. Frozen or canned fruit will usually have plenty of juice. If fresh fruit is used, add 1/2 cup milk.

Ruth Tynes

Apple Strudel

10-12 Granny Smith apples, peeled and grated
1 cup sugar, more if you like it sweeter
1 teaspoon cinnamon
1/2 cup nuts, chopped
1/2 cup golden raisins
1 (1 pound) package Phyllo dough, thawed according to package directions
1/2 pound butter or margarine, melted
1 cup cracker crumbs, bread crumbs or matzo meal
powdered sugar

In large bowl, mix together apples, sugar, cinnamon, nuts and raisins. Set aside. Remove Phyllo dough from package and unfold onto clean towel. Keep dough covered with a slightly damp cloth, to prevent drying out. Place one sheet of phyllo on work area, brush with some melted butter and sprinkle with some crumbs. Repeat 2 times. Place 1/5 of the apple mixture in a line 1 inch from the longer edge of dough. Roll up, jelly roll fashion, folding ends in to seal. Place on a buttered cookie sheet lengthwise. Make 4 more rolls. Score top of rolls diagonally 1-1/2 inches apart, for snack sizes, or score 4 inches apart for dessert sizes. Bake at 350-375 degrees until top is light golden brown. Loosen rolls carefully with spatula. Let cool. Sprinkle with powdered sugar and serve.

Rosine Chappell

Hill Country Peach Cobbler

3/4 cup flour
less than 1/8 teaspoon salt
2 teaspoons baking powder
1-3/4 cups sugar
3/4 cup milk
1/2 cup butter
3 cups fresh peaches, sliced

Mix flour, salt, baking powder and 1-1/2 cups sugar together. Slowly stir in milk. In 350 degree oven melt butter in 8x8x2 pan (a larger pan makes a thinner crust). Remove from oven. Pour batter over butter. Do not stir. Lay peaches over batter. Sprinkle with remaining 1/4 cup sugar. Bake 1 hour at 350 degrees.

Serves 6

Clara Dawson

Peach Cobbler

3 tablespoons Bisquick mix
2 tablespoons water (at least)
1/4 cup diced peaches
1 teaspoon margarine (divided)
1-1/2 teaspoons brown sugar substitute
1/4 teaspoon sugar
cinnamon to taste

Mix Bisquick and water. Put 1/2 dough in small pan, sprayed with Pam. Mix fruit with 1/2 teaspoon margarine, sugar and cinnamon. Spread on dough. Place remaining dough on top. Dot with 1/2 teaspoon margarine. Sprinkle with sugar and cinnamon. Bake 400 degrees for 10-15 minutes or until brown.

Serves 1

Leslie Hungerford

Quick Cobbler

1 large can peach halves
1 teaspoon cinnamon
1/2 stick margarine or butter
2 tablespoons sugar
1 can prepared biscuits

Place peach halves in shallow baking dish hollow side up. Sprinkle sugar and cinnamon over peaches and dot with margarine. Top with biscuits and bake in 375 degree oven until biscuits are brown. Serve warm. Also good with ice cream, if you do not mind more calories.

Serves 8

Beth Evers

Fruit Pizza

1 roll sugar cookie dough
1 (8 ounce) carton Cool Whip
1 (8 ounce) cream cheese, softened
chopped nuts
coconut, if desired
pineapple, strawberries, bananas, kiwi, or any other fruit, cut up

Slice cookie dough in 1/4 inch slices and place on jelly roll pan. Mix Cool Whip and cream cheese together. Bake cookies according to package directions. Let cool. Spread Cool Whip mixture on cookies. Add fruit and nuts. Refrigerate overnight.

Betty Tonnessen

Charlotte Rouge

2 envelopes Knox gelatin
1/2 pint hot water
1 quart whipping cream
1 cup granulated sugar
1 teaspoon vanilla
ladyfingers

Dissolve gelatin in half pint of hot water. Let cool and add whipped cream slowly. Add sugar and vanilla. Line a pan with lady fingers and pour mixture over ladyfingers. Set in refrigerator, covered, until firm. Can be made the night before.

Serves 12

Louise Breedlove

Angel Custard

3/4 cup lemon juice
1-1/2 teaspoons grated lemon rind
6 eggs, separated
3/4 cup sugar
1 tablespoon unflavored gelatin
1/4 cup water
3/4 cup sugar
1/2 Angel food cake, torn into chunks

Cook juice, rind, egg yolks and sugar in double boiler over hot, not boiling, water, stirring constantly until mixture coats spoon. Remove from heat. Dissolve gelatin in water. Add to egg yolk mixture. Cool until thickened. Beat egg whites, adding 3/4 cup sugar. Add to cooled custard. Toss with angel food cake chunks. Mold and chill.

Serves 8-10

Peggy Walker

Danish Carmelized Custard

3 eggs
1/4 cup sugar
1/8 teaspoon salt
2 cups milk
1/2 teaspoon vanilla or 1 teaspoon rum
1/2 cup brown sugar

Preheat oven to 325 degrees. Beat eggs until light. Add 1/4 cup sugar, 1/8 teaspoon salt. Scald and pour in slowly 2 cups of milk to the eggs and sugar. Add 1 teaspoon vanilla or 1 teaspoon rum. Beat until blended. Put 1/2 cup brown sugar on bottom of custard cups or baking dish. Place in bottom of pan with hot water. Bake about 50 minutes at 325 degrees until knife is inserted and the custard sticks a little.

Serves 4

George Lloyd

Lemon Sponge Custard

3/4 cup sugar
1-1/2 tablespoons butter, softened
2 teaspoons grated lemon peel
3 eggs, separated
3 tablespoons flour
1/4 cup lemon juice
1 cup milk
1/8 teaspoon salt

Cream sugar, butter and lemon peel. Add egg yolks. Stir in flour alternately with lemon juice and milk. Beat egg whites until stiff, adding salt. Fold into yolk mixture. Place in greased custard cups or 7 inch oven-proof dish. Set in a pan of water and bake 30 minutes at 325 degrees. Serve hot or ice cold — a delicious, light dessert.

Serves 6

Jeanne Dean

Creme Caramele (Flan)

1-1/2 cups sugar
2 tablespoons water
2 tablespoons lemon juice
1 can Eagle Brand condensed milk
3-1/2 cups milk
1/2 cup sugar
8 eggs, well beaten
1 teaspoon vanilla

Combine 1-1/2 cups sugar, water and lemon juice in saucepan and stir until blended and light brown in color. Pour into 1-1/2 quart bundt pan or 10 individual pyrex cups. To make custard combine rest of ingredients and pour over caramel. Place bundt pan or pyrex cups into pan with 1 inch water and bake in preheated 375 degree oven for 50-55 minutes or until knife inserted in center comes out clean. Cool, then refrigerate until ready to serve. Remove from mold onto serving plate.

Mary Bellos

Four Layer Dessert

Layer 1:
1 cup flour
1 stick margarine, softened
1/2 cup ground nuts

Mix and press into a 9x13 inch pan. Bake 15 minutes at 275 degrees. Cool.

Layer 2:
1 small container Cool Whip
1 (8 ounce) package cream cheese, softened
1 cup powdered sugar

Whip together and spread over first layer.

Layer 3:
2 packages any flavor instant pudding

Mix both packages of pudding with 3 cups of milk and pour over second layer.

Layer 4:
Cool Whip

Spread over third layer and refrigerate or can be frozen.

Lynn Miller

Miertschin's
Favorite Cream Cheese Flan

1/2 cup (heaping) sugar
1-2/3 cups sweetened condensed milk
1 cup milk
3 eggs
3 egg yolks
1 teaspoon vanilla
1 cup slivered almonds
6 ounces cream cheese, cubed and softened

Place the sugar in a 9-inch round cake pan and put over a medium heat. Using oven mitts, caramelize the sugar by shaking the pan occasionally until the sugar is melted and has turned a light golden brown. Allow to cool, the mixture may crack slightly. Place the remaining ingredients in a blender and blend on high for 20 seconds. Pour this mixture over the caramelized sugar. Cover the pan with aluminum foil and place in a larger, shallow pan containing about 1 inch of hot water. Bake at 350 degrees for 55 minutes or until a knife inserted near the center comes out clean. Remove the pan from water and uncover; let it cool on a wire rack at least 30 minutes. Loosen the edges with a spatula. Place a serving plate (with a rim) upside down on top of the cake pan and quickly invert the flan onto it. Note: If you desire more of a Cheesecake-like texture, decrease the sweetened condensed milk amount to 1 (14 ounce) can AND increase the cream cheese to 1 (8 ounce) package.

Serves 6-8

Shirin Shiekh Blackwell

Lemon Lush

1 stick butter, softened
1 cup flour
1/2 cup chopped pecans
1 (8 ounce) cream cheese
1 cup powdered sugar
1 cup Cool Whip
2 small lemon instant pudding mixes
3 cups cold milk
Cool Whip

Mix first 3 ingredients and spread in a 13x9x2 inch pan. Bake for 15 minutes at 350 degrees. Cool. Mix next 3 ingredients and spread over cooled crust. Whip together lemon instant pudding and milk and spread over cream cheese mixture. Top with Cool Whip.

Linda Blankenship

To reduce cholesterol and fat, substitute angel food cake for pound cake and low fat yogurt for ice cream.

Mary Jane Blackwell's Ice Cream Dessert

- 1 pound bag of Oreo cookies, crushed
- 1/2 cup margarine, melted
- 2 cups powdered sugar
- 1 large can evaporated milk
- 2/3 cup chocolate chips
- 1/2 cup margarine
- 1 teaspoon vanilla
- 1/2 gallon vanilla ice cream, slightly softened
- 1-1/2 cups Spanish Peanuts

Mix cookie crumbs with margarine. Press into a 9x13 inch and an 8x8 inch pan. Refrigerate for 1 hour. Combine the sugar, milk, chocolate chips and margarine in a saucepan and blend over a medium heat. Bring to a boil and boil for 8 minutes — stirring constantly. Remove from heat and stir in vanilla. Set aside to cool. Spoon the ice cream over the refrigerated cookie crumb crusts. Spread evenly. Sprinkle the peanuts over the ice cream layers. Pour the cooled chocolate mixture over the peanuts. Freeze. Serve frozen.

Shirin Shiekh Blackwell

Chocolate Mousse

- 8 ounces semi-sweet chocolate
- 1 tablespoon instant coffee dissolved in 1/4 cup hot water (can substitute Kahlua, Amaretto, etc. for water)
- 1/2 pint whipping cream
- 8 eggs, separated
- 1/8 teaspoon salt
- 2/3 cup sugar (scant)
- 1 teaspoon vanilla

Melt chocolate in double boiler (or microwave oven); add coffee mixture and stir until smooth. Cool. Whip cream and refrigerate until needed. Beat egg whites stiff; add salt and refrigerate until needed. Beat egg yolks until thick; gradually add sugar while beating slowly. Add COOLED chocolate mixture gradually into egg yolks; add vanilla. With a slotted spoon, fold 1/4 of egg whites into chocolate and blend; fold in rest of egg whites until blended. Fold whipped cream into mixture until smooth. Refrigerate in a crystal bowl. If desired, decorate with extra whipped cream and/or shaved chocolate. Can be prepared one day before serving; however, decorate same day. Two important points for success with this mouth watering temptation: Chocolate mixture must be cool and the mixture must not be over blended.

Serves 10

Lila Poland

Microwave Cherry Squares

14 graham cracker squares
1 (20 ounce) can cherry pie filling
1/4 cup nuts
1/4 cup brown sugar
1/4 teaspoon cinnamon
1/4 cup butter or margarine

Arrange 8 graham crackers in single layer over bottom of 12x8 inch dish. Spread pie filling evenly over crackers. Sprinkle nuts over filling. Crush remaining crackers until fine, then add brown sugar and cinnamon. Melt butter 1 minute on high. Mix with crumbs. Sprinkle crumb mixture evenly over pie filling. Cook on high 3 to 4 minutes. Rotate dish 1/2 turn. Cook 3 to 4 minutes longer. Cool 5 minutes before serving.

Honey Epstein

Lemon Chiffon Mousse

1 large package ladyfingers, split
2 envelopes unflavored gelatin
1 cup granulated sugar
1 teaspoon salt
8 eggs, separated
2/3 cup lemon juice
1-1/2 cups water
2 teaspoons grated lemon peel
1 cup sugar
1 cup whipping cream, whipped

Line 10 inch spring form pan (bottom and sides) with ladyfingers. Set aside. In saucepan combine gelatin, one cup sugar and salt. Beat together egg yolks, lemon juice, water and stir into gelatin mixture. Cool and stir over medium heat just until mixture comes to a boil and gelatin is dissolved. Remove from heat and stir in lemon peel. Chill mixture, stirring occasionally until mixture is partially set. Beat egg whites until soft peaks form. Gradually add 1 cup sugar, beating until stiff peaks form. Fold whites into gelatin mixture; fold in all but 1/2 cup of whipped cream. Pour mixture into springform pan. Decorate top with remaining whipped cream. Place in refrigerator until ready to serve. Unmold on plate before serving. Serves 16 to 20 people. Enjoy!

Selma Leff

Very Easy Chocolate Mousse

12 ounces chocolate chips
3/4 cup boiling water
8 eggs, separated
1 tablespoon almond extract
1 tablespoon Cointreau

In a blender, blend chocolate, water, egg yolks, almond extract and Cointreau. Pour mixture into large bowl and fold in 8 egg whites stiffly beaten. Pour into serving compote; refrigerate until ready to serve.

Mary Bellos

Diabetic Chocolate Mousse

1 envelope D-Zerta whipped topping mix
1 (6-1/2 ounce) package chocolate sugarfree Jello instant pudding
2-1/3 cups cold milk (low fat, 2% or skim)
1 tablespoon almond extract or Amaretto Liqueur, optional

Mix whipped topping per box directions and place in refrigerator while making chocolate pudding. Mix chocolate pudding per box directions except use 2-1/3 cups milk to make it thicker than normal recipe. Add optional Almond extract or Amaretto with milk when mixing. When chocolate pudding is mixed, but not firmly set, gently fold in topping mixture and serve or store covered in refrigerator. This travels well in an ice chest for picnics.

Serves 8

Tom Sellers

World's Easiest Chocolate Mousse

6-7 ounces semi-sweet chocolate bits
2 large eggs
3 tablespoons strong coffee
2 tablespoons Myers dark rum
3/4 cup scalded milk
whipped cream, optional
chocolate shavings, optional

Combine chocolate bits, eggs, coffee and rum in blender. Add the scalded milk and blend at high speed until thoroughly mixed. Pour into serving dishes (glasses or dessert ramekins) and chill in refrigerator for about eight hours. If desired, garnish with whipped cream and chocolate shavings.

Serves 4-6

George Rimmey

Pot de Creme

3/4 cups milk
1 small package chocolate chips
1/8 teaspoon salt
1 teaspoon sugar
1 egg
whipping cream

Scald milk, add chocolate chips and let sit one minute. Put in blender and add next 3 ingredients, blend one minute. Pour in Pot de Creme cups or demitasse cups. Top with whipping cream.

Yields 6 small servings

Page Lawson

Bread Pudding

2 slightly beaten eggs
2-1/4 cups milk
1 teaspoon vanilla
1/2 teaspoon ground cinnamon
1/4 teaspoon salt
2 cups (1 inch) day-old bread cubes
1/2 cup brown sugar
1/2 cup raisins

Preheat oven to 350 degrees. Combine eggs, milk, vanilla, cinnamon, and salt; stir in bread cubes. Stir in brown sugar and raisins. Pour mixture into 8x1-3/4 inch round ovenware cake dish. Place pan in larger shallow pan on oven rack; pour hot water into larger pan 1 inch deep. Bake at 350 degrees about 45 minutes or until knife inserted halfway between center and edge comes out clean.

Serves 6

Elva Lopez

Fantastic Fudge Pudding

4 cups sugar
1 cup all purpose flour
1 cup cocoa
8 large eggs
2 cups butter, melted
4 teaspoons vanilla
2 cups chopped pecans

Sift together sugar, flour and cocoa. Beat eggs in large mixing bowl. Add dry ingredients, butter and vanilla. Mix well. Stir in pecans and pour batter into 3 quart Pyrex dish. Place in a larger pan, such as a roasting pan, filled with 1 inch of water and bake at 300 degrees (preheated) on oven shelf at lowest level for 1 hour and 20 minutes. DO NOT OVERBAKE. Remove dish from water and cool completely on wire rack. Top becomes crusty as pudding cools. For a delicious, even richer treat, top with coffee ice cream.

Serves 16

Sally Root

Ricotta Pudding

1 (2 pound) container ricotta cheese
1 cup super fine sugar
1/4 cup Tia Maria
1/2 cup raisins

Combine ricotta cheese and sugar in bowl and mix well. Add Tia Maria and blend well. Fold in raisins. Divide into 6 dessert glasses or cups and refrigerate overnight.

Serves 6

Diana Horowitz

Noodle Pudding

1 package farmers cheese or ricotta cheese
4 ounces Philadelphia cream cheese
1 cup sour cream
1 stick margarine
1 teaspoon vanilla
1 teaspoon salt
6 eggs
1 cup sugar
2 cups milk
1 cup raisins
1 (8 ounce) package fine noodles
graham cracker crumbs
1 teaspoon cinnamon
2 tablespoons sugar

Combine and mix first 6 ingredients. Beat eggs with one cup sugar. Add 2 cups milk and 1 cup raisins. Add noodles. Combine and pour in a casserole. Sprinkle top with graham cracker crumbs. Mix cinnamon and sugar together and sprinkle on top of casserole. Bake 1 hour in 350 degree oven.

Serves 14

Butsey Weinstein

Quick Fudge Sundaes

1 (6 ounce) package (1 cup) semisweet chocolate pieces
1 (6 ounce) can evaporated milk
1/2 (1 pint) jar marshmallow cream
vanilla ice cream

Mix chocolate and milk in saucepan. Heat slowly, stirring to blend. Beat in marshmallow creme till blended. Serve warm or cool over ice cream. Makes 2 cups.

Elva Lopez

Lemon Souffle

1 cup sugar
2 tablespoons butter, softened
1/3 cup flour
2 eggs, separated
1 cup milk
juice and grated rind of 1 lemon
1/8 teaspoon salt

Cream sugar and butter. Cut flour into creamed mixture with a fork. Beat egg yolks; add milk to yolks and then combine with flour mixture. Add lemon juice, rind and salt. Beat egg whites until stiff and add to mixture. Pour into baking dish; set in a pan of cold water and bake, uncovered, for 1 hour at 300 degrees.

Helen Harbeson

Spiced Pears in Port Wine

4 ripe pears
1 cup red port wine
2 cups water
1/2 cup sugar
2 cinnamon sticks
1 teaspoon ground cinnamon
6-8 whole cloves
1/2 teaspoon ground cloves

Peel, half and core pears. Combine port wine, water, sugar and spices in saucepan and bring to a boil. Reduce heat, add pear halves, cover and simmer 30 minutes. Place 2 pear halves and liquid in each serving dish. Serve hot.

Serves 4

DeDe Munn

Strawberry Jello with Pretzel Crust

3 tablespoons sugar
1-1/2 sticks margarine
1-1/2 cups crushed pretzels (fine)
1 cup sugar
8 ounces cream cheese, softened
8 ounces Cool Whip
16 ounces strawberry jello (large)
2 cups boiling water
2 (10 ounce) packages frozen strawberries, thawed and undrained

Cream together sugar and margarine. Add pretzels. Mix well and press into 9x13 pan. Bake 10 minutes at 350 degrees. Cool completely. Mix sugar and cream cheese. Add Cool Whip and blend until smooth. Spread over crust. Refrigerate. In separate bowl dissolve jello in boiling water. Stir in strawberries and chill until partially congealed. Spread over refrigerated cream cheese layer. Chill until firm.

Eleanore Donnenworth

Strawberry Surprise

6 cups fresh strawberries
1-3/4 cups powdered sugar
juice of 3 oranges
juice of 3 lemons
1/2 cup Grand Marnier

Wash and hull the strawberries. Cut strawberries in half and place in large bowl. Add the powdered sugar and mix together. Squeeze the oranges and lemons; then add the juices to the strawberry mixture. Place this mixture in the blender and blend until smooth. Add the Grand Marnier and pour into large flat container or two freezer trays. Cover and freeze until partially set. Remove from freezer and place into a large bowl. Beat with electric mixer until mushy. Return to container or trays and freeze until firm. Mixture should be covered in freezer.

Serves 6

George Rimmey

Frozen Smores

- 1 package sugar free instant pudding, chocolate or banana
- 1-1/2 cups skim milk
- 1/2 cup peanut butter
- 64 squares graham crackers
- 8 ounces light whipped topping

Combine pudding, milk and peanut butter. Beat well. On 2-inch square of graham cracker, spread 1 tablespoon pudding mixture, 1 tablespoon whipped topping and top with another square of graham cracker. Repeat until all crackers are used. Wrap in plastic wrap and freeze.

Serves 32

Betty Griffith

Cheese Cake I

- 1 cup hot water
- 1 package lemon jello
- 30 graham crackers, crushed
- 1 tablespoon powdered sugar
- 1/2 pound melted butter
- 2 (8 ounce) packages cream cheese, softened
- 1/2 cup sugar
- 2 teaspoons vanilla
- 1 cup evaporated milk

Dissolve jello in hot water. Refrigerate until thickened. Mix together 1/2 of the graham crackers, the powdered sugar and the butter. Press into 8x12 pan and chill. Cream together cream cheese, sugar and vanilla. Whip cold evaporated milk. Combine cream cheese mixture, jello, evaporated milk and whip until thick. Pour over graham cracker crust. Top with 1/2 of the reserved graham cracker crumbs. Refrigerate 24 hours.

Serves 12

Marie Sullivan

Cheese Cake II

Crust:
- 1-1/2 cups graham cracker crumbs
- 1/2 cup sugar
- 2 sticks margarine
- 1/4 cups chopped nuts (optional)

Filling:
- 1/2 cup sour cream
- 2 (8 ounce) packages cream cheese, softened
- 3 eggs
- 3/4 cup sugar
- 2 teaspoons vanilla

Topping:
- 1 cup sour cream
- 3 teaspoons sugar
- 1 teaspoon vanilla

Combine crust ingredients and pat onto sides and bottom of springform pan. Bake 5 minutes at 325 degrees. Combine filling ingredients and beat until smooth. Fill crust and bake 20 minutes at 325 degrees. Let cool 15 minutes. Combine 1 cup sour cream with 3 teaspoons sugar and 1 teaspoon vanilla and spread on cake. Put back in oven for 5 minutes. Cool, then refrigerate. Freezes well. If frozen, thaw in refrigerator before cutting.

Ruth Tanner

Chocolate Chip Cheesecake

- **2 cups finely crushed cream-filled chocolate sandwich cookies (about 24)**
- **1/4 cup butter, melted**
- **3 (8 ounce) packages cream cheese, softened**
- **1 (14 ounce) can Eagle Brand sweetened condensed milk**
- **3 eggs**
- **2 teaspoons vanilla**
- **1 cup mini chocolate chips, divided use**
- **1 teaspoon flour**

Preheat oven to 350 degrees. Combine cookie crumbs and butter and press firmly on bottom of 9 inch springform pan. In large bowl beat cheese until fluffy. Gradually beat in sweetened condensed milk until smooth. Beat in eggs and vanilla. Toss 1/2 cup chips with flour and stir into cheese mixture. Pour into prepared pan. Sprinkle remaining chips over top. Bake 55 minutes or until center is set. Cool; chill in refrigerator.

Serves 10 to 12

Mary Cypert

Chocolate Chip Cookie Cheese Cake

- **2 rolls chocolate chip cookies**
- **1-1/2 cups sugar**
- **2 (8 ounce) packages cream cheese**
- **3 eggs**
- **1 teaspoon vanilla**

Preheat oven to 350 degrees. Slice 1 roll of cookies and line 9x13 inch pan. Bake 5 minutes. Cream the sugar and cream cheese. Add eggs and vanilla. Pour over cookie layer. Slice second roll of cookies and place over the top of the cream cheese mixture. Bake 30-40 minutes. Cool before slicing.

Michael Kunc

Janis' Italian Cheese Cake

- **1 pound ricotta cheese, room temperature**
- **1 pound cream cheese, room temperature**
- **4 eggs, well beaten, room temperature**
- **1-1/2 cups sugar**
- **1 stick butter, melted**
- **1 pint sour cream**
- **3 tablespoons cornstarch**
- **3 tablespoons flour**
- **2 teaspoons vanilla**
- **2 teaspoons fresh lemon juice**

Combine all ingredients in large mixing bowl and beat very well, the longer the better, but at least 10 to 15 minutes. Pour batter into greased 10 inch springform pan. Bake in preheated 325 degree oven for 1 hour and 15 minutes. Shut off oven and leave cake in oven for 1 hour. Cool and refrigerate.

Estelle Kastleman

Praline Cheesecake

Crust:
- **1 cup graham cracker crumbs**
- **3 tablespoons sugar**
- **3 tablespoons margarine, melted**

Cheesecake:
- **3 (8 ounce) packages Philadelphia cream cheese, softened**
- **1-1/4 cups dark brown sugar, packed**
- **2 tablespoons flour**
- **3 eggs**
- **1-1/2 teaspoons vanilla**
- **1/2 cup finely chopped pecans**

Heat oven to 350 degrees. Combine crumbs, sugar, and margarine; press into bottom of 9 inch springform pan. Bake 10 minutes and remove. Increase oven temperature to 450 degrees. Combine softened cream cheese, brown sugar and flour; mix at medium speed of mixer until well blended. Add eggs one at a time, mixing well after each addition. Blend in vanilla, stir in nuts. Pour mixture over crust. Bake at 450 degrees for 10 minutes. Reduce oven to 250 degrees; continue baking 30 minutes. Loosen cake from outer rim of pan with knife, cool before removing rim of pan. Chill. Brush with maple syrup and garnish with pecans halves, if desired.

Serves 12

Carolyn Hamrick

Brownie Alaska

- **1 stick margarine**
- **2 squares unsweetened chocolate**
- **1 cup sugar**
- **6 egg yolks, beaten, reserve egg whites for meringue**
- **2 tablespoons milk**
- **1/2 cup flour**
- **1/2 teaspoon baking powder**
- **1/2 cup chopped nuts**
- **1 teaspoon vanilla**
- **vanilla or butter pecan ice cream**

Melt chocolate and margarine. Blend in sugar. Add egg yolks and milk, mixing well. Stir in rest of ingredients. Spread in buttered 9x13 inch pan. Bake at 350 degrees for 20-25 minutes. Cool. Cut into 12 squares. Place on cookie sheet. Top with a mound of ice cream. Freeze approximately 2 hours. Top with meringue.

Meringue:
- **6 egg whites**
- **1/2 teaspoon cream of tartar**
- **1/8 teaspoon salt**
- **3/4 cup sugar**

Beat egg whites with cream of tartar and salt until peaks form. Gradually add sugar and beat until stiff. Cover ice cream on brownie with meringue. Return to freezer. Will keep 2-3 days. At serving time preheat oven to 450 degrees. Bake until browned, about 3 minutes.

Serves 12

Betty Tonnessen

The Brownies

- 1/2 pound sweet butter (can substitute margarine, but it won't be as good!)
- 4 ounces unsweetened baking chocolate
- 2 cups sugar (or 1-3/4)
- 1 cup all purpose flour
- 1 teaspoon baking powder
- 1 teaspoon cinnamon
- 4 eggs
- 2 teaspoons vanilla
- 3/4 cup pecans, chopped

Melt butter, chocolate, and sugar slowly stirring in double boiler (or microwave oven). Cool. Sift flour; add baking powder and cinnamon. Beat eggs, add slowly to flour mixture. Add 1/2 chocolate mixture and beat 1 minute after blended; then add rest of mixture and beat 2 minutes. Do not overbeat. Add vanilla and nuts. Bake for 18 to 20 minutes. Test with toothpick; batter should cling and be moist. Cut immediately into squares with knife dipped in warm water. Do not remove from pan until cool. Delish!! Can be frozen.

Serves 10 or more

Lila Poland

Butterscotch Brownies

- 1 stick margarine
- 2 cups brown sugar
- 2 eggs, beaten
- 2 teaspoons vanilla
- 1-1/2 cups flour
- 2 teaspoons baking powder
- 1/2 teaspoon salt
- 1 cup walnuts, broken
- powdered sugar

Melt margarine in a 2 quart saucepan. Stir in brown sugar until dissolved. Cool slightly and blend in eggs and vanilla. Sift, then measure flour on wax paper and resift with baking soda and salt. Stir these ingredients into saucepan and add walnuts. Spread into a 13x9x2 inch pan and bake at 350 degrees for 30 minutes. Cool and cut into bars. Sprinkle with powdered sugar if desired.

Leah Whitty

Better Than Sex Cake

- 1 package Duncan Hines golden butter cake mix
- 4 eggs
- 1/2 cup Crisco oil
- 8 ounces sour cream
- 1/4 cup water
- 1 box instant vanilla pudding mix
- 1 square semi-sweet grated chocolate
- 6 ounces chocolate chips
- 1/2 cup chopped nuts

Combine first 6 ingredients and beat well. Add the remaining ingredients. Pour into greased and floured tube pan. Bake 350 degrees about one hour. The chocolate chips rise to the top while baking and make icing.

Clara Dawson

Black Bottom Cupcakes

1-1/2 cups flour
1-1/3 cups sugar
1/4 cup cocoa
1 teaspoon baking soda
1/2 teaspoon salt
1 cup water
5 tablespoons oil
1 tablespoon vinegar
1 teaspoon vanilla
1 (8 ounce) package cream cheese, softened
1 egg
6 ounces chocolate chips

Preheat oven to 350 degrees. Grease muffin tins. Mix flour, 1 cup sugar, cocoa, baking soda, and salt in bowl. Make a well in center of mixture. Blend water, oil, vinegar, and vanilla. Pour into well. Gradually incorporate flour mixture into liquid, whisking until smooth. Set aside. Beat together cream cheese, remaining 1/3 cup sugar, and egg. Stir in chocolate chips. Fill muffin tins 1/2 full with batter. Drop 1 teaspoon of cream cheese mixture on top of each cupcake. Bake about 25 minutes or until done. Cool for 10 minutes and remove from tins.

Serves 20 medium cupcakes

Blanche Polunsky

Blueberry Ice Box Cake

1-1/2 cups graham cracker crumbs
1/2 cup powdered sugar
1/2 cup melted butter
2 eggs, well beaten
1 cup sugar
1 8 ounce package cream cheese, softened
1 can Comstock Blueberry Pie Mix
1/2 teaspoon lemon juice
whipped cream

Mix graham cracker crumbs, powdered sugar and melted butter. Pat into 9x13 inch pan. Beat together eggs, sugar and cream cheese. Pour over crumb mixture. Mix together 1 can Comstock Blueberry Pie Mix and lemon juice. Pour this over the cream mixture. Refrigerate for 8 hours. Serve with whipped cream topping. Can be frozen.

June Johnson

Chocolate stains may be removed with a paste of borax and water.

Brownie Trifle Turtle Cake

1 (14 ounce) package Kraft caramels
1/2 cup evaporated milk (can use skim)
1 package German chocolate cake mix, pudding type (can use devil's food or fudge)
1-1/3 cups water
3/4 cup butter, softened
3 eggs
1 cup pecan pieces
1 cup semi-sweet chocolate chips

Put caramels in top of double boiler with milk, and melt together. Set aside. In large mixer bowl combine cake mix, water, butter and eggs. Mix at low speed 1 minute. Beat at medium speed 2 minutes. Pour 1/2 batter into greased 13x9 inch dish and bake for 12 minutes at 350 degrees. Pour caramel mixture over batter, not too close to edges. Sprinkle with nuts and chips. Then pour remaining batter over. Bake 20-25 minutes. Cool. Cut into squares.

Sr. Alice Potts

Cherry Torte

1/2 cup butter or margarine, room temperature
1 cup sifted flour
2 tablespoons sugar
1/2 cup sifted flour
1 teaspoon baking powder
1 cup sugar
2 eggs
1 (No. 2) can tart, pitted cherries, drained
1/2 cup coconut
whipped cream (optional)

Mix butter with 1 cup flour plus 2 tablespoons sugar. Press mixture in bottom of 10 inch pie pan or 8 inch square pan. Bake at 350 degrees for 10-15 minutes, until light brown. Sift 1/2 cup flour, baking powder and 1 cup sugar together. Beat eggs, add dry ingredients and blend. Stir in cherries and coconut. Pour over baked crust. Bake at 350 degrees for 45 minutes. Cool. Serve with whipped cream, if desired.

Eleanore Donnenwerth

Overweight is often just desserts!

Dee-Lish Dessert

1 cup flour
1 stick butter, melted
1-1/2 cups chopped pecans
1 (8 ounce) package cream cheese, softened
1 cup powdered sugar
1 (13-1/2 ounce) carton Cool Whip
1 small box Instant Vanilla Pudding
1 small box Instant Chocolate Pudding
2-1/2 cups milk
1 (13-1/2 ounce) carton Cool Whip
1 large Hershey bar

Combine flour, butter and pecans and press in 9x13 inch pan. Bake 20 minutes at 350 degrees. Cool completely. Blend in mixer cream cheese, powdered sugar and 1 carton of Cool Whip. Spread over cooled crust. In a large mixing bowl beat until thick vanilla pudding, chocolate pudding and milk. Pour over cream cheese layer and cover with other carton of Cool Whip. Grate a large Hershey bar over the top. Chill in refrigerator at least 2-3 hours before serving. Best to make a day ahead. Entire recipe may be frozen. You may also cut into individual servings, wrap separately and freeze.

Serves 12

Pam Bankerd

Chocolate Sheet Cake

Cake:
1 stick margarine
1 cup water
1/2 cup shortening
3 tablespoons cocoa
2 cups flour
2 cups sugar
1/2 teaspoon salt
2 eggs, beaten
1 teaspoon soda
1/2 cup buttermilk
1 teaspoon vanilla

In saucepan combine first 4 ingredients and bring to a boil and let cool for 20 minutes. Mix flour, sugar, and salt in large mixer bowl. Mix eggs, soda, buttermilk, and vanilla in another bowl. Pour cooled chocolate mixture over flour mixture, then mix in rest of the ingredients. Bake in 1 inch deep jelly roll pan for 20 minutes at 350 degrees. A 13x9x2 pan takes 30-45 minutes baking time. When cake has cooled 10 minutes spread with icing.

Icing:
1 stick margarine, softened
3 tablespoons cocoa
6 tablespoons sweet milk
1 teaspoon vanilla
1 (1 pound) box powdered sugar
1 cup chopped pecans (halves preferred)

With mixer and small mixing bowl, cream softened butter and add the rest of the ingredients. Spread onto cooled cake. Very rich!

Leah Whitty
Virginia Horton
Juanita Garison

(Big Mother's) Chocolate Cake

1 stick margarine
1/2 cup Crisco
1 cup water
4 tablespoons cocoa
2 cups sugar
2 cups flour
2 eggs, beaten
1/2 cup buttermilk
1 teaspoon soda
1 teaspoon vanilla

13x9x2 inch cake pan, greased and lightly floured. In a saucepan combine first 4 ingredients and bring to a boil. Remove from heat and add next 6 ingredients. Mix all thoroughly. Bake for 40 minutes at 325 degrees. Test with finger to see if cake pops up when pressed. Cool. Ice with the following:

Icing:

1 stick margarine
6 tablespoons buttermilk
4 tablespoons cocoa
1 box powdered sugar
1 cup chopped pecans
1 teaspoon vanilla

In a saucepan combine first 3 ingredients and bring to a boil. Then add the rest of the ingredients mixing well. Sprinkle extra pecans on top.

Cher Longoria

Chocolate Potato Cake

1 cup hot mashed potatoes (unseasoned)
1/2 cup shortening
2 cups sugar
2 cups sifted flour
2 teaspoons baking powder
1/2 teaspoon salt
1 teaspoon nutmeg
1 teaspoon cinnamon
4 eggs, separated
1/2 cup milk
2 squares unsweetened chocolate, melted
1 teaspoon vanilla
1 cup pecans, chopped

Beat potatoes with shortening. Add sugar and mix well. Sift together flour, baking powder, salt and spices. Mix egg yolks with milk. Add flour mixture and egg-milk mixture to shortening mixture. Add melted chocolate, vanilla and pecans. Beat egg whites until stiff and fold into batter. Pour batter into greased and floured large tube pan. Bake at 325 degrees for about an hour or until test toothpick comes out clean. Crack in top of cake is not unusual. Cool in pan for a few minutes, then turn out on rack to cool completely. No icing necessary. Cake freezes well.

Ruth Tanner

Chocolate Turtle Cake

- German chocolate cake mix
- 1 (14 ounce) bag caramels
- 1/2 cup evaporated milk
- 3/4 cup butter
- 2 cups nuts
- 1 cup semi-sweet chocolate chips

Preheat oven to 350 degrees. Prepare cake mix as directed on box. Pour half of the batter in a greased and floured 9x13 pan. Bake for 15 minutes. Melt caramels, evaporated milk, and butter in a saucepan. Sprinkle 1 cup nuts on cake. Sprinkle with chocolate chips. Pour caramel mixture on cake. Spoon remaining cake batter into pan and top with remaining nuts. Bake an additional 15-20 minutes.

Elaine Davenport

Reva's Chocolate Velvet Cake

- 1/2 cup butter or margarine, softened
- 1 cup sugar
- 1/2 teaspoon salt
- 1 teaspoon vanilla
- 1/3 cup cold water
- 1/2 cup cocoa
- 2-1/2 cups sifted cake flour
- 1 cup cold water
- 3 egg whites
- 3/4 cup sugar
- 1-1/2 teaspoon baking soda
- 1/3 cup cold water
- Icing (recipe follows)

Cream butter. Gradually add 1 cup sugar, creaming until light and fluffy. Add salt and vanilla. Combine the 1/3 cup cold water with the cocoa; stir until smooth and beat into creamed mixture. Add flour to creamed mixture alternately with 1 cup cold water, beating well after each addition. Beat egg whites until soft peaks form; gradually add 3/4 cup sugar. Beat until stiff peaks form. Fold meringue into batter. Combine soda and 1/3 cup cold water. Stir to dissolve soda and stir into batter, mixing thoroughly. Bake in 2 well greased and floured 9 inch pans at 350 degrees for 30 minutes. Cool completely. Ice with the following:

- 6 tablespoons butter or margarine, softened
- 2-2/3 cups sifted powdered sugar
- 1/2 to 3/4 cups cocoa
- 1/3 cup milk
- 1 teaspoon vanilla

Combine powdered sugar with cocoa and add to softened butter alternately with milk. Add vanilla. Beat until of spreading consistency. This is a delicious and moist cake!

Estelle Kastleman

Chop Suey Cake

2 cups flour
2 teaspoons baking soda
2 cups sugar
1 cup pecans, chopped
1 teaspoon salt
1 (20 ounce) can crushed pineapple
2 eggs

Mix all ingredients. Bake 350 degrees in 9x13 inch pan for 45 minutes. Test with toothpick until it comes out dry. Frost with the following:

Frosting:
1 (8 ounce) package cream cheese, softened
2 cups powdered sugar
2 teaspoons margarine, softened
1 teaspoon vanilla
coconut and/or chopped pecans on top

Combine all ingredients and spread over cake in pan while still warm. This cake freezes very well.

Susan Scott

Coconut Pound Cake

6 eggs, separated, at room temperature
1 cup shortening
1/2 cup margarine
3 cups sugar
1/2 teaspoon almond extract
1/2 teaspoon coconut extract
3 cups sifted cake flour
1 cup milk
2 cups grated fresh or canned coconut

Beat egg yolks, shortening and margarine in large mixing bowl until thoroughly mixed. Gradually add sugar. Beat until mixture is light and fluffy. Add almond and coconut extracts; beat well until thoroughly mixed. Slowly add flour alternately with milk, beginning and ending with flour. Stir in coconut; beat until thoroughly combined, scraping bowl often. Set aside batter. In separate bowl beat egg whites until stiff peaks form. Gently fold into batter. Place batter in greased, floured 10 inch tube pan and place in preheated 325 degree oven. Bake until cake tester inserted in center comes out clean, checking after 1-1/2 hours. Cool on wire rack before removing from pan. This cake freezes very well by wrapping in heavy duty foil.

Estelle Kastleman

Add a little fun to leftover chocolate frosting. Scoop it up with a melon baller and roll in crushed nuts, confectioners sugar or cocoa. Voila, chocolate fudge balls!

Cream Cheese Pound Cake

1 cup margarine, softened
1/2 cup butter (real), softened
1 8 ounce pkg. cream cheese, softened
3 cups sugar
1 teaspoon salt
1 tablespoon vanilla
1 teaspoon almond extract
8 eggs
3 cups flour

Combine margarine, butter, cream cheese and sugar. Beat well. Add salt, vanilla and almond extract. Add eggs one at a time and beat well after each. Add flour and mix well. Grease and flour pan. (This recipe makes dough for large pound cake tube pan.) Put in cold oven and turn temperature to 275 degrees. Bake for 1-1/2 hours or until done.

Serves 15

Melzeria Adams

"Dump Cake"

1 can chunk pineapple, drained
1 large can prepared pie filling, any flavor
1 package yellow cake mix
2 tablespoons butter or margarine
3/4 cup chopped nuts
coconut (optional)

Preheat oven to 350 degrees. Using a 9x13 inch pan (ungreased), spread prepared pie filling on bottom and cover with pineapple. Cover the fruit with dry cake mix. Top with melted butter, poured evenly. Sprinkle with nuts and coconut. Bake for 45-55 minutes or until done. Cool completely. This is a quick and easy dessert for dinner or for last minute pot lucks! May also be topped with Cool Whip before serving.

Kathy Blevins

Earthquake Cake

Pillsbury German Chocolate Cake mix
1 can coconut
1-1/2 cups chopped pecans
1 (8 ounce) package cream cheese, softened
1 stick margarine, softened
1 box powdered sugar
1 teaspoon vanilla

Mix German chocolate cake mix according to package directions and add coconut and chopped pecans. In a separate bowl, mix together cream cheese, margarine, powdered sugar, and vanilla. Pour cake batter into a greased 15x11 inch pan sprayed with Pam. Drop cream cheese mixture in dollops over top of cake mix. Bake according to cake mix package directions.

Serves 4-6

Susan Clements

Eggnog Cake

1/4	cup finely chopped pecans	3	cups flour
1-1/4	cups margarine, softened	1/2	teaspoon salt
1-1/2	cups granulated sugar	1/2	teaspoon baking soda
4	eggs	1/4	teaspoon nutmeg
		3/4	cup eggnog
		1/4	cup brandy or rum

Generously grease 10 inch bundt pan with Crisco or other vegetable shortening; coat bottom with pecans. Beat together margarine and sugar until light and fluffy; add eggs 1 at a time, mixing well after each addition. Combine flour, salt, soda and nutmeg, and add this mixture alternately with combined eggnog and brandy or rum, beating on low speed to mix well. Spoon batter into prepared pan. Bake at 325 degrees for 1 hour or until wooden pick inserted in center of cake comes out clean. Cool 10 minutes in pan; invert onto wire rack to remove from pan and cool thoroughly on rack. Prepare glaze.

Glaze:

1	cup sifted confectioners sugar	4	teaspoons water
		2	teaspoons brandy or rum

Combine confectioners sugar, water, and brandy or rum; mix until smooth. Drizzle over cake. Can garnish with candied fruit if desired.

Mark E. Schier

Elton's Snowball Cake

1	(9 inch) Angel food cake	1	(10 ounce) package frozen strawberries
1	cup sugar	3	envelopes Dream Whip
2	envelopes Knox gelatin	1-1/2	cups milk
1	tablespoon lemon juice	1/2	teaspoon salt
1	(7 ounce) can coconut		

Crumble cake and set aside. Mix strawberries, salt, sugar and lemon juice together and chill. Soften gelatin in 1/4 cup tap water, add one cup boiling tap water and stir until dissolved. Pour into strawberry mixture and chill again. Mix 2 packages of Dream Whip as directed on package and mix with strawberry mixture. Line a 2-1/2 quart round bottom bowl with Handi-wrap, letting ends fall over edge of bowl. Pour mixture into bowl alternating cake crumbs and strawberry mixture. Make sure that the first and last layers are strawberry mix. Put in refrigerator and let sit about one hour or until firm. Turn out on cake plate. Ice with 1 package of Dream Whip, mixed as directed on package, and sprinkle with coconut. Cover with Handi-wrap and keep in refrigerator until ready to serve.

Serves 8

Elton Kytle

Raisin Cake

- **1 (15 ounce) box raisins**
- **1 cup sugar**
- **1-1/3 cups water**
- **1/3 cup butter or margarine, softened**
- **2 cups sifted all purpose flour**
- **1 teaspoon baking soda**
- **3/4 teaspoon ground cinnamon**
- **1/4 teaspoon ground cloves**
- **1/2 teaspoon salt**
- **3/4 cup walnuts, chopped**
- **1 teaspoon vanilla extract**

In a large saucepan combine raisins, sugar, water and butter. Mix well. Bring to boil; remove from heat; let cool 30 minutes. Lightly grease and flour a 9x5x3 inch loaf pan. Preheat oven to 350 degrees. Sift flour with soda, spices, and salt. Add to cooled raisin mixture. Add walnuts and vanilla and with a wooden spoon mix until well blended. Bake about 1 hour or until cake tester comes out clean. Cool on a wire rack. Note: May use a bundt pan. Bake at lower temperature and shorter time.

Serves 12

Stella Abney

Hot Milk Cake

- **3 eggs**
- **2 cups sugar**
- **1 stick margarine or butter**
- **1 cup milk**
- **2 cups flour**
- **1 teaspoon vanilla**
- **pinch of salt**
- **2 teaspoons baking powder**

Beat eggs. Add sugar, gradually. Set aside. In saucepan, bring butter and milk to a boil. Remove from heat. Add the flour and hot milk gradually to the egg and sugar mixture. Add vanilla and salt. Add baking powder and blend well. Pour evenly into 3 greased and floured 8 inch layer pans or one 13x9 inch sheet cake pan. Bake at 350 degrees until done. Note: It is very important to add baking powder last, as it reacts immediately when added to hot mixture.

Jane Wells West

" 'Tis an ill cook that cannot lick his own fingers."
— Shakespeare, Romeo and Juliet

Grandmother's English Nut Cake

4 cups flour
1/2 teaspoon salt
2-1/2 cups sugar
1 tablespoon pumpkin pie spice
4 cups, or more, broken walnuts
2 packages seeded dark raisins
1 pound butter
6 eggs, well beaten

Use large mixing bowl for recipe preparation. Sift flour, then add salt, sugar, spice, nuts and raisins and mix well. Melt butter and set aside to cool a few minutes, then pour over dry mixture. Add eggs and mix well, using hands instead of a spoon to save time. Pour batter into a tube pan which has been greased and lined with greased wax paper. Bake 3 hours at 325 degrees. Indulge for the holidays — this is better than fruitcake! Store in cake tin with an apple half, changing as needed. Slices better when refrigerated.

Serves 16-20

Leah Whitty

Hummingbird Cake (No Mixer)

3 cups flour
1 teaspoon soda
1 teaspoon salt
2 teaspoons cinnamon
2 cups sugar
3 eggs
1 can (large) crushed pineapple, undrained
1-1/2 cups butter flavor vegetable oil*
1 cup chopped nuts
2-3 mashed bananas

Combine all dry ingredients and sift 2-3 times until well blended. Add eggs, crushed pineapple, oil and mix well. Add nuts and mashed bananas. Pour into greased and floured tube pan. Bake 350 degrees for one hour and five minutes. Let cool before removing. Frost or glaze, if desired. Freezes well. *Add 1-1/2 teaspoons butter flavoring to one cup of regular vegetable oil to make butter flavor vegetable oil.

Marie Brown

Most times very hot water will revive your wilted flowers.

Mandarin Orange Cake I

1 Duncan Hines Butter Golden Cake Mix
1 cup oil
2 cups mandarin orange slices
4 eggs
Icing recipe follows

Combine cake mix, oil, oranges, and eggs. Pour into 3-8 inch cake pans. Bake 350 degrees for 15-18 minutes. Cool and frost. Can be frozen or served.

Icing:
1 cup crushed pineapple
1 large vanilla instant pudding
1 (12 ounce) Cool Whip

Combine icing ingredients and mix well.

Michael Kunc

Lemon Jello Cake

1 white or yellow cake mix
1 (3 ounce) package lemon jello
3/4 cup salad oil
3/4 cup water
4 eggs

Spray bundt pan or tube pan (7-1/2x3) with Bakers Joy and set aside. Mix cake mix, jello, oil and water well. Add eggs one at a time beating well after each addition. Pour into pan. Bake at 350 degrees for 45 minutes. While cake is warm, pierce with a fork and glaze with the following:

Glaze:
1/4 cup lemon juice
1/2 cup sugar

To prepare glaze, mix lemon juice and sugar stirring well. Drizzle glaze over top.

Juliana Ortegon

Italian Cream Cake

1 stick margarine, softened
1/2 cup Crisco
2 cups sugar
5 eggs, separated
2 cups flour
1 teaspoon baking soda
1 cup buttermilk
1 teaspoon vanilla
1 small can coconut
1 cup pecans, chopped

Preheat oven to 350 degrees. Cream margarine, Crisco and sugar. Add egg yolks and beat well. Combine flour and soda. Add to creamed mixture alternating with buttermilk. Add vanilla, coconut and pecans. Fold in stiffly beaten egg whites. Use cookie sheet that has sides or 3 layer pans greased. Bake 350 degrees for 25-30 minutes. Cool completely and frost.

Cream Frosting:
1/2 cup margarine, softened
1 (8 ounce) package cream cheese, softened
1 box powdered sugar
1 teaspoon vanilla

Beat margarine and cream cheese until smooth. Add powdered sugar and vanilla. Spread on cooled cake. Garnish with pecans and coconut.

Lynn Miller

Mandarin Orange Cake II

- 1 package Butter Cake Mix
- 1/2 cup margarine, softened
- 3 eggs
- 3/4 cup milk
- 1 (11 ounce) can mandarin oranges, drained and chopped; leave a few oranges whole to be used later as garnish on icing
- Icing (recipe follows)

Mix all cake ingredients together and pour into 2 lightly greased 8 or 9 inch round cake pans. Bake 325 degrees or until done. Cool completely. Ice.

Icing:

- 1 pint Cool Whip
- 1 (20 ounce) can crushed pineapple, undrained
- 1 package vanilla instant pudding mix

Mix ingredients together and spread between layers, on tops and sides. Garnish with leftover mandarin orange slices if desired. Refrigerate cake until ready to serve.

Doris Blumenthal

Mississippi Mud Cake

- 4 eggs
- 2 cups sugar
- 1 cup margarine, melted
- 1-1/2 cups flour
- 1/3 cup cocoa
- 1 teaspoon vanilla
- 1 cup coconut
- 1/2 cup chopped pecans
- 1 (7 ounce) jar marshmallow cream
- Frosting, recipe follows

Beat eggs until thick about 5-7 minutes. Gradually add sugar. Combine margarine with flour, cocoa, vanilla, coconut and pecans. Add egg mixture to flour mixture. Stir well with a spoon. Pour into 13x9 inch greased pan and bake 30 minutes at 350 degrees. Remove cake from oven immediately spread with marshmallow cream on top of cake. Prepare frosting.

Frosting:

- 1/2 cup margarine, melted
- 1/3 cup cocoa
- 1 teaspoon vanilla
- 6 tablespoons milk
- 1 box powdered sugar

Mix all ingredients. Spread over warm marshmallow cream. Swirl to marble. Top with 1 cup chopped pecans.

Kathy O'Brien

Mother's Pound Cake

1 cup butter (real), softened
1-3/4 cups sugar
5 eggs
2 cups flour, sifted
1 teaspoon vanilla

Cream butter and sugar. Add eggs and then flour, mixing well. Add vanilla. Pour into greased and floured 10 inch tube or bundt pan. Bake 325 degrees for 45-55 minutes.

Serves 10

Virginia Van Horn

Nut Torte

2 cups crushed Zwieback crumbs
2 cups chopped pecans
1/2 teaspoon cinnamon
1/2 teaspoon salt
2 teaspoons baking powder
2 teaspoons brandy (or vanilla)
6 eggs, separated
1 cup sugar
3 cups water
2 cups sugar
1 slice lemon
1 stick cinnamon

Mix together first 5 ingredients; add brandy or vanilla. Beat egg yolks until light; add sugar and continue beating until light lemon colored. Add to dry ingredients, mixing thoroughly. Beat egg whites until stiff and fold into mixture. Pour into greased 8x12 inch pan. Bake in 325 degree oven for 30 minutes or until toothpick inserted comes out clean. Remove from oven. To make syrup boil 3 cups water, 2 cups sugar, 1 slice lemon and 1 stick cinnamon for 30 minutes. Cool. Pour syrup over torte slowly so that it may be completely absorbed. Let stand for 6 hours (or overnight) before serving.

Serves: 20

Sophia Papas

To get the corn silk off of corn on the cob, brush downward with a paper towel.

Perry's White Lemon Fruitcake

- 1 pound white raisins
- 1 pound candied pineapple
- 1/2 pound candied cherries
- 4 cups flour
- 1 pound butter (do not substitute margarine), melted
- 2-1/2 cups white sugar
- 4 egg yolks, lightly beaten
- 2 ounces lemon extract
- 1 pound pecans

Cut up all fruits and mix with one cup of the flour. Let stand, covered, overnight, in the refrigerator. The next day add remaining ingredients, mixing in enough water to make batter manageable (it will be very stiff). Pour batter into three 9x5 inch loaf pans with a large pan of water under the loaf pans. Bake at 225 degrees for 3 hours.

J. F. DeCell

Oma Brandtner's Kugelhupf

- 1 package active dry yeast
- 1/4 cup warm water (105-115 degrees)
- 1/2 cup lukewarm milk (scalded then cooled)
- 1/2 cup sugar
- 1/2 cup butter or margarine, softened
- 1/2 teaspoon salt
- 3 eggs
- 2-3/4 cups all purpose flour
- 1/2 cup golden raisins
- grated peel of 1 lemon
- 1/3 cup cornflake crumbs
- 12 to 16 whole blanched almonds

Dissolve yeast in warm water in large mixing bowl. Beat in milk, sugar, margarine, salt, eggs and 1-1/4 cups of the flour on low speed, scraping bowl constantly, about 30 seconds. Beat on medium speed, scraping bowl occasionally, 4 minutes. Stir in raisins, lemon peel and the remaining flour. Scrape batter from side of bowl. Cover; let rise in warm place until double, about 1-1/2 hours. Grease bottom and side of bundt or kugelhupf pan; sprinkle with cornflake crumbs. Arrange whole almonds evenly in bottom of pan. Stir down batter by beating about 25 strokes. Spoon batter into pan. Let rise until double, about 1 hour. Heat oven to 350 degrees. Bake until golden brown, about 50 minutes. Immediately remove from pan. This is a great brunch cake, as it is not too sweet. It is also good toasted.

Shirin Shiekh Blackwell

Fresh Apple Cake

3 cups flour
1 teaspoon baking soda
1/2 teaspoon salt
1 teaspoon cinnamon
2 cups sugar
2 eggs, well beaten
1-1/4 cups Wesson oil
3 cups diced fresh apples
1 cup chopped nuts, if desired

In a large bowl, combine dry ingredients. Make a well in the center of dry ingredients and add the eggs, oil and apples (and nuts, if desired). Mix with a spoon and pour batter into a 13x9 inch pan and bake at 325 degrees for 1 hour and 5 minutes. Stays moist for days.

Regina Werner
Susan Scott

Pineapple Pudding Cake

1 package yellow cake mix
1 package vanilla pudding (6 serving size)
1 (20 ounce) can crushed pineapple, undrained
1 cup sugar
2 cups whipping cream, whipped and sweetened to taste
flaked coconut

Mix and bake cake in a 13x9x2 inch pan according to package directions. Prepare vanilla pudding according to package directions and set aside. Bring undrained pineapple and sugar to a boil, then let cool. When baked cake has cooled, poke holes in it with a fork and pour pineapple mixture over it. Spread prepared pudding over top of pineapple layer. Refrigerate. Shortly before serving, cover cake with whipped cream and sprinkle with coconut.

Wayne McHatton

The recipe that is not shared with others will soon be forgotten, but when it is shared, it will be enjoyed by future generations.

Pound Cake

- 2 cups shortening
- 3-1/2 cups sugar
- 10 eggs
- 4 cups flour, sifted
- 1 lemon, juice and grated rind

Beat the shortening for 10 minutes. Add the sugar, beating until extremely fluffy (about 10 to 15 minutes). Add the eggs, one at a time, beating well after each. Add the flour, lemon juice and grated rind and beat until smooth. Pour batter into a greased and floured tube pan or two greased and waxpaper-lined loaf pans and bake at 325 degrees for 1-1/2 hours.

Jane McFaddin

"Puddin" Cake

- 1 cup flour
- 1 stick butter, softened
- 1 cup chopped pecans
- 1 (8 ounce) package cream cheese, softened
- 1 cup powdered sugar
- 1 (9 ounce) carton Cool Whip
- 1 (3 ounce) package Instant Chocolate Pudding
- 1 (3 ounce) package Instant Vanilla Pudding
- 2 cups milk
- grated chocolate

Combine flour, butter and pecans; press on bottom of 9x13 pan; bake 12-15 minutes at 325 degrees. Cool. Cream together cream cheese, powdered sugar and 1/2 carton Cool Whip and spread over cooled crust. Mix together pudding mixes and milk and spread over cheese mixture. Spread with remaining Cool Whip and top with grated chocolate.

Serves 8-12

Mary Cypert

Rum Cake

- 1 package yellow cake mix
- 1 small package instant vanilla pudding
- 4 eggs
- 1/2 cup salad oil
- 1/2 cup water
- 1/2 cup rum
- 1/2 cup chopped pecans
- Glaze (recipe follows)

Mix first 6 ingredients about 2 minutes. Sprinkle pecans on bottom of greased tube pan or bundt pan. Pour batter over nuts and bake at 325 degrees about 1 hour. Remove from oven and pierce top thoroughly with handle of wooden spoon. Immediately pour glaze over top. Cool completely before removing from pan.

Glaze:

- 1 stick butter
- 1/4 cup water
- 1 cup sugar
- 1 ounce rum

Boil butter, sugar and water for 1 minute. Remove from heat and add rum.

Betty Tonnessen

Rave Reviews Cake

1 (2 layer size) package white or yellow cake mix
1 (4 serving size) package JELLO Vanilla Flavor Instant Pudding
1-1/3 cups water
4 eggs
1/4 cup oil
1-1/3 cups Baker's Angel Flake Coconut
1 cup chopped nuts

Coconut Cream Cheese Frosting:
1/3 cup butter, softened
2 (3 ounce) packages cream cheese, softened
1 (16 ounce) box confectioners sugar
4 teaspoons milk
1/2 teaspoon vanilla
1 cup Baker's Angel Flake Coconut

Combine cake mix, pudding mix, water, eggs and oil in large mixer bowl. Blend; beat at medium speed for 4 minutes. Stir in coconut and nuts. Pour into greased and floured 10 inch tube pan. Bake at 325 degrees for 60 minutes. Cool 15 minutes. Remove from pan and cool on rack. When cake is cool make icing as follows: Cream butter; blend in cream cheese. Add confectioners sugar alternately with milk, beating well after each addition. Add vanilla. Spread frosting over top and sides of cake. Sprinkle coconut over frosting.

Sr. Alice Potts

Sandy's Coffee Cake

Cake:
1 box yellow cake mix
1 small package coconut instant pudding
1/2 cup oil
4 eggs
1 large carton sour cream
1 teaspoon vanilla

Topping:
2/3 cup sugar
1 cup chopped pecans
1 teaspoon cinnamon

Mix all cake ingredients together. Pour 1/2 of the batter into a greased and floured 9x11 pan. Mix topping ingredients together and sprinkle half into pan. Add remaining cake batter. Add remaining topping. Bake at 350 degrees for about 40 to 45 minutes.

Sandy Schmelzer

Sherry Cake

1 box yellow cake mix (not with pudding added)
1 small package vanilla flavored instant pudding
4 eggs
3/4 cup oil
3/4 cup sherry
1 cup pecan halves
Glaze recipe:
1 cup powdered sugar
3-4 tablespoons sherry

Combine mix, pudding, eggs, oil and sherry in large mixing bowl. Beat for 10 minutes. Pour batter into buttered bundt pan sprinkled with 1 cup pecans. Bake at 350 degrees for 40-45 minutes. Cool in pan 10 minutes. To make glaze, mix sherry with powdered sugar and stir until well combined. Drizzle over cake.

Serves 12

Pat Gruenert

Strawberries and Angel Food Cake

1 (3 ounce) package strawberry jello
1-1/2 cups boiling water
1 (10 ounce) box frozen strawberries, thawed
1 tablespoon sugar
pinch of salt
1/2 pint whipping cream
1 Angel Food Cake, baked or store-bought

Dissolve jello in boiling water. Add strawberries, sugar and salt. Let chill at least one hour or until partially congealed. Whip cream and fold into strawberry mixture. Break angel food cake into bite-size pieces and cover bottom of oblong pan. Pour strawberry mixture over cake pieces and chill. Serve when the mixture has set.

Sandy Schmelzer

Strawberry Cake

1 yellow cake mix
1 package strawberry jello
4 eggs, beaten
1 cup Mazola oil
1/2 cup cold water
3/4 package frozen strawberries, thawed

Mix cake mix and jello together. Add beaten eggs, oil, water and strawberries. Pour into 3-9 inch layer pans. Cook about 20-25 minutes at 350 degrees. Cool and ice with the following:

Icing:
2 cups powdered sugar
1/2 cup margarine, melted
1/4 package or less strawberries

Mix ingredients in the order given.

Serves 18

Mrs. Roy Williams

Sock-It-To-Me Cake

1 package Duncan Hines Butter Recipe Golden Cake Mix, divided
1 cup dairy sour cream
1/3 cup Crisco oil or Puritan oil
1/4 cup sugar
1/4 cup water
4 eggs

Filling:
2 tablespoons reserved cake mix
2 teaspoons cinnamon
2 tablespoons brown sugar
1 cup finely chopped pecans

Glaze:
1 cup confectioners sugar
2 tablespoons milk

Preheat oven to 375 degrees. Combine filling ingredients and set aside. In a large bowl blend cake mix, sour cream, oil, sugar, water and eggs together. Beat at high speed for 2 minutes. Pour 2/3 of the batter into a greased and floured 10 inch tube or bundt pan. Sprinkle filling ingredients over batter in pan. Spread remaining batter evenly over filling mixture. Bake for 45-55 minutes, or until cake springs back when touched lightly. Cool right side up for about 25 minutes, then remove from pan. Make glaze by blending 1 cup confectioners sugar with 2 tablespoons milk. Drizzle over cake.

Serves 12

Sr. Alice Potts

Tally's Scrumptious Red Birthday Cake

1-1/2 cups sugar
1/2 cup Crisco
2 eggs
1 teaspoon vanilla
1 ounce red food coloring
1 ounce water
1 teaspoon salt
2 cups flour, sifted
2 tablespoons cocoa
1 cup buttermilk
1 teaspoon baking soda
1 tablespoon vinegar

Cream sugar and Crisco. Add eggs, vanilla, coloring and water. Sift together salt, flour and cocoa. Add the sifted ingredients alternately with buttermilk. Beat ten minutes. Dissolve soda in vinegar and fold into the batter. DO NOT BEAT. Fold batter into two 9 inch round pans or 9 inch square pans. Bake at 350 degrees for 30-35 minutes.

Frosting:
1 cup milk
1 cup flour
pinch of salt
1 cup sugar
1/2 cup Crisco
1 stick margarine, softened
1 teaspoon vanilla

Cook first two ingredients until paste, add a pinch of salt. Set aside and cool. Cream sugar, Crisco and margarine until fluffy, then add flour mixture plus vanilla. Beat at high speed until ready for spreading. Can be garnished with coconut or toasted almonds.

Bob Burrill

"Three Milks" Cake (Nicaraguan)

Cake:

- **2 cups sugar**
- **9 eggs, separated**
- **1 teaspoon vanilla**
- **2 cups flour**
- **1 tablespoon baking powder**
- **1/2 cup milk**

Topping/Filling:

- **3 egg yolks**
- **2 cans evaporated milk**
- **1 pint cream**
- **1 teaspoon vanilla**

Cake: Beat sugar and egg yolks until light. Add vanilla, flour, baking powder and milk. Beat egg whites until stiff and fold into mixture. Pour into a greased 9x13 glass casserole dish and bake in preheated 350 degrees oven for 30-40 minutes. Let cool. Make topping. When cake has cooled, unmold onto a large platter. Pierce all over with fork and pour filling mixture over and over the cake so it absorbs all the filling. Topping/filling: Beat 3 egg yolks for 1 minute at high speed of mixer. Add the three kinds of milk and beat thoroughly. Add vanilla. Refrigerate at least two hours but best if set overnight.

Kathy Blevins

Very Berry Coffee Cake

Cake:

- **7/8 cup sugar**
- **1 stick margarine**
- **2 eggs**
- **1 teaspoon almond extract**
- **1 teaspoon rum extract**
- **2 cups sifted flour**
- **1 teaspoon baking powder**
- **1 teaspoon baking soda**
- **1 (8 ounce) carton blueberry or raspberry yogurt**

Filling and Topping:

- **2 tablespoons brown sugar**
- **2 tablespoons white sugar**
- **1 tablespoon cocoa**
- **3 tablespoons almonds or pecans, chopped**
- **grated rind of half lemon**

Cream margarine and sugar; add eggs and flavorings and beat until smooth. Sift dry ingredients together and add alternately with yogurt to creamed mixture, beginning and ending with the flour. Grease a bundt pan. Combine all ingredients for topping and sprinkle half the mixture on bottom of pan. Add half the batter; sprinkle the rest of topping mixture on batter. Cover with remaining batter. Bake in preheated 350 degree oven for 40-45 minutes.

Serves 10-12

George Rabson

Vanilla Wafer Cake

2 sticks butter or margarine
2 cups sugar
6 eggs
1/2 cup milk
1 teaspoon vanilla
1 (12 ounce) box vanilla or lemon wafers, crushed
1 cup coconut
1 cup pecans

Cream butter and sugar. Add eggs, one at a time, then add milk and vanilla. Add wafers and mix well. Last, add coconut and pecans. Pour into greased tube pan lined on bottom with waxed paper and bake at 325 degrees for 1 to 1-1/4 hours. Turn out on rack to cool.

Ruth Crowe

Wacky, Wacky Chocolate Cake

3 cups flour
2/3 cup cocoa
2 cups sugar
2 teaspoons soda
1 teaspoon salt
2 cups water
2 teaspoons vinegar
2 teaspoons vanilla
1 cup Wesson oil

Mix first 5 ingredients; add the next four ingredients and mix well. Bake in 350-375 degree oven until straw comes out clean. I'm not wacky, the cake is, no eggs, no milk!

Beth Evers

Any housewife, no matter how large her family, can always get some time alone by doing the dishes.

HODGEPODGE

Mock "Baby Ruth"

1 package chocolate or vanilla Alba drink mix
3 tablespoons peanut butter
3/4 ounce grapenut cereal
1 package sweetener
1 tablespoon hot water (or little more)
1 teaspoon vanilla

Mix all together well. Shape into log or small balls. Refrigerate or freeze 1 to 3 hours.

Serves 1

Betty Griffith

Boiling Water

cold water

Fill to 3/4 full any pot, whistling kettle, etc. Place on burner at highest heat. Heat until water boils. Add tea, coffee or cocoa to taste. Multiple servings.

Winnie Welch
Linda Young

"Luncheon" Cocktail
Fun — Fast — Good

1 can limeade
2 cans sherry
1 tray ice cubes

Dump ingredients in blender. Pour in wine or cocktail glasses and then drink it.

Serves 12 to 16

Thommye Stewart

Golden Punch

6 bananas (pureed)
3 cups sugar
6 cups water
3 cups orange juice
1/2 cup lemon juice
2 large cans pineapple juice
4 (1 litre) jugs of ginger ale or lemon/lime soda.

Blend all ingredients except soda. Refrigerate. Add soda when ready to serve.

Kathy Blevins

Jim Thompson's Apricot Brandy

1-1/2 pounds dried apricots
1-3/4 cups sugar
1 quart Vodka

Combine all ingredients in a large jar with a TIGHT FITTING top. Shake well. Let the jar sit for a MINIMUM of 4 weeks, inverting once EVERY day. Strain off the clear liquid and store tightly covered. The apricots CAN be reused. This makes a great hostess gift — decorate a bottle and fill with the brandy.

Shirin Shiekh Blackwell

Pan Am Sangria

1 quart Yago Sangria
1 quart ginger ale
1 cup brandy
slices of citrus fruit

Mix all liquids, float fruit and serve over ice.

Serves 12

Karen Ortegon

Peach Fuzz

1 (6 ounce) can frozen lemonade or limeade
4-6 ounces vodka
2-3 medium size peaches, pitted, unpeeled and cubed
ice cubes

Put lemonade, vodka and peaches into blender; fill to the top with ice cubes. On high speed, blend until mixture is of "slush" consistency. This is a delicious, refreshing beverage and can be stored in the freezer. If frozen, let it sit in the refrigerator for a few hours before serving. Note: Fresh strawberries can be substituted for peaches.

Estelle Kastleman

Russian Tea

2 cups Tang
1 cup sugar
1 cup instant tea
1 teaspoon cinnamon
1/2 teaspoon cloves
1/2 (3 ounce) package lemonade mix
1 teaspoon lemon peel

Combine all ingredients and store in airtight container. When ready to serve, use 2 teaspoons of mixture to 1 cup of boiling water.

Joyce A. Wagner

Cece's Spiced Tea

- 2/3 cup instant tea with lemon
- 2 cups Tang
- 2 cups sugar
- 1 teaspoon cinnamon
- 1 teaspoon cloves
- 1/4 teaspoon nutmeg (optional)

Mix all ingredients together. Store in large jar or "divvy up" for gift-giving. For one serving use 3 teaspoons mixture added to one cup boiling water.

Thommye Stewart

Spiced Tea

- 4 cups water
- 2 teaspoons whole cloves
- 4 tea bags
- 3 tablespoons lemon juice
- 1 cup pineapple juice
- 2 sticks cinnamon
- 1-1/2 cups sugar
- 1 (12 ounce) can frozen orange juice

Boil 4 cups water with cloves, cinnamon and tea for 4 minutes. Strain over sugar and add juice. Add enough water to make 1 gallon of tea.

Betty Tonnessen

Wassail

- 2 quarts sweet apple cider
- 2 cups pineapple juice
- 1-1/2 cups orange juice
- 1 cup granulated sugar
- 2 sticks whole cinnamon
- 1 teaspoon whole cloves
- 3/4 cup lemon juice

Combine all ingredients in a large saucepan and bring to a boil. Serve hot. Can be put in a crockpot to keep warm. Serves 12-15. Note: For easy removal of cinnamon and cloves, tie them in a small piece of cheesecloth.

Lea Jones

Barbecue Sauce

- 1 (28 ounce) bottle catsup
- 1 (8 ounce) bottle Lea and Perrin Sauce
- 6 ounces garlic vinegar (use white vinegar in which garlic has been soaked at least 72 hours)
- 1/3 bottle Red Hot sauce

Mix all ingredients together and refrigerate until ready to use.

Lou Bruno

Patty's Bar-B-Q Sauce

- 2 teaspoons flour
- 1 teaspoon salt
- 1/2 teaspoon black pepper
- 1/2 teaspoon red pepper
- 1 teaspoon garlic powder
- 2 teaspoons mustard
- 4 tablespoons lemon juice
- vinegar
- 2 sticks of butter or margarine

Mix first 6 ingredients well in a cup. Add lemon juice and fill remainder of cup with vinegar. Add butter and simmer over low heat.

Dora Hughes

Clam Sauce for Linguine

- 1/4 cup olive oil
- 1/2 cup butter or margarine
- 3 cloves garlic, crushed
- 1/4 cup finely chopped parsley
- 1 tablespoon dried or 3 tablespoons fresh chopped basil
- 3 tablespoons Parmesan cheese
- dash cayenne
- dash pepper
- 1-2 cans clams with liquid, chopped

Heat oil in saucepan. Add butter, simmer 2 minutes. Add garlic, parsley, basil, cheese and peppers. Bring to a boil and stir in clams with liquid. Return to a gentle boil. Serve over 3/4 pound linguine. Top with freshly shredded Parmesan.

Serves 4

Michelle K. Hohnke

Meat Marinade

- 3/4 cup Lea and Perrin or Worcestershire sauce
- 1 clove garlic, minced
- 1/8 cup vegetable oil
- 1/4 cup water
- salt and pepper, optional

Blend all ingredients and pour over any roast before baking. Especially good on beef tender or rib eye roast.

Selma Leff

Will power is the ability to eat one salted peanut or one potato chip.

Parsley Sauce (Pesto)

1 garlic clove-minced
4 canned flat anchovies
1/4 cup fresh parsley half a bunch (Italian Parsley)
2 tablespoons lemon juice
5 large fresh basil leaves
6 tablespoons olive oil (extra virgin)

Place all ingredients in a blender and blend until smooth.

Chris Salazar

Remoulade Sauce I

4 hard boiled egg yolks
3 tablespoons Dijon mustard
3 tablespoons horseradish
4 tablespoons lemon juice
dash of Tabasco
1 clove garlic
2 tablespoons paprika
2 tablespoons Worcestershire sauce
4 tablespoons chopped parsley
salt and pepper to taste
3 cups mayonnaise

Combine in blender or food processor. Good with shrimp, crab or saltines.

Michael Kunc

Remoulade Sauce (For Shrimp) II

1 or 2 hard cooked eggs
2 shallots
4 cloves garlic
1/4 cup mayonnaise
1 tablespoon Worcestershire sauce
1 tablespoon creole mustard
1 tablespoon fresh lemon juice
3 anchovy fillets
dash of Tabasco sauce

Process all ingredients, except hard cooked eggs, in blender or food processor until minced well. Grate hard cooked eggs and incorporate well. Serve with boiled shrimp. The Best

Beverly Loftis

Rum Dum

1 small onion, chopped fine
butter
1/4 teaspoon dry mustard
1 pound Cheddar or rat cheese, cut into chunks
1 can cream of tomato soup
1 egg, beaten
dash of Worcestershire sauce, if desired
toast, lightly buttered

Brown onion in butter and add mustard. Add cheese and melt with onion mixture. Add undiluted tomato soup; add egg just before serving. Add Worcestershire sauce, if desired. Serve over toast.

Lucretia "Mimi" Gardner

Shrimp Cocktail Sauce

1/2 pint fresh ground horseradish
1/2 cup sugar
1 small can evaporated milk
1 (12 ounce) bottle Heinz catsup
1 (12 ounce) bottle chili sauce
2/3 bottle white vinegar

Combine all ingredients, reserving 1/3 bottle of vinegar. After ingredients have been mixed, rinse catsup and chili sauce bottles with the remaining 1/3 cup vinegar and pour into mixture. Mix well and refrigerate until ready to be used.

Lou Bruno

A Real Quick Tomato Sauce

oil
1 small onion
1 clove garlic, chopped
1 (32 ounce) jar of Prego, Ragu, or other
1 (14 ounce) jar pizza sauce
1 can Italian stewed tomatoes
parsley, to taste
basil, to taste
oregano, to taste
Parmesan cheese, to taste

Put some oil in saucepan and saute onions and garlic. Add sauces and stewed tomatoes. Stir well. Cook for an hour or two. After it has cooked for an hour, put in some parsley, basil, oregano, and Parmesan cheese to taste. If sauce gets too thick, add a little water. Note: Meatballs, sausage, etc. may be added to sauce mixture before simmering for an hour.

Lou Bruno

Fudge Frosting

2 cups sugar
1 stick margarine
2 squares chocolate, baking
2/3 cup evaporated milk, undiluted
dash salt
1 teaspoon vanilla

Boil all ingredients except vanilla one minute after coming to a full boil. (1-1/2 minutes on a damp day). Add vanilla and leave until lukewarm. My mother always said leave until you can place your hands on side of pan. Then beat until consistency is spreadable. Serves 2 layer cakes or 2 sheet cakes.

Jane Wells West

Crunchy Fudge
The way Grandma used to make it!

2 (1 ounce) squares unsweetened chocolate
2 cups sugar
1/8 teaspoon salt
3/4 cup milk or cream
2 tablespoons light corn syrup
2 tablespoons real butter
1 tablespoon vanilla extract

First, attach a good, readable thermometer to a large pot. Next, dump chocolate squares, sugar, salt, milk and corn syrup into the pot. Place over medium heat and stir enough to mix ingredients. When chocolate is melted, turn heat down, stirring occasionally (You can watch TV for 10-minute intervals between stirring), keeping an eye on the thermometer. It will quickly rise to 210 degrees, then temperature will rise more slowly. Keep stirring occasionally until the temperature gets up to 238 degrees. Remove from heat and add butter and vanilla, stirring for about 10 minutes as butter melts and fudge cools. Have a pyrex square dish very slightly greased and ready. When fudge starts to harden, pour into dish and let it sit until it hardens sufficiently to be cut into squares. Serves 1 to 30 people. Note: Double recipe for true fudge lovers. 1/3 cup pecans can be added for nut nuts who don't fully appreciate pure, crunch calorie-laden fudge!

George Vietor

Debbie's Refrigerator Fudge

1/2 pound margarine, softened
2-3 cups pecans
3 teaspoons vanilla
18 ounces semi-sweet chocolate morsels
4-1/2 cups sugar
1 large can evaporated milk

Mix in large bowl first four ingredients. In saucepan, mix and bring to a full boil the sugar and milk. Boil for exactly six minutes once it has reached a full boil. After sugar mixture has boiled for six minutes, pour over ingredients in bowl and stir to mix well. Pour into 2-9 inch buttered pans or one 13x9x2 inch pan. Refrigerate until solid. Serves approximately 48 one inch squares.

Diana Horowitz

Housework is something you do that nobody notices unless you don't do it.

Rich Chocolate Fudge

4-1/2 cups sugar
1 stick butter
1 large can Pet milk
1 teaspoon vanilla
1 (12 ounce) bag of semi-sweet chocolate chips
6 Hershey bars
2 cups pecans
1 (8 ounce) jar of marshmallow

Combine first 3 ingredients together and boil for 5-7 minutes, stirring occasionally. Add remaining ingredients and stir until chocolate chips and Hershey bars are dissolved. Pour into a 13x9 pan to cool — when slightly cool — put into refrigerator. Wait several hours before cutting.

Gerry and Barbara Berard

Mexican Fudge

1/2 pound grated sharp Cheddar cheese
1/2 pound grated Monterey Jack cheese
1/4 cup Jimenez green sauce
3 eggs, beaten

Mix the grated cheeses together. In a 13x9 inch pan spread 1/2 the mixed cheeses. Combine eggs and green sauce. Spread over cheese. Sprinkle remainder of cheeses over all. Bake 350 degrees for 30 minutes.

Diana Horowitz

Peanut Butter Skillet Fudge

2 cups sugar
1 cup evaporated milk
1 tablespoon butter
1 (12 ounce) jar peanut butter
1 teaspoon vanilla
1 cup miniature marshmallows

In a large skillet, combine first 3 ingredients and cook until it boils and then boil 7-8 minutes until thick. Take off the stove and add the remaining ingredients stirring until combined and pour into buttered dish.

Linda Blankenship

Nuked M&M's

1 (1.69 ounce) package plain M&M's
1 (1.63 ounce) package peanut butter M&M's

Heat plain M&M's in microwave for 30-45 seconds. Outside shell will crack. Leave in for about 15 seconds longer. Heat peanut butter M&M's in microwave for 1 minute. Outside shell will crack. Peanut butter M&M's are tastier when warm.

Serves 1

Mark E. Shier

Apricot Coconut Balls

1-1/2 cups dried apricots, ground
2 cups shredded coconut
2/3 cup Eagle brand sweetened condensed milk
1 tablespoon orange juice
1 teaspoon grated orange rind
powdered sugar

Mix and form all ingredients, except powdered sugar, into 1-1/2 inch balls. Roll in powdered sugar. Make ahead of time and store in an air-tight container. Makes 32 balls.

Ruth Crowe

Date Comfits

1 pound pitted dates
1 cup chopped walnuts or other nuts
3 tablespoons candied ginger, chopped or ground
confectioners sugar

Force dates through coarse blade of food chopper. Combine dates with walnuts and chopped or ground ginger. Dust hands with confectioners sugar and knead mixture until well blended. Roll mixture into a 7x2 inch sausage shape; chill. Slice thin and serve.

Ruth Crowe

Date Roll

1/2 pound marshmallows, chopped fine
1/2 pound chopped nuts
1/2 pound chopped dates
10 maraschino cherries, chopped
1-1/2 cups milk
1/2 pound graham crackers, crushed
whipped cream or Cool Whip

Combine first 5 ingredients. Place graham cracker crumbs on wax paper. Put marshmallow mixture onto cracker crumbs and work into a roll shape. Cover completely with cracker crumbs. Store in refrigerator overnight. Serve with whipped cream or Cool Whip.

Margo Cannom

Kentucky Bourbon Balls

1 package vanilla wafers
1 cup chopped pecans
1 cup powdered sugar
2 tablespoons cocoa
2 tablespoons white Karo syrup
1/2 cup (at least) Kentucky Bourbon, more if desired

Use food processor to grind vanilla wafers until fine. Process pecans just a bit coarser. Mix vanilla wafer crumbs with nuts, powdered sugar, and cocoa. Dissolve Karo syrup in the bourbon and add to the dry ingredients. Mix well to blend. The mixture must be moist enough to hold together. Form into balls about the size of an English walnut and roll in powdered sugar. When adding the bourbon you should add enough to make the mixture just a little too "loose" to form balls, then let set for approximately 30 minutes to "firm up".

Moonbeam Humphrey

NOTE: Each holiday season, a decorating contest is held on the hospital and clinic floors with local media personalities serving as judges. A gift box of Bourbon Balls from Moonbeam keeps them coming back!!

Mama's Bleu Cheese Dressing

3 ounces bleu cheese, crumbled
1 cup sour cream
1 cup mayonnaise
juice of 1 lemon
2 teaspoons soy sauce
1/4 teaspoon mixed salad herbs or Italian seasoning
1/4 teaspoon garlic powder
1/4 teaspoon pepper
salt to taste

Combine all ingredients and mix well. Chill. Yields about 2-1/2 cups. Shake well before serving.

Liza Wright

Feta Dressing (Saltsa Feta)

2 cups crushed feta cheese
2 garlic cloves, minced
1 teaspoon salad herbs
2 tablespoons olive oil
2 cups mayonnaise
1/2 cup red wine vinegar
1 teaspoon oregano

Combine all ingredients in a blender and mix until smooth. Refrigerate. Variations: For a chunky dressing, mash the cheese with a fork. Combine all ingredients in a jar, shake well and chill. For a quick dressing, combine 1 cup feta cheese (crushed) with 1 cup bottled herb salad dressing. Place in a bottle, shake well and chill. This will keep for weeks in the refrigerator. Pour over salad and serve.

Sophia Papas

French Dressing

1/2 cup salad oil
2 tablespoons vinegar
2 tablespoons lemon juice
1 teaspoon sugar
3/4 teaspoon dry mustard
1/2 teaspoon salt
1/8 teaspoon paprika
dash cayenne

Combine ingredients in jar; cover and shake well before using. Makes 3/4 cup.

Elva Lopez

Oriental Salad Dressing

4 tablespoons oil
1 teaspoon chicken bouillon granules dissolved in 1/2 cup hot water
4 teaspoons sesame oil
2 tablespoons +2 teaspoons rice wine vinegar
6 teaspoons sugar
1 tablespoon soy sauce

Whisk together with wire whisk.

Nathan Huang

Red Pop Homemade Ice Cream

36 ounces strawberry pop
2 cans Eagle Brand condensed milk
1 package frozen strawberries or fresh
2 large cans pet milk

Mix ingredients in alternating layers in electric ice cream maker. Makes 1/2 gallon of ice cream.

Pearlie Leger

Ro's Peach Ice Cream

3-4 pounds very ripe peaches
3 cups sugar
1/2 cup lemon juice
2/3 large can (1203) evaporated milk
1/2 pint whipping cream
1 quart homogenized milk

Peel and mash peaches in a large bowl. Add sugar and lemon juice and stir until sugar is completely dissolved. Pour into 1 gallon electric freezer container. Add evaporated milk and whipping cream. Fill container with homogenized milk. Freeze. Remove dasher, add more ice and salt. Let it set for a few hours before serving. Makes one gallon.

Serves 10

Roberta Torn

Bread and Butter Pickles

4 quarts thinly sliced cucumbers
3 white onions, peeled and sliced
1/2 cup pickle salt
1 quart cracked ice
5 cups sugar
1-1/2 teaspoons turmeric
1 teaspoon celery seed
2 tablespoons mustard seeds
5 cups cider vinegar

Mix the cucumbers and onions with the salt and let stand for 3 hours in 1 quart of cracked ice. Cover with weighted lid. Drain and put cucumbers and onions in a large kettle. Add remaining ingredients and bring almost to a boil, stirring often with a wooden spoon. Pack the pickles into hot jars and seal.

Serves: 4 quarts

Dianne Ibenthal

Sweet Bread and Butter Pickles

7 pounds sliced cucumbers
2 cups pickling lime
2 gallons water

Syrup:
2 quarts vinegar
9 cups sugar
2 tablespoons picking spices
green food coloring

Slice cucumbers. Cover with water to which lime had been added. Let them soak 24 hours in crockery or enamel ware. Stir occasionally. After 24 hours rinse several times in cool water. Soak 3 hours in ice water. Remove carefully to drain. In saucepan, over medium heat, mix together vinegar and sugar. Tie spices in cheesecloth or other lightweight material. Add to vinegar mixture. Once the mixture has begun to boil, add a few drops of green food coloring. Add cucumbers and cook approximately 45 minutes, stirring occasionally. Fill jars and seal. If canning jars are not used, keep refrigerated. Makes 10-11 pints.

Rebecca Phifer

Moonbeam's Pickles

1 jar, any size, whole dill pickles
granulated sugar (enough to cover pickles in jar)

Drain pickles and remove from jar. Rinse jar and set aside. Wash the pickles in cold water and pat dry with a paper towel. Slice pickles into 1/2 to 3/4 inch chunks. Return chunks to rinsed jar. Pour sugar over pickles in jar, shaking often, until jar is completely full of sugar. Let sit until sugar dissolves into a clear liquid. Invert jar about once per hour. Let sit at least 12 hours. Happy crunching!

Moonbeam Humphrey

MacDonald Marmalade

7 medium oranges
1 grapefruit
1 lemon
water
sugar
pectin

Wash fruit, leave rind on, slice thin. Add one pint of water to one pint of fruit. Let stand 24 hours. Boil 2-3 hours or until rather thick. Add 1 pint of sugar and one box of pectin to one pint of fruit. Let stand 24 hours, stirring occasionally. Boil until thick enough to gel. Put into glasses. Use enamel kettle.

Serves 10-12 jars

Ann A. Corscaden

Play Dough

1/2 cup salt
2 teaspoons cream of tartar
1 tablespoon oil in 1 cup water
1 cup flour
food color

Cook one minute. Knead one minute. Store in plastic bag.

Rebecca Phifer

A neighbor asked a small boy if his family said prayers before the meals. "No," he replied, "We don't have to. My mother is a good cook."

HEALTHY EATING

HEALTHY EATING

Not only is healthy eating good for you, it can be FUN! Favorite foods and recipes can often be changed to be healthier and still retain familiar flavors. And — with imagination and an adventuresome spirit, exciting new taste experiences and foods can be discovered.

The Department of Nutrition and Food Service at M. D. Anderson Cancer Center has developed a healthy eating program for visitors and staff. Some of the recipes used by the department are featured here, as well as ideas for changing recipes to make them healthier. The guidelines used by this department represent current recommendations for Healthy Eating suggested by leading scientific and health organizations.

Guidelines for Healthy Eating

Maintain ideal body weight

Cut down on total fat intake, as well as saturated fat

Reduce foods high in cholesterol

Eat more high-fiber foods, such as whole grain breads and cereals

Include a variety of vegetables and fruits daily

Use less salt

Cut down on salt-cured, smoked and nitrite-cured foods

Keep alcohol consumption moderate, if you do drink.

Chicken in Almond Plum Sauce

3/4 cup water
1/3 cup lemon juice
2 tablespoons soy sauce
1/2 bulb garlic, chopped
1-1/4 teaspoons cornstarch
1/4 teaspoon white pepper
cayenne pepper to taste
10 (6 ounce) chicken breasts, boneless, skinless
1 tablespoon + 2 teaspoons corn oil
3/4 cup red plum jam
5/8 cup sliced almonds
5/8 cup onions green, washed, chopped

Combine water, lemon juice, soy sauce, garlic, cornstarch, white pepper, and cayenne. Marinate chicken in mixture 1 hour. Remove chicken reserving marinade. Saute chicken in oil over high heat 1 minute on each side. Add marinade and plum jam to pan and reduce over high heat until sauce thickens to a syrupy consistency. Top each chicken breast with 1 tablespoon almonds. Pour sauce over chicken. Bake at 350 degrees for 8-10 minutes or until chicken is tender. Before serving, sprinkle each breast with 1 tablespoon green onion. Serving size: 1 chicken breast with sauce. Yield: 10 servings (390 calories, 56 grams protein, 14 grams fat, 145 mg cholesterol, and 870 mg sodium per serving).

Department of Nutrition and Food Service

Chinese Sweet and Sour Chicken

2-1/2 pounds chicken tenderloins
5 tablespoons sugar
1/2 teaspoon salt
1/4 cup white vinegar
1 tablespoon soy sauce
2 tablespoons cooking sherry
2 tablespoons + 1-1/2 teaspoons catsup
1/4 teaspoon garlic, chopped
2 cups sliced green peppers
2 tablespoons + 1-1/2 teaspoons cornstarch
3 tablespoons water
2 cups pineapple tidbits, drained
1 (13 ounce) can mandarin orange sections, drained
2 (6 ounce) cans water chestnuts, sliced, drained
2 cups sweet red peppers, sliced
1-3/4 cups sweet and sour sauce

Cut chicken into strips. Combine the next 6 items; stir to dissolve sugar. Reserve. In hot vegetable oil, stir-fry chicken. Add garlic and green pepper and saute. Add reserved liquid, and heat to simmering. Combine cornstarch and water until smooth. Add to simmering liquid, stirring constantly. Cook to thicken. Add remaining ingredients and chicken to simmering liquid and cook just until heated. Serve over steamed rice, 1/2 cup rice per serving. Yield: 12 servings (413 calories, 33 grams protein, 3 grams fat, 80 mg cholesterol, and 890 mg sodium per serving).

Fish with Tomato and Broccoli

4 pounds flounder filets
3 medium tomatoes, whole, washed
3/4 pound broccoli florets
9 tablespoons lemon juice
1 teaspoon thyme
2 tablespoons + 1-1/2 teaspoons oil, cottonseed
1 tablespoon + 1 teaspoon Spanish paprika
1/4 teaspoon garlic powder
1 teaspoon black pepper
3/4 cup onions, chopped

Cut tomato into wedges, combine 2 tablespoons oil and lemon juice and brush on filets, bake at 350 degrees until just done. Heat remaining oil in pan and add onions; when onions are soft, add spices and broccoli. When broccoli turns bright green, add tomatoes, cook about 2 minutes, then remove from heat. Spoon over fish and serve. Yield: 10 servings (210 calories, 33 grams protein, 6 grams fat, 65 mg cholesterol, and 155 mg sodium).

Department of Nutrition and Food Service

Orange-Baked Pork Chops

10 (4 ounce) pork loin chops
1-1/2 cups orange juice, unsweetened
2-1/2 tablespoons honey
1/4 teaspoon dried thyme
1-1/4 teaspoons grated orange peel
3/4 teaspoon dry mustard
1 teaspoon onion powder
1 tablespoon soy sauce

Trim fat from meat. Broil chops on a rack in preheated broiler, turning once, until lightly browned. Place chops on a rack in shallow baking pan. Preheat oven to 350 degrees. Combine remaining ingredients; pour over chops. Cover and bake 1 hour. Yield: 10 servings (269 calories, 27 grams protein, 13 grams of fat, 83 mg cholesterol, 97 mg sodium per serving).

Department of Nutrition and Food Service

Cinnamon Apples

2-1/2 quarts sliced fresh apples
1 tablespoon honey
2 tablespoons granulated sugar
1/3 cup orange juice
1 teaspoon white vinegar
2 teaspoons lemon juice
1/8 teaspoon ground cloves
1/4 teaspoon cinnamon

Mix all ingredients, except apples, and cook to make syrup. Add apples and cook until tender, about 20 minutes. Serving size: 4 ounce. Yield: 11 servings (78 calories, 0 protein, 0 fat, 0 cholesterol, 1 mg sodium per serving).

Department of Nutrition and Food Service

Soft Turkey Tacos

- **2 cups chopped tomatoes**
- **3 tablespoons chopped green pepper**
- **1/3 cup diced onions**
- **1/4 cup mashed, cooked pinto beans**
- **5 ounces ground turkey**
- **1 (1 ounce) package taco seasoning mix**
- **10 flour tortillas, 6 inch size**
- **1-3/4 cups shredded low-fat Cheddar cheese**
- **3 cups lettuce, shredded**
- **3/4 cup diced tomatoes**

In a large skillet, combine chopped tomatoes, green peppers and onions; simmer for 10-15 minutes. Add beans, ground turkey and taco seasoning mix; blend well, bring to a boil and simmer 10 minutes. Heat tortillas according to package directions; keep warm. For each taco, place 3 tablespoons of filling on tortilla, top with lettuce, tomatoes, and cheese. Yield: 10 tacos (179 calories, 12 grams protein, 5 grams of fat, 30 mg cholesterol, 370 mg sodium per serving).

Department of Nutrition and Food Service

Spiced Peachy Chicken

- **10 (5 ounce) chicken breasts, boneless, skinless**
- **4 cups sliced peaches**
- **1-1/2 cups orange juice**
- **2 tablespoons + 1-1/2 teaspoons wine vinegar**
- **1-1/4 teaspoons nutmeg**
- **1-1/4 teaspoons basil**
- **1/4 teaspoon garlic powder**
- **3 tablespoons corn oil**
- **2 teaspoons margarine**
- **2 tablespoons + 1-1/2 teaspoons dark brown sugar**

Several hours before baking, place chicken in an 8 inch square baking pan that has been sprayed with a nonstick cooking spray. Combine peaches with remaining ingredients. Pour mixture over chicken, marinate in the refrigerator for several hours. Return to room temperature. Preheat oven to 350 degrees, cover chicken and bake 1 hour. Serving size: 1 chicken breast with sauce. Yield: 10 servings (360 calories, 39 grams protein, 11 grams fat, 106 grams cholesterol, and 88 mg sodium per serving).

Department of Nutrition and Food Service

Creole Sauce

- 3 medium tomatoes, chopped
- 1 can tomato sauce
- 1-1/2 cups water
- 3/8 cup onions, chopped
- 1/4 cup sliced green pepper
- 1/4 cup celery, diced
- 3 tablespoons flour
- 2 tablespoons margarine
- 1 tablespoon dark brown sugar, packed
- 1 teaspoon salt
- black pepper to taste
- chili powder to taste
- parsley flakes to taste
- garlic powder to taste

Make roux by browning flour in margarine. Add tomatoes, tomato sauce, and water. Bring to a boil, reduce heat and simmer. Add onions, celery, and green pepper. Add seasoning and simmer for 1 hour, stirring occasionally.

Department of Nutrition and Food Service

Creole Squash

- 2-3/4 pounds yellow squash, sliced, fresh
- 1 tablespoon water
- 2-1/4 cups creole sauce

Simmer or steam sliced squash until tender. Add hot creole sauce. Mix well and serve. Serving size: 4 ounce. Yield: 15 servings (36 calories, 1 gram protein, 1 gram fat, 0 cholesterol, 112 mg sodium per serving).

Department of Nutrition and Food Service

Green Beans with New Potatoes

- 1 (1 pound) package frozen whole green beans
- 1 teaspoon margarine
- 1/8 teaspoon salt
- 1/2 cup water
- 3/4 pound small red potatoes, scrubbed

Steam or simmer about 20 minutes until potatoes are done. Add margarine and salt. Serving size: 4 ounce. Yield: 8 servings (56 calories, 2 grams protein, 1 gram fat, 0 cholesterol, 60 mg sodium per serving).

Department of Nutrition and Food Service

Zucchini with Herbs

1-1/2 pounds zucchini squash, fresh
1 tablespoon margarine
1/2 teaspoon Italian seasoning
1/4 teaspoon salt
1/2 teaspoon white pepper
1 cup water

Slice zucchini; add water. Steam or simmer until tender; then drain. Add remaining ingredients and mix well. Serving size: 4 ounce. Yield: 8 servings (27 calories, 1 gram protein, 1 gram fat per serving).

Department of Nutrition and Food Service

Broccoli and Tomato Salad

1 pound broccoli florets
1/2 pound fresh cherry tomatoes
1 pound caulifloretts, fresh
1/2 cup ripe olives, pitted
3/4 cup lite Italian dressing

Wash and drain broccoli, tomatoes, and cauliflower. Cut cherry tomatoes in half. Drain olives and slice. Mix all ingredients together and chill. Yield: 12 servings (47 calories, 2 grams protein, 3 grams fat, 1 mg cholesterol, and 16 mg sodium per serving).

Department of Nutrition and Food Service

Sesame Slaw

1 pound (about 8 cups) cabbage, shredded
1/2 pound (about 1-1/2 cups) carrots, grated
1/2 pound radishes, sliced
3 tablespoons white vinegar
3 tablespoons corn oil
1 teaspoon sesame oil
1 teaspoon Dijon mustard
3 tablespoons sesame seeds, toasted

Combine cabbage, carrots, and radishes in a large bowl. Combine vinegar, oils, and mustard in a small bowl; stir with a wire whisk until well blended. Pour over cabbage mixture; toss lightly. Cover and refrigerate 8 hours. To serve, add sesame seeds; toss gently. Serving size: 4 ounce. Yield: 9 servings (87 calories, 1 gram protein, 7 grams fat, 0 cholesterol, 31 mg sodium per serving).

Department of Nutrition and Food Service

Hot Fruit Compote

- 1 (#303) can sliced peaches
- 1 (#303) can pear halves
- 1 (#303) can unpeeled apricot halves
- 1 (#303) can pineapple tidbits
- 1 (8 ounce) jar maraschino cherry halves
- 1/4 cup dark brown sugar
- 3/4 teaspoon allspice
- 1 tablespoon margarine, melted

Drain fruits and save juice, combine juices in saucepan. Add brown sugar, margarine, and allspice, bring to boil until sugar is dissolved, pour over fruit. Serving size: 4 ounce. Yield: 18 servings (105 calories, 0 protein, 1 gram fat, 0 cholesterol, and 12 mg sodium per serving).

Department of Nutrition and Food Service

Italian Cake

- 1 (10 inch) pre-made Angel Food Cake

Icing:

- 1-1/2 cups low salt, low fat ricotta cheese
- 8 ounces light cream cheese
- 1/4 cup orange juice
- 1-1/2 cups powdered sugar
- 1 teaspoon vanilla
- 1 tablespoon skim milk
- grated rind of 1 lemon
- grated rind of 1 orange

Raspberry Sauce:

- 2 cups red raspberries (fresh or frozen)
- 1/4 cup sugar
- 2 tablespoons cornstarch

Icing: In a mixer, beat together all icing ingredients until fluffy. Set aside. Raspberry Sauce: In a blender, combine all sauce ingredients and puree. Strain sauce through a sieve to remove raspberry seeds. (Discard seeds.) Cake: Slice cake horizontally with a serrated knife into three layers. Spread icing between layers as well as the rest of the cake. Slice the cake and serve over the raspberry sauce. Yield: 16 servings (235 calories, 8 grams protein, 4 grams fat, 9 mg cholesterol, 148 mg sodium per serving).

Department of Nutrition and Food Service

HELPFUL HINTS FOR HEALTHY CHANGES

Shopping Tips

When Shopping, buy...

1% or skim milk instead of whole milk products

More chicken and fresh fish instead of untrimmed meat

Whole grain products instead of products made from refined flours

Fruit instead of chips and candy

Prepared foods without sauces instead of those with sauces

Reduced fat or fat-free salad dressings

Cooking Tips

When cooking...

Bake, broil, microwave, steam, roast, or poach instead of frying

Trim all visible fat from meat

Remove skin from poultry

Season with herbs and spices instead of butter or fats

Cook meat on a rack to let fat drain

Baste poultry and meat with fruit juices or broth instead of drippings

Skim fat from soups and gravies

Use less fat, oil, or margarine than recipe states; fat can be cut by 1/3 to 1/2 in most quickbreads and casseroles

Use vegetable cooking sprays instead of frying in fat

In soups, stews, casseroles, decrease meat or poultry and add extra vegetables or legumes.

Use skim milk in recipes that call for milk

Recipe Substitutions

Instead of	*Use*
Sour Cream	One cup of lowfat cottage cheese, two tablespoons of lowfat buttermilk, and 2 or 3 teaspoons of lemon juice, beaten until smooth. In cooking, plain yogurt can be substituted for sour cream if you add 1 tablespoon of cornstarch to every cup of yogurt to prevent separation.
Heavy Cream	Equal parts of part skim milk, ricotta cheese and nonfat yogurt, beaten until smooth. This mixture cannot be heated because of separation. In cooking, evaporated skim milk.
Eggs	In baking, use 2 egg whites for 1 whole egg. Egg substitutes may be used for baking and for making egg dishes, such as scrambled eggs.
Non Dairy Creamer	Nonfat Powdered Milk
Fudge Topping	Chocolate Syrup

Better Dessert Ideas

Use angel food cake instead of high fat cakes made with butter and shortening.

In many recipes, cocoa powder can be substituted for chocolate squares to reduce the fat.

Two egg whites can be substituted for each whole egg in many baked recipes.

Much of the fat in a cake is in the frosting. Try omitting frosting and top with fresh fruit, fruit sauce, or sprinkle of confectioner's sugar.

Eliminate nuts, which are high in fat, or use them in small quantities.

GOOD NUTRITION DURING CANCER TREATMENT

Patients receiving cancer treatment have special nutritional needs. In order to maintain weight and obtain adequate protein, patients may need to include foods which are high in calories and protein. Thus, some of the healthy eating guidelines may not apply during treatment. Featured here are nourishing beverage recipes which were developed especially for our patients by the clinical dietitians at The University of Texas M. D. Anderson Cancer Center.

Banana Nut Milkshake

1 cup vanilla ice cream
1 package vanilla instant breakfast powder
1/2 cup Half and Half
1/4 teaspoon black walnut extract
1/2 ripe banana

Blend until smooth. Serve immediately. 600 Calories; 15 grams protein.

Chocolate Mint Milkshake

1 cup vanilla ice cream
1 package chocolate instant breakfast powder
1 cup Half and Half
1/4 teaspoon mint or peppermint extract

Blend until smooth. Serve immediately. 560 Calories; 15 grams protein.

Raspberry Fluff
Patients tired of sweet drinks enjoy this tart drink!

8 ounces raspberry yogurt
1/2 cup Half and Half
1/4 cup cranberry juice

Blend until smooth and serve. 430 Calories; 12 grams protein.

High Protein Milk

1 cup whole milk
4 tablespoons instant non-fat dry milk powder

Note: Protein can be boosted by enriching milk with the addition of nonfat dry milk, using this recipe.

Stir until dissolved. Refrigerate. 211 Calories; 14 grams protein.

PROFESSIONAL
CHEFS

Barbara Bush
First Lady
United States of America

Blackened Redfish

3	pounds redfish, fileted
	melted butter or margarine
1	tablespoon paprika
2-1/2	teaspoons salt
1	teaspoon onion powder
1	teaspoon red pepper
1	teaspoon garlic powder
3/4	teaspoon white pepper
3/4	teaspoon black pepper
1/2	teaspoon dry thyme
1/2	teaspoon oregano

Dip fish in melted butter or margarine and then in mixture of seasonings. Cook in cast iron skillet, preheated until pan is very hot. Cook 2 minutes on one side, turn, and cook for another minute. This dish is very smoky to prepare; it cooks well outside on a grill or campstove.

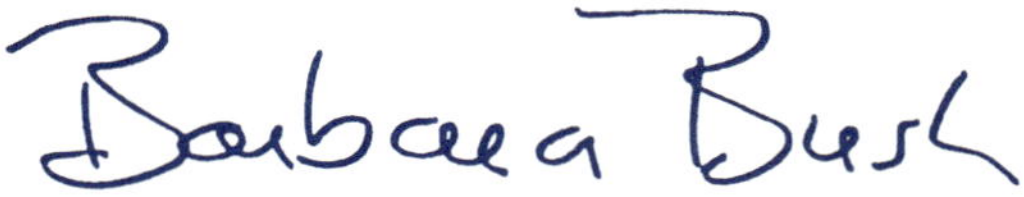

Note: Mrs. Bush may not be a "professional chef", but in the hearts of America, she's a First Lady Chef!

Daniel Boulud, Executive Chef
Le Cirque Restaurant
New York, New York

Roasted Black Sea-Bass with a Herb Crust and Salsify

4 (7 ounce) filets of black sea-bass (or red snapper)
3 ounces mixed fresh herbs: chive, chervil, parsley, and a little rosemary
2 slices white bread, slightly dried
6 ounces sweet butter, softened
1 pound salsify, peeled and sliced
1 tablespoon corn oil
salt, pepper

Place the fresh herbs in a food processor and chop finely. Set 1 tablespoon of herbs aside for the salsify. Remove and discard the crusts of the bread. Add the bread to the herbs in the food processor and chop finely. Add 5 ounces of butter, salt and pepper and blend until smooth. Set aside. Boil the salsify in salted water until cooked, about 5 to 7 minutes. Drain and toss the salsify in 1 ounce butter in a pan over medium heat. Add the 1 tablespoon of fresh herbs, salt and pepper to taste. Salt and pepper the filets of sea-bass. Warm 1 tablespoon of oil in a pan over high heat. Place the fish skin-side down and sear for 2 minutes. Turn the filets over and cook for another minute. Transfer the filets to a broiling pan skin-side up and let cool. Spread the bread and herb butter mixture evenly on the skin of each filet of sea-bass. When ready to serve, preheat the broiler. Broil the fish for 2 minutes or until the herb crust starts browning. Serves 4. Presentation: Arrange the salsify on a serving platter. Place the filets of sea-bass over, and drizzle the melted butter from the broiler pan all around. Decorate with sprigs of chervil.

Jeff Clark, Executive Chef
Holiday Inn Oceanfront
Hilton Head Island, South Carolina

Chicken and Sausage Contidina

- 1 raw potato, skinned and cubed
- 1 red pepper, seeded and cubed
- 1/2 cup olive oil
- 4 ounces boneless chicken breasts, cubed
- 4 ounces Italian sausage, pre-cooked and cubed
- 2 cloves garlic, chopped
- 8-10 mushrooms, sliced thin
- salt
- pepper
- parsley
- oregano

Fry potato and pepper in olive oil (enough to cover potato) until cooked. Remove from oil; set aside. Saute chicken breasts in olive oil until cooked. Add potato, peppers and other ingredients. Saute for 3 minutes or until all ingredients are hot. Drain off excess oil and serve.

Crawfish and Tasso Ham with Linguine

- 1 ounce butter
- 1 tablespoon chopped green onions
- 1/2 teaspoon garlic, chopped, pressed
- 1 ounce Tasso ham (or you may substitute Prosciutto or Capacola ham)
- 5 ounces crawfish tails and fat
- 1 cup heavy cream
- 1 tablespoon Parmesan cheese
- 8 ounces cooked linguine
- 1/2 tablespoon parsley
- Cajun seasoning, to taste

Add butter to skillet; when butter is hot, add green onions, garlic and Tasso ham; saute until vegetables are cooked. Add crawfish and fat; add heavy cream; reduce heat for about 4 to 5 minutes or until sauce is thick enough to coat the back of a spoon. Add Parmesan cheese and parsley; blend; add pasta and toss. Add Cajun seasoning and toss.

Shrimp Angelina

Romano Batter:

- 1 tablespoon parsley
- juice of 1/2 lemon
- Romano cheese
- 1 tablespoon white wine
- 1 teaspoon granulated garlic
- 3 eggs

Shrimp:

- 16-20 shrimp, cleaned and deveined
- flour to coat shrimp
- 1 teaspoon garlic
- 2 ounces mushrooms, sliced
- 4 artichoke hearts, quartered
- 1 ounce white wine
- juice of 1/2 lemon
- 1 tablespoon parsley
- 1 ounce whipped butter
- 1 ounce melted butter

Mix all Romano batter ingredients together and set aside. Heat melted butter in a skillet. While butter is hot in skillet, dredge shrimp in flour, shaking off excess. Then, dip in Romano batter — let excess batter drain off shrimp. Place shrimp in skillet with butter. When butter cooks on one side of shrimp, turn shrimp to other side, add garlic, mushrooms and artichoke hearts. When batter is cooked on other side of shrimp, remove shrimp and place on platter. Place in 400 degree oven for 4 to 5 minutes, or until shrimp are cooked. Add wine and juice of 1/2 lemon, reduce to one-half. Remove skillet from flame and add parsley. When skillet has cooled some, add whipped butter. Shake skillet and add creamed butter with other ingredients. Pour sauce over shrimp.

Tarragon added to melted butter makes a nice sauce for fresh seafood or vegetables.

Mark Cox, Executive Chef
Tony's Restaurant
Houston, Texas

Fedelini Bayou with Crawfish and Cognac Sauce

1	pound live crawfish, perged and cleaned in salt water (drain and dry reserve)
4	ounces olive oil
1/4	cup garlic
1	small onion, minced
2	stalks celery, minced
1	teaspoon seasoned salt
1	tablespoon paprika
	freshly ground white pepper
4	tablespoons tomato paste
16	ounces chicken stock
3	tablespoons butter
3	tablespoons flour
1/4	cup Cognac
1	cup heavy cream
	Worcestershire sauce and Tabasco to taste
	salt and pepper
1	pound fedelini
2	cups fresh mushrooms
1/4	cup black olives, sliced
1/4	cup basil
4	tablespoons unsalted butter
	basil, chopped
	red pepper flakes, crushed

Puree crawfish in food processor and reserve. In a saucepan over medium heat add olive oil, garlic, onions, celery, seasoned salt, paprika and freshly ground white pepper. Saute for 7 to 8 minutes until cooked. Add crushed crawfish, tomato paste and chicken stock. Simmer for 10 to 15 minutes. Strain liquids through a china cap strainer or a cheese cloth.

In another saucepan, melt 3 tablespoons butter. When the butter begins to foam add the 3 tablespoons flour. Continue stirring until incorporated. Add the prepared crawfish stock. Continue to stir until slightly thickened. Add cognac, heavy cream and stir. Season with Tabasco, Worcestershire sauce, salt and pepper to taste. Reserve sauce until it is needed.

Cook fedelini in 3 quarts of salted boiling water with a few drops of olive oil for about 1-1/2 minutes if fresh, or 5 to 6 minutes if dried. Drain well. In a saucepan over medium heat melt unsalted butter and saute crawfish. Add remaining ingredients and stir until mixture is hot. Add 3 cups of the prepared sauce to mixture. Place cooked pasta into serving bowls. Spoon crawfish mixture over pasta. Sprinkle with chopped basil and crushed red pepper flakes. Serves 6.

Lemon Mousse with Raspberry Sauce

- 6 large eggs
- 6 large egg yolks
- 1-1/2 cups sugar
- 1 cup fresh lemon juice, strained
- 2 tablespoons minced lemon peel
- 14 tablespoons (1-3/4 sticks) chilled, unsalted butter cut into small pieces
- 3/4 cup chilled whipping cream
- 1-1/2 cups fresh raspberries or frozen unsweetened, thawed
- 2 tablespoons or more sugar
- fresh mint sprigs for garnish

Whisk eggs and yolks in heavy non-aluminum saucepan until foamy. Whisk in 1-1/2 cups sugar, then lemon juice, then peel. Stir over low heat until mixture thickens to consistency of a heavy custard (about 10 minutes). Do not boil. Remove from heat and whisk in butter. Transfer mixture to bowl and cool until very thick, stirring occasionally (50-60 minutes). Whip cream in a medium sized bowl to soft peaks. Fold cream into lemon mixture just until combined. Spoon mousse into individual serving glasses. Cover and refrigerate until set (about 2 - 2-1/2 hours). In a small bowl mash berries with a fork or barely puree them in a processor. Mix in 2 tablespoons sugar or more if desired. Cover and refrigerate for one hour. Mix the sauce before using. Spoon sauce over center of mousse and garnish with mint sprigs. Serves 8-10.

Jackson Hicks
JAGS/Jackson and Company
Houston, Texas

Gazpacho Rio Grande

- 5 large, ripe tomatoes, peeled, seeded and chopped
- 1 large cucumber, peeled, seeded and chopped
- 1/2 cup green pepper, chopped
- 1 large ripe avocado, peeled and diced
- 5 tablespoons sherry wine vinegar (Posada)
- 2 tablespoons fresh lime juice
- 1-1/2 cups good quality tomato juice
- 2 teaspoons grated onion
- 1/2 teaspoon dill weed
- 1/2 teaspoon Tabasco sauce
- freshly ground black pepper to taste
- salt to taste (add after chilling)
- 1/8 cup extra virgin olive oil
- sour cream and fresh dill weed to garnish

Combine all ingredients. (Leave avocado pit in soup to keep avocado from turning brown.) Chill for at least 24 hours. When ready to serve, remove pit, place in bowls, garnish with dollop of sour cream and top with sprig of dill weed. Makes six 3/4 cup servings.

When buying mushrooms, look for tightly closed caps. It is better not to wash mushrooms; wipe them with a damp paper towel.

Scott Foster, Executive Chef
the ECCENTRIC
Chicago, Illinois

Legato of Roasted Red Bell Peppers

10-15 red bell peppers
1-1/2 pounds yellow Spanish onions
3/4 quart Chardonnay wine
2-1/2 quarts heavy whipping cream
4 ounces whole unsalted butter, cut into cubes
1/3 teaspoon cayenne pepper, or to taste
2 teaspoons salt, or to taste
3 ounces clarified butter

Place whole peppers on a sheet tray in a 400 degree preheated oven. Rotate peppers every 10 minutes; cook for approximately 20-30 minutes. Remove peppers and place in a large mixing bowl and wrap with plastic wrap, making sure it is tight. This is "sweating" the peppers thus making it easier to remove the bitter skins. "Sweat" peppers for approximately 1 hour. Then run each pepper under cool water to remove the skin, seeds and stem. Place cleaned pepper flesh in blender and puree very fine. While the peppers are baking, start the base. Chop onions and place in a large pan, preferably a low and wide base saucepan. Gently saute the onions with clarified butter. Keep a low flame as to avoid browning or any burn on the onions. When onions become transparent and soft, add the Chardonnay wine. Reduce by two-thirds, then add heavy cream. Reduce by two-thirds, then add heavy cream. Reduce by approximately half on medium heat, then add the red pepper puree. Stir well. Cook for approximately 10 minutes on low heat. Remove base from stove and puree in a blender cup two-thirds full at a time. Puree on low speed. Add bits of butter, salt and cayenne, a little at a time for each cupful, until all the base is pureed.

Michigan Bing Cherry Chutney

9 cups fresh ripe cherries, pitted
3/4 cup apple cider vinegar
1/2 cup dark brown sugar
1/4 cup molasses
4-5 cloves (depending on freshness)
3/4 teaspoon ground cinnamon
1/2 teaspoon nutmeg
1 teaspoon salt
1/2 teaspoon ground white pepper

Bring vinegar to a boil and add brown sugar, molasses, cloves, cinnamon and nutmeg. Reduce to a medium thickness and fold in fresh pitted cherries. Cook 10 minutes. Remove from heat and chill quickly over ice in a mixing bowl. Pick out whole cloves. Season.

Jackson Hicks
JAGS/Jackson and Company
Houston, Texas

Gazpacho Rio Grande

5 large, ripe tomatoes, peeled, seeded and chopped
1 large cucumber, peeled, seeded and chopped
1/2 cup green pepper, chopped
1 large ripe avocado, peeled and diced
5 tablespoons sherry wine vinegar (Posada)
2 tablespoons fresh lime juice
1-1/2 cups good quality tomato juice
2 teaspoons grated onion
1/2 teaspoon dill weed
1/2 teaspoon Tabasco sauce
freshly ground black pepper to taste
salt to taste (add after chilling)
1/8 cup extra virgin olive oil
sour cream and fresh dill weed to garnish

Combine all ingredients. (Leave avocado pit in soup to keep avocado from turning brown.) Chill for at least 24 hours. When ready to serve, remove pit, place in bowls, garnish with dollop of sour cream and top with sprig of dill weed. Makes six 3/4 cup servings.

To absorb grease from the top of soup, drop a leaf of lettuce into the pot. Remove and throw away when it has served its purpose.

Griff Brazil, Chef/Owner
Hotel Mac
Point Richmond, California

Spicy 3 Pepper Chicken

4 (8 ounce) chicken breasts cut into 1" strips
1 cup soy sauce
2 cups rice wine
1/2 cup minced fresh ginger
1 tablespoon cornstarch
1/2 cup red pepper flakes
1 small package whole walnuts
1 tablespoon salad oil
Sprinkle of sugar
1 each of yellow, green, red bell peppers cut into 1" chunks
2 ounces chicken stock

Marinate chicken in soy sauce, rice wine, ginger, cornstarch and pepper flakes for 30 minutes (save marinade). Stir fry walnuts in oil for 1 minute. Remove and sprinkle with sugar (save oil). Stir fry chicken in salad oil until cooked through. Add bell peppers and cook until crisp-tender. Add 2 ounces of marinade and chicken stock. Cook until sauce thickens into a glaze. Toss walnuts into chicken and serve over white rice. Serves 8.

Vanilla flavor evaporates when it is boiled. Add vanilla extract to candies and desserts after they have been removed from heat.

Wolfgang Puck, Owner
Spago's
West Hollywood, California

Regular Pasta Dough

1-1/2 cups semolina flour, finest grind
1-1/2 cups all-purpose flour
2 teaspoons salt
4 eggs
2 tablespoons extra-virgin olive oil

Place the flours in a food processor fitted with a metal blade. Add the salt, eggs and olive oil. Process until the dough begins to mass on the blade (about 1-2 minutes). Remove the dough from the processor and press it into a ball. Wrap in plastic and let rest at least 2 hours in the refrigerator before rolling and cutting. (Rolling the dough by hand is extremely tedious; with a small pasta machine and cutting attachment you will save time and produce a much more uniform product.) Makes 1-1/2 pounds. Note: The pasta can also be made by hand or in an electric mixer fitted with a dough hook. For each of these methods, mix the dry ingredients together first, make a well in the center, add the wet ingredients and mix them together slowly until everything is combined well. Wrap the dough in plastic. It is best to have the pasta dough as dry as possible because the noodles have a better texture. If the dough is too soft, knead in some semolina or all-purpose flour until the dough becomes quite firm. Since it is hard for small machines to roll pasta that is very firm, the pasta may have to be dried after rolling on a rack made for that purpose or over a broomstick that hangs between 2 chairs.

Candles will burn longer and slower if stored in the refrigerator before using.

Angel Hair Pasta With Goat Cheese and Broccoli

At Spago in the summertime we use fresh basil in this recipe instead of thyme.

12 ounces Regular Pasta Dough, cut into 1/8 inch noodles (see index)
extra-virgin olive oil
1/2 pound tiny broccoli flowerettes
3/4 cup double-strength chicken stock
1 teaspoon thyme leaves, plus 4 to 6 sprigs for garnish
freshly ground pepper
3 tablespoons unsalted butter
4 ounces chevre (goat cheese), crumbled
salt
1 tablespoon toasted pine nuts

Bring a large pot of water to a boil with a little olive oil. In a skillet, saute the broccoli in a little olive oil for 1 minute, or until just crispy and add the stock. Bring it to a boil. Add the thyme leaves, pepper, butter and goat cheese and whisk together until the cheese melts. Remove the skillet from the heat and keep the sauce warm. Add some salt to the boiling water, then the pasta and cook it until al dente. Drain the pasta and rinse it under hot water. Add the pasta to the sauce and toss to distribute the sauce and broccoli evenly. Season to taste with salt and pepper. Serves 4 to 6. Presentation: Divide the pasta among warm appetizer plates. Garnish each serving with a sprig of thyme and some of the toasted pine nuts.

Anton Walker, Executive Chef
Stouffer Center Plaza Hotel
Dayton, Ohio

Pork Tenderloin with Thyme Lemon Sauce

4 whole pork tenderloins
salt and pepper
2 tablespoons olive oil
1 tablespoon Dijon mustard
2 cloves garlic, minced
1/4 ounce thyme leaves
2 tablespoons lime juice
2 ounces white wine
2 ounces pork stock
2 ounces heavy cream
1 lemon

Season the well trimmed pork tenderloins with salt and pepper. Combine the oil, mustard, minced garlic, 1/2 of the thyme leaves and 1 tablespoon of the lime juice. Place the tenderloins in the marinade, allowing it to sit in the refrigerator for 2-3 hours. Remove from pan. Brown well in saute pan. Hold the marinade and place in a pre-heated oven at 350 degrees for 15-20 minutes. Remove the meat and keep warm. Remove the fat. Deglaze with white wine and 1 tablespoon of the lime juice. Make a reduction, then add pork stock and cream. Reduce and adjust seasoning as required. Arrange the meat and pour the sauce over it. Garnish with blanched julienne of lemon zest and fresh thyme leaves. Serve with basil fettuccine. Serves 12.

Pirates Chicken A La Caribbean

4 chicken breasts
1 clove garlic, cut in half
3 tablespoons sugar
1/3 cup water
1 stalk celery, chopped
1/4 cup green pepper, chopped
1 carrot, chopped
1 onion, chopped
1 garlic clove, minced
2 teaspoons parsley, chopped
1/4 teaspoon crushed thyme
1/4 teaspoon ground cumin
1/4 teaspoon ground coriander
1/4 teaspoon ground tumeric
1/4 teaspoon curry powder
1/2 teaspoon pepper

Rub chicken pieces with garlic; set aside. Place sugar in large heavy pot over medium-high heat. When sugar is melted and turns dark brown, turn heat to low and slowly stir in water. Place chicken in pot, skin side down. Add the rest of the ingredients. Cover and cook chicken for 15 minutes. Turn chicken, cover and cook 15 more minutes. Place chicken on a serving dish and keep warm. Cook sauce in pan for 5 minutes longer; pour over chicken. Sprinkle with parsley and serve with rice.

Conversions

Measures	Weights
3 teaspoons	= 1 tablespoon
8 tablespoons	= 1/2 cup
16 tablespoons	= 1 cup
5-1/3 tablespoons	= 1/3 cup
4 tablespoons	= 1/4 cup
2 cups	= 1 pint
2 pints	= 1 quart
4 quarts	= 1 gallon
4 ounces	= 1/4 pound
8 ounces	= 1/2 pound
16 ounces	= 1 pound

Yield from Citrus Fruits

3 medium oranges yield 1 cup of juice
1 medium orange yields 4 teaspoons grated rind
1 medium orange yields 10-12 sections
1 medium grapefruit yields 2/3 cup juice
1 grapefruit yields 10-12 sections
6 medium lemons yield 1 cup of juice
1 medium lemon yields 1 tablespoon grated rind

Hint:
Citrus fruits yield more juice if they stand in boiling water a few minutes before squeezing. If you are going to use the rind in some way, always grate or peel before placing fruit in boiling water.

Food Equivalents

Butter	1 pound	= 2 cups
Cheese	4 ounces	= 1 cup
Chocolate morsels	6 ounces	= 1 cup
Cream	1/2 pint	= 1 cup liquid, 2 cups whipped
Crumbs:		
graham	14 squares	= 1 cup
saltine	28 squares	= 1 cup
Flour	1 pound	= 3-1/2 cups
Rice (long grain)	1 cup	= 2-3 cups cooked
Spaghetti	7 ounces	= about 4 cups
Bread	2 slices	= 1 cup crumbs
Chocolate	1 square	= 1 ounce

Substitutions

Instead of:	*Use:*
1 teaspoon baking powder	1/4 teaspoon baking soda + 1/2 teaspoon cream of tartar
1 cup buttermilk	1 cup milk + 1 tablespoon lemon juice or vinegar (let stand 5 minutes, stir well)
1 square unsweetened chocolate	3 tablespoons cocoa + 1 tablespoon butter or margarine
1 cup corn syrup	3/4 cup granulated sugar + 1/2 cup water
1 cup cake flour	1 cup all purpose flour minus 2 tablespoons
1 medium size garlic clove	1/8 teaspoon garlic powder
1 tablespoon prepared mustard	1 teaspoon dry mustard + 1 tablespoon vinegar
1 (6 ounce) can tomato paste	2 (8 ounce) cans tomato sauce (reduce other liquids)
1 tablespoon cornstarch	2 tablespoons flour

INDEX

Volunteer Services
M.D. Anderson Cancer Center
1515 Holcombe, #115
Houston, Texas 77030

Please send _____ copy(ies) @ $15.00 each _________
Postage and handling @ $3.00 each _________
Total _________

Name ____
Address ______________________________________
City ______________ State ______________ Zip ______________

Make checks payable to *M.D. Anderson Volunteer Cookbook*

- -

Volunteer Services
M.D. Anderson Cancer Center
1515 Holcombe, #115
Houston, Texas 77030

Please send _____ copy(ies) @ $15.00 each _________
Postage and handling @ $3.00 each _________
Total _________

Name ____
Address ______________________________________
City ______________ State ______________ Zip ______________

Make checks payable to *M.D. Anderson Volunteer Cookbook*

- -

Volunteer Services
M.D. Anderson Cancer Center
1515 Holcombe, #115
Houston, Texas 77030

Please send _____ copy(ies) @ $15.00 each _________
Postage and handling @ $3.00 each _________
Total _________

Name ____
Address ______________________________________
City ______________ State ______________ Zip ______________

Make checks payable to *M.D. Anderson Volunteer Cookbook*

Volunteer Services
M.D. Anderson Cancer Center
1515 Holcombe, #115
Houston, Texas 77030

Please send _____ copy(ies) @ $15.00 each _________
Postage and handling @ $3.00 each _________
Total _________

Name ____
Address ____
City _______________ State _______________ Zip _______________

Make checks payable to *M.D. Anderson Volunteer Cookbook*

- -

Volunteer Services
M.D. Anderson Cancer Center
1515 Holcombe, #115
Houston, Texas 77030

Please send _____ copy(ies) @ $15.00 each _________
Postage and handling @ $3.00 each _________
Total _________

Name ____
Address ____
City _______________ State _______________ Zip _______________

Make checks payable to *M.D. Anderson Volunteer Cookbook*

- -

Volunteer Services
M.D. Anderson Cancer Center
1515 Holcombe, #115
Houston, Texas 77030

Please send _____ copy(ies) @ $15.00 each _________
Postage and handling @ $3.00 each _________
Total _________

Name ____
Address ____
City _______________ State _______________ Zip _______________

Make checks payable to *M.D. Anderson Volunteer Cookbook*